THE STATUE OF LIBERTY
ENCYCLOPEDIA

BARRY MORENO

SIMON & SCHUSTER

New York London Toronto Sydney Singapore

SIMON & SCHUSTER
Rockefeller Center
1230 Avenue of the Americas
New York, NY 10020

Copyright © 2000 by Barry Moreno

Designed by Jeanette Olender
Manufactured in the United States of America

10 9 8 7 6 5 4 3 2 1

Library of Congress Cataloging-in-Publication Data
Moreno, Barry.
The Statue of Liberty encyclopedia / Barry Moreno.
p.   cm.
Includes index.
1. Statue of Liberty (New York, N.Y.)—Encyclopedias.   2. New York (N.Y.)—
Buildings, structures, etc.—Encyclopedias.   I. Title.
F128.64.L6 M67 2000
974.7'1—dc21   00-044006
ISBN 0-684-86227-1

The illustrations in this book are reproduced by courtesy of the Statue of Liberty
National Monument, with the exception of the following: The American Numismatic
Society, p. 143; HABS/HAER, National Park Service, pp. 22, 110, 174; James and Bradford
Hill, p. 112; JB Pictures, Ltd., p. 102; Theodore Roosevelt Birthplace, p. 207; Author's
collection, pp. 8, 62, 164, 168, 170, 216, 217; Kevin Daley, National Park Service, p. 83.

ACKNOWLEDGMENTS

The idea of writing this book first came to me in July 1994. I had long been conscious of the difficulty in finding information on the Statue of Liberty conveniently and easily, and so I wrote the first outline for *The Statue of Liberty Encyclopedia*. My hope was to include as much in it as possible and, through an alphabetical arrangement and an index, to ensure for its readers quick accessibility to the statue's rich history.

Two institutions were invaluable to me in researching the history of the Statue of Liberty: the library at the Statue of Liberty National Monument, and the New York Public Library's Main Branch at 42nd Street and Fifth Avenue as well as its St. George Branch on Staten Island. The New York Public Library's large collection of reference materials in the French, Spanish, Dutch, German, and Italian languages was especially valuable.

I should like to express my profound gratitude to those who assisted and encouraged me in this project. First and foremost I must thank Denise Roy, my editor at Simon & Schuster, whose astuteness, professionalism, and thoughtfulness were so important in the completion of this volume. I should also like to thank all those at Simon & Schuster who contributed to the production of this book, including Tara Parsons, Loretta Denner, and Jeanette Olender. At the Statue of Liberty National Monument, I thank Diana R. Pardue, Jeffrey S. Dosik, Frank W. Mills, David H. Cassells, Charles B. Lemonick, North Peterson, Marcus Smith, Eric Byron, Sydney Onikul, Paul Sigrist, Janet Levine, Kevin Daley, George Tselos, Kenneth Glasgow, Peter Stolz, Andrea Boney, Robert D. Peterson, James Elkin, Eugene Kuziw, Dave McCutcheon, Steven Divivier, Mario Torricella, David Haynes, Richard Koester, Timothy Romaine, Michael Monaghan, Charlie DeLeo, James I. Hill, Bradford Hill, Jose Sepulveda, and others too numerous to mention.

I am also grateful to the following: Charles Markis of Theodore Roosevelt Birthplace; Arthur Lawrence of the Union League Club; Nancy Johnson of the Lotos Club; Joy Rich of the New York Genealogical and Biographical Society; Richard Moylan of Greenwood Cemetery, Brooklyn; the French Senate Archives, Paris; The Metropolitan Museum of Art; the Library of Congress; the New-York Historical Society; and the Butler Historical Society, in New Jersey. I should also like to thank Joseph Michalak, Laura Langlie, Dorothy Hoobler, John F. Small, Kevin C. Buckley, Robert M. Stanton and Joan Banks (NPS Washington, D.C.), Philip Lax, Lawrence Bellante, Peg Zitko, Chief Inspector Philip Wheeler of Scotland Yard, Jack Gomez, Alex Villar, and Angela Siciliano.

I should also like to thank my parents and grandparents, and all of my family.

TO THE PERSONNEL

OF THE STATUE OF LIBERTY

NATIONAL MONUMENT—

PAST, PRESENT, AND FUTURE

THE STATUE OF LIBERTY
ENCYCLOPEDIA

THE
NATIONAL PARK SERVICE
WELCOMES YOU
TO THE

STATUE OF LIBERTY
NATIONAL MONUMENT

A

About, Edmond François Valentin (*b.* 14 February 1828, Dieuze, Lorraine, France; *d.* 16 January 1885, Paris, France). Author and journalist. About was a friend of Auguste Bartholdi and came to know and admire the sculptor's mother, Madame Charlotte Bartholdi, whom he met during his many visits to the family's house in Colmar. In his book *Alsace,* About wrote glowingly and extensively of Madame Bartholdi: *"Je vois encore la maîtresse du logis debout . . . semblable à une statue de l'hospitalité. C'était une grande femme d'environ soixante ans; sa physionomie, voilée . . . annonçait beaucoup de courage et infiniment de bonté"* ("I then saw the mistress of the house standing . . . like a statue of hospitality. She was a tall woman of about sixty; her face, [though] veiled . . . revealed great courage and infinite goodwill"). He also was impressed by the family's long history of bourgeois respectability.

Although a student of archaeology at Athens from 1851 through 1853, upon returning to France, About switched to literature. He produced such novels as *Tolla* (1855), *Le Roi des montagnes* (1856), *Le Nez d'un notaire* (1862), and *Madelon* (1863), which won him a public reputation as a sharp polemicist and a brilliant and fantastic storyteller. His work was strongly anticlerical. The Franco-Prussian War, which resulted in the loss of his country house in Lorraine, provoked him to write the pro-French book *Alsace* (1872). The political nature of the book cost him a week's confinement in a German-run prison. His other works include *Le Fellah* (1869), about Egypt; *Le Roman d'un brave homme* (1880), a patriotic work; and *De Pontoise à Stamboul* (1884), a charming travel book about Istanbul. His stage plays were *Guillery* (1857), *Risette* (1859), and *Gaëtano* (1862). He was elected to the French Academy in 1884.

Adamic, Louis (*b.* 23 March 1899, Blato, Slovenia; *d.* 4 September 1951, Milford, New Jersey). Author. Adamic came to America in 1913, undergoing immigration inspection at Ellis Island. For many years he wandered through towns and rural areas finding work at odd jobs. During these years, he formed contrasting views, some idealistic and others critical, about his new country. He frequently expressed a hope that America would learn to tolerate and even value the infinite variety of its people. In 1934, he boldly launched a publicity campaign to elevate the social position of immigrants and ethnic minorities. Realizing that a legitimizing symbol might strengthen his cause, he enlisted the potent imagery of the Statue of Liberty and the inspiring words of Emma Lazarus's eloquent sonnet, *The New Colossus.* Throughout the 1930s and early 1940s, Adamic and others recited it in radio broadcasts, making its words known to millions of listeners. Educators eventually adopted it for teaching students patriotism and the plight of immigrants. Adamic's many published works include *Dynamite* (1931), *Laughing in the Jungle* (1932), *The Native's Return* (1934), *My America* (1938), and *From Many Lands* (1940). Adamic's life ended in tragedy. In 1951, he was found dead of a gunshot wound in his head, and buildings on his property were ablaze. Initially, police suspected murder (his widow had testified that his socialist political leanings provoked threats against his life), but finally ruled his death a suicide, although lingering doubts could never be dispelled. At the time of his death, political tension in the Yugoslav immigrant exile community was high due to powerful factions, especially those that supported Yugoslavia's communist dictator, Marshal Joseph Tito, and those that still favored the restoration of the country's overthrown king, Peter II. The author's widow, Stella Adamic, was dissatisfied with the ruling about her husband's end. She died in 1964. *See also* New Colossus.

Adams, Charles Francis (*b.* 18 August 1807, Boston, Massachusetts; *d.* 21 November 1886, Boston, Massachusetts). Politician and diplomat. Member of the Boston Committee, Franco-American Union. Unsuccessful candidate for U.S. vice president (Free Soil party), 1848; U.S. congressman, 1859–61; minister to Great Britain, 1861–68.

Advertising. Liberty is indisputably the most popular image used in American advertising. Its proliferation in commercial, government, and other types of advertising and propaganda is unparalleled; artists have recreated it in astonishing ways. The earliest widely seen images of Liberty appeared in periodicals of the 1880s such as *L'Illustration* in Paris and *Frank Leslie's Illustrated Newspaper, Harper's Weekly,* and the *Daily Graphic* in New York. Statue of Liberty lithographs, produced by such firms as Root & Tinker (which was officially commissioned to make them by the American Committee, 1883) and Currier & Ives further popularized the image. Commercial firms quickly saw possibilities in the image. In 1884, one company substituted the torch for its Star Lamp and another company adopted the pedestal to represent its Astral Oil container. Trade cards were got up by firms as well, and so appeared many different versions of

PUCK.

LET THE ADVERTISING AGENTS TAKE CHARGE OF THE BARTHOLDI BUSINESS,
AND THE MONEY WILL BE RAISED WITHOUT DELAY.

(facing) Commercialization of Liberty decried, c. 1883

(left) French tourism advertisement

(right) Beverage advertisement, 1940s

Liberty standing in the harbor for products such as Dr. Haas Hog & Poultry Remedy (1884), Parisian Sauce (c. 1886), G. A. Shoudy & Son's Wonderful Soap (a washerwoman poses as Liberty with a cake of Wonderful soap as her torch), and Liberty in a clothier's changing room for the T. W. Perry firm (c. 1886). The name "Liberty Enlightening the World" has been altered by advertisers and cartoonists, reappearing as "Liberty Feeding the World," "Liberty Cleaning the World," and "Liberty Frightening the World." *Puck* magazine produced a cartoon criticizing the commercial abuse of the image; its caption read, "Let Advertising Agents Take Charge of the Bartholdi Business." Liberty was used widely in cartoons illustrating or expressing opinion or criticizing public policy. Thomas Nast substituted Liberty's head for a skeleton's in "Leave All Hope, Ye That Enter Here," a cartoon about New York's March 1881 cholera scare. The *Evening Telegram* (New York) produced an anti-immigration cartoon in which the "Dregs of Europe" surround Liberty; she is depicted pinching her nose tightly to keep out the stench, while grasping a bottle of carbolic acid and supporting her tablet, which is inscribed with a new message: "Immigration Stopped for Twenty Days. Why Not Twenty Years?" (Immigration had been temporarily halted at Ellis Island due to fear of a cholera epidemic.) Also effective was Grant Hamilton's cartoon showing an idealized Liberty and torch, with the caption "A Republic"; while on the opposite side was the image of a Roman statue of war. The new statue had usurped Liberty's place on the pedestal, leaving the copper goddess on the ground with remains of the torn Declaration of Independence and U.S. Constitution (Hamilton got the idea for it from Democratic politician William Jennings Bryan, who had opposed America's acquisition of Cuba, Puerto Rico, and the Philippines following the U.S. victory in the Spanish-American War of 1898).

Liberty was suited to patriotic art during World War I (1914–18). In 1914, the artist Sem produced his powerful Statue of Liberty poster, *Pour la Liberté du Monde,* to sell French war bonds. Upon America's entry in the conflagration in 1917, J. C. Leyendecker and other artists produced equally effective patriotic art to sell American war bonds, known as the Liberty Loan. In the interwar years, 1919–39, Liberty returned to peaceful advertising and publicity uses, such as for Haig's Whisky (1928), the Works Projects Administration's "Liberty for All—Keep 'em Flying" (1932); the French State Railways poster welcoming visitors to the Paris International Exposition (1937); and "War's First Casualty," a 1939 antiwar advertisement from the America First Committee. During World War II (1939–45), Liberty appeared in defense bond and stamp posters (such as Pepsi

(left) Holmes and Coutts Wafers, 1880s

(below) Soapine, 1880s

(opposite page) Louis Agassiz

Cola's). During the cold war, the Soviet caricaturist Kukrinisky produced a cartoon in 1968 showing the statue as an imposter for an axe-wielding U.S. military officer (with a faint resemblance to General Douglas MacArthur). This poster shows the officer breaking away the plasterwork statue that hides him, while the tablet, 'Democracy,' lies at his feet. The caption reads, "American Liberty."

Agassiz, Louis Rodolphe (*b.* 28 May 1807, Môtier-en-Vuly, Fribourg, Switzerland; *d.* 4 December 1873, Cambridge, Massachusetts).

Naturalist, geologist, and author. Agassiz began teaching at Neufchâtel University in 1832, where he gained international renown for his geological theories. While on a lecture tour of the United States between 1846 and 1848, he accepted the offer of a professorship in natural history at Harvard University. Edouard de Laboulaye gave Bartholdi a letter of introduction to present to the naturalist (1871), cannily observing, "To know Agassiz is to know everyone." In turn, Agassiz arranged for Bartholdi to meet the poet Henry Wadsworth Longfellow. Agassiz is famous for expounding the theory of

the Ice Age. He also vigorously opposed theories of evolution. His publications included *Recherches sur les poisson fossiles* (1833), *Etudes sur les glaciers* (1840), *Contributions to the Natural History of the United States* (1857–62), and *A Journey to Brazil* (1867).

Alsace. Auguste Bartholdi's beloved native province. Alsace became a province of France in 1678 when King Louis XIV acquired the territory under the Treaty of Nimègue. In 1871, Prussian chancellor Otto von Bismarck claimed Alsace as a spoil of war and compelled France to surrender it to the German empire; this profoundly distressed the sculptor. The Cuban exile writer José Martí interpreted Bartholdi's Statue of Liberty as a cry of liberation for Alsace and Lorraine, the "lost daughters of France." In October 1886, he wrote, "No man ever made truly beautiful works without much sorrow. It is the hope of his country's restoration which inspired Bartholdi's sovereign statue. This is why she advances as if to enter the Promised land, why her head is bowed like a widow's and her beacon arm aims proudly at the sky. 'A l'Alsace!, à l'Alsace!,' she cries—a dolorous maiden come to demand Alsace back to France rather than illuminate the freedom of the world." Bartholdi certainly expressed his feelings about the Franco-Prussian War and the position of his native province in such French sculptural works as the *Curse of Alsace;* a funerary monument in memory of three Alsatian National Guardsmen, including Joseph-Edme Voulminot (inscribed: "Morts en Combattant, 14 Sept. 1870"); and the *Lion of Belfort*. In America—especially among French Americans—there was some understanding of his sensibilities, symbolized by the inclusion of an Alsatian float in the inaugural parade of the Statue of Liberty. When France reconquered the province in 1918, a Bartholdi cult emerged as a part of a politically pro-French movement. Several places such as the Lycée Bartholdi (a high school) were named in the sculptor's honor. Further, in 1934 (Bartholdi's centennial

year), the Alsatian Theatre presented a dramatic play about him. Its title, *Bartholdi un sin Rabmanella,* refers to Bartholdi's *Jeune Vigneron Alsacien* (1869). With the return of the Germans in 1940, the movement was suppressed, the Lycée Bartholdi was given a new name, and pro-French sculptures were ordered to be taken apart. Bartholdi works to be removed were a full-scale sculpture of Count Jean de Rapp, the Bruat fountain, and the National Guard monument in the cemetery. They were rebuilt after the war. Aside from Bartholdi, noted Alsatians include Rapp, Baron Georges Haussmann, and Albert Schweitzer.

Alsace-Lorraine. French provinces located at the Franco-German border that together form the administrative departments of Lower Rhine, Upper Rhine, and Mulhouse. The people of Alsace have by tradition been Alsatian speaking, and those of Lorraine have been mixed. France ceded Alsace and Lorraine to Germany under the terms of the Treaty of

(below) Alsatian National Guard funerary monument, Colmar (sculptor: A. Bartholdi, 1872)

(opposite page) Notice of a meeting of the Alsace-Lorraine Masonic lodge, Paris, 1884

Frankfurt (May 1871), but retained two successfully defended adjacent territories, Belfort and Moselle. The Germans united Alsace and Lorraine to form the Reichsland of Elsass-Lothringen. As such, the "lost daughters of France" became part of the newly created Second Reich ruled by Emperor Wilhelm I and his "iron chancellor," Prince Otto von Bismarck. The new Reichsland elected deputies to the Imperial Reichstag in Berlin (an Alsatian deputy would be present at the funeral of Auguste Bartholdi in Paris in 1904). The province was made up of three districts, each with a governing council of ten. The councillors elected the thirty-seat Consultative Assembly (Landesausschuss) to govern the province.

As time passed, three new political groups emerged in Alsace-Lorraine: pragmatists who accept the union with Germany, autonomists who rejected either French or German sovereignty, and socialists who tried to concentrate public attention on economic inequalities. In 1911, Emperor Wilhelm II gave Alsace-Lorraine a constitution that introduced responsible government and granted autonomy to the province. This cleverly weakened the demands for complete autonomy. With a new two-chamber assembly, the province henceforth controlled its own finances and made its own laws. In addition, considerable economic development greatly energized the province.

Following the German declaration of war against France on 3 August 1914, French troops invaded Upper Alsace. This war put the whole province in an unenviable situation, for the German and French forces sought traitors everywhere. With the armistice of November 1918, the French army seized complete control of Alsace-Lorraine. Subsequently, the Treaty of Versailles (1919) returned the "lost provinces" to France. Auguste Bartholdi's dream at last came true: Alsace-Lorraine was French once more.

Alsace-Lorraine lodge. Masonic lodge instituted by the Grand Orient of France in 1872 to serve as a gathering place for pro-French Alsa-

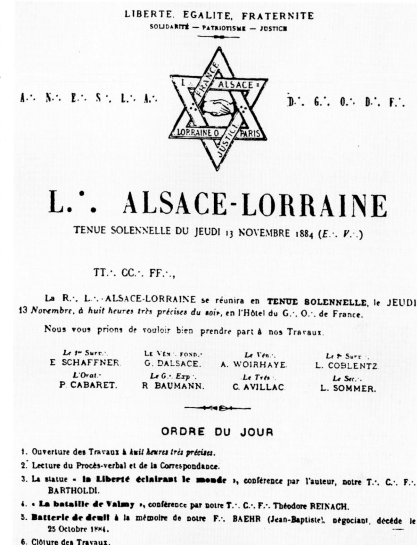

tians and Lorrainers who lived a life of self-imposed exile in Paris. Auguste Bartholdi was initiated into this lodge on 14 October 1875. Educator Jean Macé, who worked with Bartholdi to complete the Statue of Liberty project, was also a member of the Alsace-Lorraine lodge. On 19 June 1884, the lodge members visited the newly completed Statue of Liberty as Bartholdi's guests, and the sculptor later delivered a lecture on the statue to lodge members.

Alsatian. Low Alemannic German dialect traditionally spoken in Alsace and the name for the region's inhabitants. In the nineteenth century, Alsatian was the primary spoken language of the province, while High German was preferred for most literary expression. French was used for administrative purposes and was taught in all schools. However, during the province's period of union with Germany (1871–1918), German was aggressively promoted and the use of French officially discouraged. Alsatian, previously regarded as a folk dialect, became the preferred language for groups that promoted Alsatian autonomy. An example of Alsatian is seen in these lines of the Colmarian poet Jean-Thomas Mangold:

> D'r Freïheits-Genie
>   Monümànt vom
>   Herr Auguste Bartholdi
>   Fér's hundertjàhrige
>   Befreïungs-Fest von Amerika
> Amerika uf alle Flanke
>   Bésch du jo s'wahre Züefluchtsland
>   Ewral gét's Völker wo noch zanke,
>   Wàm reich sie enander d'Hand?
>   Génie, loss Colmar stoltz erklènge,
>   Em Herr Bartholdi si Wàrk umrénge
>   Un lowe's grosse Meisterstéck.
> (On America's One-Hundredth Anniversary
>   of Independence: The Genius-of-Liberty
>   Monument by August Bartholdi
> America, the world's true corner of refuge/
>   Everywhere people quarrel; when will
>   they shake hands? / O Genius, let Colmar
>   unite in pride and let Bartholdi's great
>   masterwork be ringed round with praise.)
> [*B. Moreno, translator*]

The use of Alsatian has declined, although it remains the language of preference among staunch Lutherans, especially in Strasbourg.

American Committee ("Pedestal Committee"). American branch of the Franco-American Union. This fund-raising committee or board was launched in New York City by William M. Evarts, John Jay, Samuel Babcock, William H. Wickham, and William Appleton at the request of Edouard de Laboulaye, who had already formed both the central umbrella organization, the Franco-American Union, and a fund-raising board known as the French Committee (Comité français). Evarts chaired the main American Committee in New York and was assisted by small American committees in other cities, known respectively as the Boston Committee, Philadelphia Committee, and Brooklyn Committee. The chief task of these committees was to inform Americans of the Statue of Liberty project, secure federal acceptance of it (1877), and, especially, to raise funds to build the statue's pedestal. At the January 1877 meeting, Evarts put the cost of the pedestal at $125,000. He described the French enthusiasm of the fund-raising drive and expected a similar response from the American people. He drew the group's attention to Edward Moran's painting, *The Nations Paying Homage to Liberty,* which depicted foreign steamships entering New York harbor and boatloads of tourists visiting Bedloe's Island to pay homage to the goddess Liberty. J. Seaver Page then read a poem written by John Moran. Richard Butler next took the floor. He stated that the intention in calling the meeting was to select a committee of twenty to lead the subscription campaign and raise the necessary $125,000. F. R. Coudert of the French Committee of New York, Auguste Bartholdi, Rush Hawkins, and Theodore Roosevelt, Sr., each delivered a brief address. The assembled company then elected Evarts chairman and authorized him to appoint the committee of twenty. Evarts eventually selected twenty-two members, whose names were announced in March 1877: William M. Evarts (chairman); James W. Pinchot (treasurer, 1877–83); Henry F. Spaulding (who also later served as treasurer, 1883–86); Richard Butler (secretary, 1877–1902), William H. Appleton, Samuel P. Avery, Samuel D. Babcock, Clark Bell, William Cullen Bryant, Frédéric Coudert, John T. Denny, Parke Godwin, John Jay, John Taylor Johnston, V. Mumford Moore, Edwin

(opposite page) American Museum of Immigration commemorative medal, 1965

Morgan, J. Seaver Page, Theodore Roosevelt, Anson Phelps Stokes, Theodore Weston, Worthington Whittredge, and William Wickham. The American Committee was enlarged to four hundred members in 1882–83 and included a new executive committee chaired by Joseph W. Drexel. Prominent among new members were Daniel Appleton, G. R. Blanchard, Noah Davis, M. B. Fielding, Henry Hentz, John H. Inman, Henry Hilton, James F. Dwight, Algernon S. Sullivan, and Frederick Potts. In 1885 there were yet more changes in the American Committee's composition, when wealthy businessmen were brought in to bolster the finance subcommittee in its last major fund-raising campaign: Louis de Bebien, Edward Kemp, Charles Lanier, Henry Marquand, William L. Strong, and Stephen V. White. Other key people associated with the American Committee through the years were August Belmont, Cornelius Bliss, Joseph Choate, George W. Curtis, Chauncey M. Depew, Christian Detmold, Cyrus Field, Georges Glaenzer, Richard Morris Hunt, John La Farge, Joseph Pulitzer, and Carl Schurz. After the Statue of Liberty's completion and dedication, the American Committee (also known as the Citizens' Committee) maintained a successful ferry service to Bedloe's Island. The committee used the profits from the ferry operation to set up a beautification fund to pay for minor repairs at the monument and to keep on duty a caretaker who swept out the monument and kept paraffin oil lamps burning inside the dark interior of the pedestal and statue during the day. The American Committee's New York City locations were 67 Madison Avenue (1877–81), 33 Mercer Street (1881–84), 55 Liberty Street (1884–85) and, once again, 33 Mercer Street (1885–1902). *See also* Boston; Franco-American Union; French Committee (New York); Pedestal Campaign; Philadelphia Committee.

American Museum of Immigration. Museum in operation on Liberty Island in the base of the pedestal from 1972 until 1991. In 1951, William H. Baldwin, a trustee of the American Scenic

President Franklin D. Roosevelt at the Statue of Liberty's Golden Jubilee, 1936

and Historic Preservation Society (ASHPS), suggested to his colleagues the idea of building a museum dedicated to the memory of immigrants. Consensus held that Castle Clinton, in Battery Park, lower Manhattan, would make an ideal location. However, the National Park Service (NPS) disagreed, finding the Statue of Liberty at Bedloe's Island a more suitable site.

By 1954, prominent backers led by Pierre S. DuPont III, Alexander Hamilton, and General Ulysses S. Grant III won the support of President Dwight D. Eisenhower and his secretary of the interior, Douglas McKay. In 1955, the American Museum of Immigration (AMI) was incorporated as a nonprofit, educational organization. In 1957, with the fund-raising campaign lagging, AMI officials enlisted the aid of Vice President Richard Nixon. But the total cost of the museum—$5 million—was eventually met through funds allocated by Congress. Alexander Hamilton laid the cornerstone for the AMI on 28 October 1962. A committee of historians—John A. Krout, Theodore Blegen, Allan Nevins, Carl Wittke, John Hope Franklin, Elsie M. Lewis, Oscar Handlin, John Higham, and Rudolph J. Vecoli—advised the AMI, and NPS historians Thomas M. Pitkin and George J. Svejda oversaw the planning of the galleries. Viola Scott Thomas acted as secretary. Although Lady Bird Johnson, wife of President Lyndon Johnson, opened a temporary AMI exhibit on Liberty Island on 17 May 1968, it was not until the 1970s that the AMI was at last complete. On 26 September 1972, only weeks before his election to a second term, President Richard M. Nixon formally inaugurated the museum at Liberty Island in the presence of Pierre S. DuPont and its other founders.

The museum exhibits, arranged chronologically, depicted the causes of emigration, mapped the areas of immigrant settlement throughout the United States, and displayed cultural artifacts brought from the countries of origin. The controversial theory of America as a melting pot was much in evidence, and such nationalities as English, Scottish, German, and Chinese were featured, as well as Native American peoples, black African slaves, and Mormon migrants. Loyalty and patriotism, technological and scientific achievements, and social and cultural gifts of immigrants were emphasized, and famous immigrants were celebrated—including Tadeusz Kosciuszko, Franz Siegel, Carl Schurz, Andrew Carnegie, Bert Williams, Al Jolson, I. M. Pei, Wanda Landowska, and Nikola Tesla. As an afterthought, AMI officials included a small Statue of Liberty exhibit known as the Statue of Liberty Story Room. AMI chief curators, all NPS personnel, were consecutively Edward L. Kallop, Jr., Paul O. Weinbaum, Paul Kinney, and Diana R. Pardue. The AMI failed as a permanent museum because its private founders did not provide a financial endowment to ensure its future. It was officially closed by the NPS in January 1991, shortly after the inauguration of the Ellis Island Immigration Museum.

Anchorage. Two massive cross beams intersected vertically by enormous tension bars embedded in the pedestal's interior concrete walls, continuing downward into the masonry foundation. Horizontal pairs of steel I-beams are embedded within the pedestal's inner concrete walls. The anchorage is reinforced by steel girders that embrace the concrete walls. Liberty's skeleton frame is secured by bolts into the upper cross beams. This extraordinary system holds Liberty firmly in place and prevents the statue from collapsing. Designed in 1885 by chief engineer Charles P. Stone, the contractor for its installation was Andrew Carnegie's Keystone Bridge Company, with engineer C. C. Schneider performing inspections.

Anniversaries. Celebrations commemorating the Statue of Liberty's inaugural date of 28 October 1886. The first major event of this kind was the Thirtieth Anniversary in 1916, for which President Woodrow Wilson illuminated the monument's new floodlighting system. The New York *World* newspaper launched a fund-raising campaign that successfully raised $30,000 to pay the

General Electric Company for the new system. Famous actors such as vaudeville star Claire Rochester went on a motor tour of the country dressed as "Miss Liberty," while Liberty Girls collected donations stored in "Liberty banks." A grand finale banquet, held in December 1916 at the Waldorf Astoria Hotel, was hosted by President Wilson, with French ambassador Jules Jusserand, Chauncey M. Depew, and Ralph Pulitzer, publisher of the *World,* as honored guests.

The Golden Jubilee Anniversary (28 October 1936) culminated in extensive restoration work between 1937 and 1941 on the statue and Bedloe's Island. The celebration itself took place on Bedloe's Island and in New York harbor; it was presided over by President Franklin Delano Roosevelt and included French ambassador André de Laboulaye (a grandson of Edouard de Laboulaye) and Albert Bartholdi, an American kinsman of the sculptor. The battleship *U.S.S. Indianapolis* led the naval display.

As part of the Seventieth Anniversary festivities in 1956, Congress changed the name Bedloe's Island to Liberty Island.

During the American Bicentennial in 1976, the Statue of Liberty became a focus of patriotic fervor. On the Fourth of July, Liberty and New York harbor witnessed Operation Sail, one of the greatest of naval parades of the century and a grand display of fireworks.

The 1986 Centennial Anniversary of the Statue of Liberty, hosted by President Ronald Reagan, with President François Mitterand of France, was equally magnificent. Preparations for it were undertaken between 1982 and 1986 and included extensive restoration work on the Statue of Liberty itself, as well as important improvements on Liberty Island.

The Ladies Auxiliary of the Veterans of Foreign Wars, which has participated in all of the major anniversaries since 1936, has annually donated items to enhance the enjoyment of visitors to the monument. *See also* Liberty Weekend.

Antiquities Act. Legislation passed by Congress and signed into law by President Theodore Roosevelt in 1906. This law grants the president authority to create national monuments by proclamation. President Calvin Coolidge utilized the law to proclaim the Statue of Liberty a national monument on 15 October 1924, and President Lyndon B. Johnson used it to declare Ellis Island part of the Statue of Liberty National Monument on 11 May 1965. The Antiquities Act guarantees federal protection of antiquities and monuments. *See also* Legislation.

Architectural view of Liberty's pedestal

Appleton, Daniel (*b.* 24 February 1852, New York, New York; *d.* 16 March 1929, North Andover, Massachusetts). New York publisher who was a member of the American Committee of New York, 1883–86. He was a grandson of the founder of D. Appleton & Company.

Appleton, Nathan, Jr. (*b.* 1843, Boston, Massachusetts; *d.* 1906, Boston, Massachusetts). International banker and member of the French Committee of the Franco-American Union in Paris, 1875–81, and the American Committee of Boston, 1881–86. Appleton and his half-brother, Thomas G. Appleton, were scions of an old New England family. In 1868, Appleton joined the Paris branch of Bowles Brothers, an investment firm. He represented a variety of American commercial interests in Paris and, with fellow Bostonian Joseph Iasigi, the Board of Trade. Appleton was the author of *Sketch of Life* (1873), *Centennial Movement* (1877), and *Russian Life and Society in 1866–67* (1904).

Appleton, Thomas Gold (*b.* 31 March 1812, Boston, Massachusetts; *d.* 17 April 1884, New York, New York). Essayist, poet, and artist who was a member of the French Committee, Franco-American Union, Paris, and the American Committee of Boston, 1876–84. He was the half-brother of Nathan Appleton, Jr. A resident of Paris, Appleton was a prominent literary figure in the American community. Among his works were *Faded Leaves* (poems, 1872), *Fresh Leaves* (poems, 1874), *A Sheaf of Papers* (1875), *Windfalls* (1878), and *Chequer-Work* (1879).

Appleton, William Henry (*b.* 27 January 1814, Haverhill, Massachusetts; *d.* 19 October 1899, Riverdale, New York). New York publisher who became a member of the American Committee in New York in 1877 and served on its Contributions and Press subcommittees. The son of pioneer book publisher Daniel Appleton, William succeeded his father as head of the publishing house of D. Appleton in 1849. During his years of ownership, William Appleton published a wide variety of books, from scientific works to sentimental novels.

Architecture. The primary architectural feature of the Statue of Liberty National Monument is the pedestal, designed by Richard Morris Hunt. In the 1880s, it was referred to as the Pharos design due to its resemblance to the lighthouse (*pharos*) of Alexandria, one of the seven wonders of the ancient world. It was constructed between 1884 and 1886. The pedestal sits within the walls of Fort Wood, an eleven-pointed star-shaped fortress built between 1807 and 1811. *See also* Fort Wood; Hunt, Richard Morris; Master Plan of 1939; Newton, Norman; Pedestal.

Arm. The right arm of the Statue of Liberty, bearing the torch and flame, is 42 feet in length (12.8 meters). The upper portion of the arm, in-

Liberty's right arm

cluding torch and flame, was completed in Paris in August 1876 and sent immediately to the Philadelphia Centennial Exhibition, where it became a leading attraction. At the end of the exhibition, Frédéric Coudert's French Committee raised funds to ship it to New York, and, at the expense of the City Department of Public Works, it was mounted for display in Madison Square in February 1877. The arm was shipped back to France to be assembled with the rest of the statue in August 1882. During the restoration of the 1980s, it was found that one of the spikes or rays of the crown was in contact with the upraised arm. Engineers solved the problem by shifting the spike a few degrees. Due to corrosion, the 1876 torch and flame were replaced in 1986. Liberty's left arm bears a tablet with the Latin inscription "July 4, 1776," the date of the signing of America's Declaration of Independence. *See also* Flame; Torch.

Armature. Liberty's vast network of steel bars. A total of 1,830 armature bars form horizontal and vertical patterns carefully shaped to match the contours of the copper plates, and are designed to expand or contract easily in response to heat and cold without causing metallic stress. The steel bars and copper plates are joined indirectly by steel brackets known as saddles. Twelve thousand rivets secure the armature network in place. The armature bars then connect to the interior skeletal framework by means of 325 flat bars or springs. This relieves the statue of rigidity, transferring excess pressure, generated by such forces as the wind, to the central framework.

Army (War Department). Caretaker of the goddess *Liberty Enlightening the World* from 1902 to 1933. The army administered Bedloe's Island as a military reservation from 1811 to 1937. In 1811, a star-shaped fort (or battery) of masonry was constructed, with thirty heavy cannons capable of firing twenty-four-pound cannonballs mounted in the masonry. Additional defenses included a stone magazine large enough for two

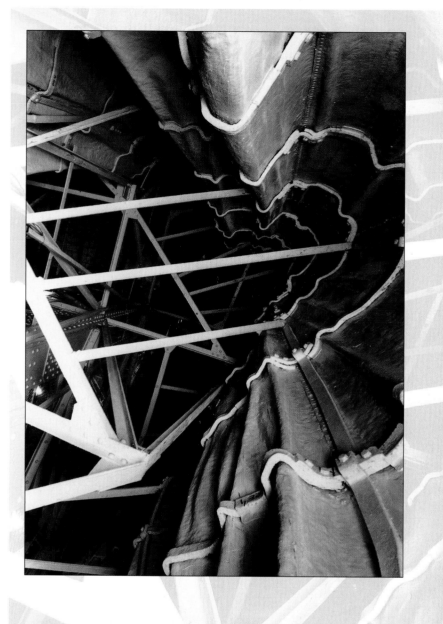

hundred barrels of gunpowder and a brick arsenal. The military site was officially known as the "works on Bedlow's Island" until 9 November 1814, when Governor Daniel D. Tompkins of New York renamed the battery Fort Wood, in memory of Lieutenant Colonel Eleazer D. Wood, the famous hero who lost his life during the Battle of Fort Erie in September 1814.

In the first few years following the War of 1812, an artillery corps was stationed at the fortress. In 1817, a certain Captain Romayne had seventy-four soldiers under his command there. In the next year, Lieutenant Colonel House commanded 306 men.

From 1820 to 1824, a small but overzealous garrison permitted no unauthorized parties to approach the island. At least this was the claim of a petition submitted to the New York City Common Council on 19 February 1821. The local oystermen accused the "United States Troops stationed on Bedlow's Island" of obstructing them in the pursuit of their occupation, "by taking them out of their Boats, and even threaten-ing to fire upon them if they followed their occupation nigh the said Island." The council referred the complaint to its Police Committee.

Beginning in 1848, the newly established New York State commissioners of emigration set up a convalescent hospital on Bedloe's Island for immigrants recovering from contagious diseases after release from quarantine. By 1851, the garrison at Fort Wood had been enlarged. The army surgeon of the period was Doctor Josiah Simpson, who lived there with his wife, Harriet St. John Simpson. An excerpt of a letter that she

(opposite page) Partial view of Liberty's inner armature structure

(below) Aerial view of the army post on Bedloe's Island, 1933

wrote on 23 September 1851 describes life on Bedloe's Island:

Doctor is busy enough with the Command so large as it is. He had between fifty and sixty men in the hospital. Some of them very ill and has had a number of deaths. One man was buried to-day. A man who used to milk Mrs. Brown's cows. We had taken a good deal of interest in his case, sent him down a number of things to tempt his appetite, but it was of no avail. Doctor has got into his new hospital. Indeed, he says, he does not know what he should have done if it had not been ready for him. There are now on the island some 600 men, if not more. The ramparts are half covered with tents and still none are sent off. I am getting tired myself seeing so many men around.

By 26 November 1852, Mrs. Simpson had learned of

a moving of Troops all round the harbour. The depot is ordered over to Fort Columbus, the companies then go to Fort Hamilton and the company at Fort Hamilton comes here to Bedloe's Island. I felt some anxiety to know our destination, but Doctor is not included in the order and remains here. . . . The men have already gone and the place looks quite deserted. . . . As a company is only fifty men, the Doctor says he can fold his hands this winter. We both feel this movement very much lessens our chances of remaining here. They will hardly keep an able-bodied man like the Doctor here when some old man not able to do much duty, will answer just as well. . . . However, they may take it into their heads to let the Doctor alone.

During the Civil War, Bedloe's Island and Fort Wood were used primarily as a recruiting station and ordnance depot, although the hospital was kept up. Over the years, the army remained active, and when the Statue of Liberty was being built in the 1880s, soldiers were assigned guard duty at the construction site.

In 1905, the War Department sent engineer Sedley Chapin to inspect the condition of the Statue of Liberty. Chapin prepared a lengthy report, estimating that $6,400 would be required for planned maintenance work, which included regrading; sodding and seeding the grounds surrounding the statue; building a new stone entrance stairway, lavatories, and a visitors' waiting room; interior painting of the pedestal; and the installation of an electrical passenger elevator in the pedestal. Chapin rejected the suggestion of painting the statue, although he favored the notion of gilding the torch (it was never done). The work was completed between 1907 and 1909. Army maintenance work in subsequent years included the replacement of broken saddles (1911), copper skin repair (1920s), and lighting changes (1909 [the statue was electrified for the Hudson-Fulton Celebration]; 1916, 1931).

From 1904 until 1923, the Army Signal Corps replaced the regular army on the island. When the Signal Corps was withdrawn in 1923, it was replaced by the Military Police, which occupied the site until September 1937, when the Secretary of War turned Bedloe's Island over to the National Park Service, U.S. Department of the Interior. *See also* Army Signal Corps; Bedloe's Island; Congressional Joint Resolution of 1877; Governor's Island; Military Police.

Army Signal Corps. U.S. Army unit stationed on Bedloe's Island, 1904–23. In 1905, a permanent communication cable was laid in a previously dredged water pipe trench between the island and Black Tom Wharf, New Jersey, on 5–6 October 1905, at a cost of $150. A telegraph station was in operation until it was replaced by a wireless radio station, c. 1921. The latter station remained at Bedloe's Island until 1941, when it was removed to Governor's Island.

Asbestos. During the Statue of Liberty restoration project of the 1980s, workers found that asbestos had been used as an insulator on the iron armature bars; Gustave Eiffel would have been responsible for the choice of asbestos. Its purpose was to prevent an electrolytic reaction of the copper and the iron. Restorers removed the bars and stripped them of paint and asbestos. Stainless steel duplicate bars were made and installed. Because steel and copper are known to produce a galvanic effect under extreme conditions, the restorers selected Teflon tape with a pressure-sensitive silicone backing as the insulator.

Atrium Libertatis (Atrium of Liberty). Public building in ancient Rome established in the third century B.C.; it was consecrated to the goddess Libertas and stood near the Forum. The atrium housed the office and archives of the censor, a position that carried considerable moral authority, for the censor not only counted the population of Rome every five years but drew up official lists of the nobility and controlled the public treasury. The Atrium Libertatis also has the distinction of being the site of the first public library at Rome. Gaius Asinius Pollio, a friend of the poets Virgil and Horace, founded the library in 39 B.C. with booty from his Illyrian campaign. The collection primarily consisted of the works of old Greek and Latin writers and contained only one set of books by a living author. This was the Latin writer Varro, whose portrait was kept on display. In addition, the atrium functioned as a sort of police station and detention hall [Livy (25.7.12) and Cicero (*Pro Milone* 59–60)]. *See also* Libertas.

Auguste Bartholdi, Rue. Street in Paris named in honor of the sculptor. Located in the Fifteenth Arrondissement, between the Boulevard de Grenelle and Avenue de Suffren, it is quite close to the Place Dupleix. Also within walking distance is the Pont Grenelle, the bridge leading to the Ile de Cygnes, where the thirty-six-foot bronze replica of the Statue of Liberty overlooks the Seine River and gazes westward toward her big sister in America.

Avery, Henry Ogden (*b.* 31 January 1852, Brooklyn, New York; *d.* 30 April 1890, New York, New York). Draughtsman and assistant architect in the offices of Richard Morris Hunt, 1879–83; son of Samuel P. Avery. Young Avery made many distinctive drawings of alternative pedestal ideas for the Statue of Liberty, but in the end, the American Committee selected a sketch made by Richard Morris Hunt. He also assisted Hunt in designing private residences. Avery studied architecture at the Ecole des Beaux-Arts in Paris between 1872 and 1879. His best-known design is that of the Union Prisoner of War Monument in Washington, D.C. Columbia University's Avery Architectural Library in New York City is named in his memory.

Avery, Samuel Putnam (*b.* 17 March 1822, New York, New York; *d.* 11 August 1904, New York, New York). An art dealer and engraver; member of the American Committee of the Franco-American Union in New York. Avery was director of the American Committee's publicity campaign and also served on the Artistic subcommittee. He played an especially active role during the 1883 Pedestal Art Loan Exhibition, a fund-raising event for Liberty's pedestal. A pioneer in selling both European and American art in New York City, Avery had a predilection for French paintings, for which he made annual buying trips to Europe in the 1870s. His wealthy American clients included William H. Vanderbilt, Edwin D. Morgan, William W. Corcoran, and James J. Hill. Avery was also a wood engraver and illustrated the following books: *The American Joe Miller* (1853), *Laughing Gas: An Encyclopedia of Wit, Wisdom and Wind by Sam Slick, Jr.* (1854), and *The Harp of a Thousand Strings* (1858). As the secretary of the Art Committee of the Union League Club, he was present for the first discussion of founding a Metropolitan Museum of Art for New York City. Avery was eventually to serve as a lifelong trustee of that institution. In his later years, he returned to his first love: that of collecting old prints and rare books. In 1900, he donated nineteen thousand rare prints to the New York Public Library. He also founded the Avery Architectural Library at

Columbia University in memory of his son, Henry Ogden Avery.

Aviation. Aeronauts have long been attracted to the 151-foot-tall Goddess of Liberty and have flown around her in airplanes, dirigibles, and helicopters. In 1909, pioneer aviator Wilbur Wright flew from Governor's Island and then circled around the Statue of Liberty to mark the Henry Hudson–Robert Fulton anniversaries. It was the first time an American had flown over a body of water. In 1910, aviator Glenn H. Curtiss, following the route of Robert Fulton's famous steamboat, the *Clermont,* finished the performance by dramatically circling the Statue of Liberty. In the same year, the Belmont Park air exposition included a spectacular Statue of Liberty air race, won by the American aviator John Moisant. To celebrate Liberty's new floodlights, the aviatrix Ruth Law flew over the monument; on the bottom of her airplane were affixed electric lights spelling out the word "Liberty." In 1928, Lieutenants John A. Macready and Oakley G. Kelly used the Statue of Liberty as a beacon in their transcontinental race. During the gyroplane craze of the late 1920s and early 1930s, several "autogyros" circumnavigated the statue.

In the post–World War II years, helicopters have more often been seen near the statue. A dramatic occasion for this was the demonstration of the technologically advanced French helicopter *Alouette* in 1957. Americans were astonished by its ability to hover gracefully next to the Statue of Liberty's head. In 1978, the U.S. Army parachute team known as the Golden Knights staged a picturesque performance of their capabilities in front of the Statue of Liberty. Throughout his two terms of office, President Ronald Reagan contributed to the aviation heritage of the statue by arranging for his helicopter pilots to fly close to Lady Liberty on his visits to New York.

A U.S. Army Golden Knights
parachute team performance,
1978

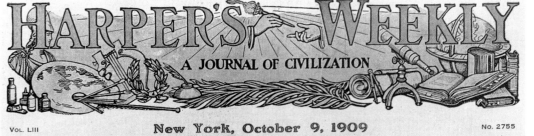

Vol. LIII   New York, October 9, 1909   No. 2755

(opposite page, right)
Autogyros of the early 1930s

(opposite page, left)
Helicopters and Liberty,
1940s

(left) Wilbur Wright's historic air flight over water,
September 1909

B

Babcock, Samuel Denison (*d.* 1902, New York, New York). Financier and member of the American Committee, Franco-American Union. During an extensive career in business, Babcock held the presidency of the International Bell Telephone Company and was also director of the American Exchange.

Bacon, Henry (*b.* 1839, Haverhill, Massachusetts; *d.* 13 March 1912, Cairo, Egypt). Painter and member of the French Committee, Franco-American Union; served on the Statue of Liberty Lottery Commission, 1879. Bacon went to France in 1864 to study painting techniques. Drawn to the orientalist tradition, he became known for his oil and watercolor paintings depicting Egyptian scenes. Exemplary works are *Church and Lake, The Erechtheum,* and *General View of the Acropolis* and *Sunset.*

Baldwin, William Henry (*b.* 17 September 1891, Saginaw, Michigan; *d.* 17 May 1980, Pennsylvania). Public relations counselor and fund raiser; a founder of the American Museum of Immigration. In 1951, the American Scenic and Historic Preservation Society (ASHPS), after having prevented the demolition of Castle Clinton, now sought ways of revitalizing the fort. Baldwin, a preservation society trustee, recom-

mended that because of its former role as an immigration depot, an immigration museum be established at the fort. The National Park Service approved of the museum idea but not the proposed location; it preferred locating the museum at the Statue of Liberty. In April 1952, Baldwin attended a meeting at which all parties accepted the new proposal. The public relations firm that Baldwin had founded in 1926 agreed to launch a publicity campaign. The preservation society was succeeded as sponsor of the project in 1953, when Baldwin and his fellow trustees formed the National Committee for the American Museum of Immigration; it was incorporated as a nonprofit organization in 1955. Two years later, Baldwin's firm was dropped as the AMI's paid publicity firm because of financial difficulties; however, Baldwin agreed to remain on the AMI board as vice-president.

Baldwin began his career in New York City as a newspaper reporter in 1914. After working in military censorship during World War I, he became a public relations counselor and fund raiser. Perhaps the greatest achievement of his career came in the 1920s, when he raised a $1 million endowment fund for Fisk University. He was elected chairman of the National Association of Public Relations Counselors in 1942. Baldwin was also active in the Democratic party.

Barbedienne, Ferdinand (*b*. 10 January 1810, Calvados, France; *d*. 1892, Paris, France). Founder. Auguste Bartholdi engaged Barbedienne's foundry to produce several works, including the statue of *Lafayette Arriving in America,* which has stood in New York City's Union Square since September 1876; it was cast in bronze by Barbedienne in 1874–75. The Barbedienne foundry, specializing in the reproduction in bronze of ancient and modern statuary, was established in 1841. Barbedienne's associate, Achille Collas (1795–1859), was the inventor of an ingenious machine for reduction of sculpture (1836), which allowed the firm to sell affordable imitations of statuary drawn from the great museums of Europe.

Bartholdi, (Anne-Marie-Auguste-) Charlotte, née Beysser (*b*. 29 September 1801, Ribeauvillé, Upper Alsace, France; *d*. 25 October 1891, Paris, France). Mother of sculptor Auguste Bartholdi. She was the daughter of the merchant Simon Beysser (1762–1829) and his wife, Marguerite Graf. Her father was mayor of Ribeauvillé, a village just north of Colmar. She had two older sisters, Frédérique and Henriette, and a brother, Charles. Frédérique Beysser married the writer Charles Jundt of Strasbourg; Henriette Beysser was married twice, first to Daniel Arnold (d. 1829) and then to Frédéric Rauter, both of them Strasbourg lawyers.

Charlotte married Jean-Charles Bartholdi (1791–1836), the prefecturate's legal counselor, on 3 December 1829; the couple lived in his charming old house at 30 Rue des Marchands, Colmar. They had four children: Jean-Charles (1830–85), Frédéric-Auguste (1831–32), Auguste-Charlotte (1833–33), and Frédéric-Auguste (1834–1904). Charlotte's husband died suddenly in 1836, leaving her alone to care for the two surviving children. In 1837, the Widow Bartholdi, as she would be known for the rest of her life, took the boys to Paris with her to live with her late husband's first cousin, the Countess Walther. She decided on this course because she thought that the city would offer greater ed-

ucational and career opportunities for them. However, she made certain that they spent each summer in Colmar, where she maintained the family house and property.

In sculpturing the Statue of Liberty, Auguste Bartholdi used his mother as the model. This was revealed in 1876 when Bartholdi invited Senator Jean Bozérian to his box at the Opéra. He said, "You will understand later the reason for my invitation." On drawing the curtains aside and entering, Bozérian was stunned to see the Statue of Liberty in the form of a dignified old lady. Bartholdi was there, and the senator turned to him and exclaimed, "That's the Statue of Liberty!" The sculptor pressed his hand warmly and replied, "Yes, it is. But do you know who this lady is? She's my mother."

As she grew older, Charlotte Bartholdi spent more and more time in her beloved Colmar. When her health began to decline noticeably by 1884, she once again took up permanent residence in Paris, this time in the home of her son

Auguste and his wife. In November 1884, Madame Bartholdi went to the Gaget and Gauthier foundry in the Rue des Chazelles to greet Victor Hugo and glimpse the Goddess of Liberty. She died in Paris, leaving her son in an "agony" of sorrow, and was buried in Montparnasse Cemetery.

Bartholdi, (Frédéric-) Auguste (*b.* 2 August 1834, Colmar, Alsace, France; *d.* 4 October 1904, Paris, France). Sculptor of *Liberty Enlightening the World,* his most celebrated work. Born the second son of Jean-Charles and Charlotte Bartholdi, he was christened at Saint Matthew's Church, in the Lutheran faith. Following his father's premature death in 1836, Auguste accompanied his mother, the Widow Bartholdi, to Paris. He was educated at the Lycée Louis-le-Grand in the 1840s and during holidays went to Alsace, where he was instructed in drawing by Martin Rossbach, a teacher at the Collège de Colmar. Bartholdi made sketches during holidays on the Normandy coast in 1847 and in London in 1851. In the late 1840s, he frequented the studio of Antoine Etex and studied painting under the Dutch artist Ary Scheffer. Scheffer advised him to become a sculptor, so Bartholdi began studying that art form under Jean-François Soitoux. In addition, he took lessons in architecture from Eugène Viollet-le-Duc. From October 1855 to July 1856, Bartholdi traveled with the painters Léon Gérôme, Narcisse Berchère, Léon Belly, and Edouard Imer to Egypt, Nubia, Arabia, and Ethiopia. Like many other Frenchmen of his time, Bartholdi was deeply influenced by the archaeological discoveries of Napoleon Bonaparte's expedition in Egypt and Jean-François Champollion's decipherment of the hieroglyphic inscriptions on the Rosetta Stone. He was similarly inspired by the colossal monuments of the ancient Egyptians, particularly the pyramids at Gizeh, the Colossi of Memnon, and the Great Sphinx.

Count Jean de Rapp was the subject of Bartholdi's first important sculpture, inaugurated on 31 August 1856 and presented at the

(opposite page) Charlotte Bartholdi (artist: Ary Scheffer, oil on canvas, 1855)

Paris Salon of 1857. This very large statue established the young sculptor's artistic reputation. Several other works followed, including the *Berber's Lyre* (1857) and the *Admiral Bruat* fountain (1863) in Colmar.

In 1865, Bartholdi attended a dinner party given by Professor Edouard de Laboulaye and his circle of fellow liberal intellectuals and politicians; at this dinner, Laboulaye began formulating a plan to build a monument to celebrate American independence and liberty. Laboulaye commissioned Bartholdi to execute a bust of the scholar, which was completed in 1866. The next year, Bartholdi met the Egyptian khedive, Isma'il Pasha, in Paris, and developed his idea for a Suez lighthouse, *Egypte apportant la lumière a l'Asie*. In 1869, Bartholdi went to Egypt for the opening of the Suez Canal by the khedive and Ferdinand de Lesseps, only to be disappointed when the khedive informed him that he would not commission the project. Back in France, Bartholdi joined the National Guard to fight in the disastrous Franco-Prussian War of 1870–71, in which Alsace was ceded to Germany as a spoil of war.

Discharged with the rank of major in 1871, Bartholdi returned to Laboulaye, now free to take up Laboulaye's Statue of Liberty project. The scholar sent him to the United States to sound out American support for the idea; this proved successful. Bartholdi also found a desirable site for the statue at Bedloe's Island in New York harbor and made maquettes of Liberty, the last of which was approved by Laboulaye in 1875. Following his return to Paris, Bartholdi was commissioned by the new French government to sculpt a statue of the marquis de Lafayette as a gift to the United States. Known as *Lafayette Arriving in America,* it was unveiled in New York with considerable fanfare in 1876.

Laboulaye, with his friends and political allies, launched the Statue of Liberty fund-raising campaign with the creation of the Franco-American Union in 1875, the goal of which was to raise 400,000 francs ($250,000). Laboulaye arranged Bartholdi's second trip to the United

States in 1876, to participate in the Philadelphia Centennial Exhibition and exhibit the colossal arm and torch of Liberty (which remained in the United States for fund-raising purposes until 1882); and to attend the unveiling of the Lafayette statue. Further, the sculptor married Jeanne-Emilie Baheux de Puysieux in Newport, Rhode Island. He unveiled the colossal head of Liberty at the Paris Universal Exposition in 1878. The fund-raising campaign for Liberty was completed in 1880, and work resumed on the statue at the foundry of Gaget, Gauthier and Company in the Rue de Chazelles, Paris. It was completed and formally presented to Levi Parsons Morton, the U.S. minister representing President Chester Arthur, on 4 July 1884. Viscount Ferdinand de Lesseps had by then succeeded the deceased Laboulaye as president of the Franco-American Union. Liberty was transported to the United States in 1885 and unveiled on Bedloe's Island in 1886. The Americans had agreed to build the statue's pedestal.

Auguste Bartholdi's other noteworthy works include a bust of Edouard Laboulaye (1866); a statue of the hero of the Gauls, Vercingétorix, at Clermont-Ferrand (1870); his engravings, *Old California* and *New California* (c. 1871–72); *The Curse of Alsace,* a statue (1872); *The Four Steps of Christian Life,* a bas-relief at Boston (1874); a statue of Champollion in Paris (1875); a bust of Léon Belly (1877); his colossal war memorial, the *Lion of Belfort* (1880); a bust of William Maxwell Evarts (1883); a smaller statue of *Liberty Enlightening the World* for Paris (1889); a statue of Gambetta (1891); and a sculptural group, *The Swiss Aiding Strasbourg* (1895). He produced some one hundred works of art in his fifty-two years as an artist: statues, bas-reliefs, sculptural groups, medallions, busts, fountains, tombs, and engravings. Much of the later work was influenced by his experiences in and views of the Franco-Prussian War. Bartholdi was decorated with the Legion of Honor as *chevalier* (1864), *officier* (1882), and *commandeur* (December 1886). He was also a Grand Orient Order Freemason (1875). He died in Paris of tubercu-

(opposite page) Auguste Bartholdi

(top) American adulation for Bartholdi is evident in this engraving c. 1886

(below) The Auguste Bartholdi Statue in Colmar (sculptor: Louis-Noel, 1907)

losis on 4 October 1904 and was buried in Montparnasse Cemetery on 7 October.

Bartholdi genealogy. Earliest known records of the family come from Germany. Veit Barthold, a Lutheran minister, was born in Monheim, in the Palatinate, in 1578 and died in 1630. He married Walburge Döderlein. Their son, also named Veit Barthold (1608–71), was a tailor in Aberzhausen, Bavaria. He married Anna Maria Heck and died in Frankfurt. Their son, Wilhelm Barthold (1637–90), lived in Frankfurt. He married Maria Juliana Welcker. Their son, Hans Georg Barthold, born in Höringhausen, Hesse, in 1674, was a Lutheran minister. He went to Strasbourg to study theology in 1694 and was graduated four years later. In 1713, he was appointed pastor of Wissembourg, a small town in northern Alsace; he died there in 1733. At some time, he gallicized his name to Jean-Georges Bartholdi. In Wissembourg, he married Marie-Dorothée Boell. She bore him eight children, of whom the seventh, Gilles-François, continues the line leading to our sculptor. Gilles-François Bartholdi (1723–87) became an apothecary. He met another apothecary, Jean-Charles Sonntag of Colmar, and married the latter's daughter, Marie-Ursule, in 1755. The couple had three sons—Jean-Charles, Gilles-Engelhard, and Jacques-Frédéric—each of whom was born in Colmar. Gilles-François Bartholdi's father-in-law persuaded him to move to Colmar in 1760. In 1766, a year after his father-in-law's death, Gilles-François took over the pharmacy, known as Le Soleil. The marriage into the Sonntag family and the operation of the pharmacy gained Bartholdi easy acceptance into the upper-middle-class households of Colmar. The eldest of the couple's children, Jean-Charles Bartholdi (1756–1830), became a doctor. He married Catherine-Dorothée, daughter of the architect Etienne Meyer, who was also Colmar's mayor (*stettmester*). At about this time, Jean-Charles Bartholdi obtained the dwelling at 30 Rue des Marchands, which the family would continue to own until Madame

Auguste Bartholdi gave it to the town of Colmar in 1907 as a museum to honor her husband. Jean-Charles and Catherine-Dorothée Bartholdi's son, also named Jean-Charles Bartholdi (1791–1836), was the father of Auguste Bartholdi. Their other children were Gilles-Engelhard Bartholdi (1759–1822), a bachelor apothecary, and Jacques-Frédéric Bartholdi (1763–1844), a prosperous banker.

Bartholdi, Jacques-Frédéric (*b.* 1763, Colmar, Alsace, France; *d.* 1844, Paris, France). Merchant and banker. He was the son of Gilles-François Bartholdi and granduncle of Auguste Bartholdi. In 1787, he married Catherine-Elisabeth Soehnée, daughter of a wealthy merchant. He entered the cotton business and moved to Paris in 1797 as a manager in the Soehnée firm. In about 1820, he opened a bank in the Rue Richelieu. In 1827, he became president of the Royal General Assurance Company. A devoted Lutheran, he served as vice president of the Paris Bible Society. His daughter Marie-Elisabeth married twice—first to a general and, following his death, to the marquis de Boubers, with whom she had two daughters, Clementine, viscountess Renouard de Bussière, and Marie-Louise, Madame Law de Lauriston. His son, Jean-Frédéric Bartholdi, followed in his father's footsteps and was created a peer of France.

Bartholdi, (Jean-)Charles (*b.* 20 December 1791, Colmar, Alsace, France; *d.* 16 August 1836, Colmar, Alsace, France). French civil servant. Charles Bartholdi was the husband of Charlotte Beysser Bartholdi and father of Charles and Auguste Bartholdi. He was apprenticed to his uncle, the merchant Jacques-François Bartholdi, in Paris. He returned to Alsace to complete his military service, attaining the rank of adjutant officer in the Legion du Berry Lancers. In 1829, he married Charlotte Beysser, a daughter of the mayor of Ribeauvillé. Charles Bartholdi spent the remainder of his brief life in Colmar in the high bureaucratic post of prefecture's counsellor.

Bartholdi, (Jean-)Charles (*b.* 1 November 1830, Colmar, Alsace, France; *d.* 1 April 1885, Vanves, France). Lawyer, genealogist, and scholar. Charles Bartholdi was the elder brother of Auguste Bartholdi. He studied art at the studio of Ary Scheffer but changed to law and was graduated from the Paris Faculty of Law in 1855. Although successful as a lawyer, he gained a reputation as an eccentric, especially in genealogy, in which he attempted to discover family connections with counts of the Holy Roman Empire and Italian nobility. He was also an amateur scholar and edited an archaeological and historical review, *Curiosités d'Alsace.* He suffered a nervous breakdown in 1862. A lifelong bachelor, he lived his last years in Vanves, near Paris.

Bartholdi, Jean-Frédéric, cr. First Baron Bartholdi, 1830 (*b.* 1794, Paris, France; *d.* 1839, Tours, France). Merchant and banker, son of Jacques-Frédéric Bartholdi (1763–1844). He married the Countess Louise-Catherine Walther. Their sons were Frédéric-Henri, Second Baron Bartholdi (1823–93), a high civil servant, and Philippe-Amédée Bartholdi (1830–1904), a diplomat who served as minister to the United States, 1875–78.

Bartholdi, Jeanne-Emilie, née Baheux (*b.* 25 October 1829, Bar-le-Duc, Lorraine, France; *d.* 12 October 1914, Paris, France). Wife of Auguste Bartholdi. Daughter of Pierre-Joseph Baheux, an impoverished spinning mill owner, and his wife, Louise Nestier Baheux, who died when Emilie was six. She had two sisters—one who lived in Australia and the other in Marseilles. She was adopted by a rich Canadian named Mrs. Walker, who brought her to Paris and retained her as a companion. Due to the Franco-Prussian War and the Paris Commune, Mrs. Walker, with Miss Baheux in tow, returned to her family in Montreal in 1871, but then went to Newport, Rhode Island, where they met Auguste Bartholdi. (It has been speculated that Bartholdi and Emilie Baheux may have first met in Nancy or in Paris.) Mrs. Walker died the next year, leaving Miss Baheux penniless. However, her heirs gave Emilie Baheux $3,000 invested in U.S. stocks as a source of income. As an adult, Emilie had altered her surname to the aristocratic "Baheux de Puysieux." She came to know Bartholdi better during his 1876 trip to the United States, and it was then that they resolved to wed. In this, they were assisted and en-

couraged by Miss Baheux's "cousin," Margaret LaFarge, and her husband, John. Bartholdi wrote to his mother to request permission to marry her and received written consent in November 1876. A civil marriage was recorded in the Newport town hall on 15 December, and on 20 December 1876, the couple were joined in holy wedlock by Unitarian pastor Charles F. Brooks at the LaFarges' house in Newport. They had a brief honeymoon in Niagara Falls and then went to New York for the New Year's celebration. They embarked for France on 26 January 1877. Jeanne-Emilie Bartholdi returned to the United States in 1886 and 1893, on both occasions in the company of her husband. After Auguste Bartholdi's death in 1904, she lived in their Paris house for the remainder of her life.

Bartholdi, Philippe-Amedée (*b.* 1830, Paris, France; *d.* 1904, Paris, France). French diplomat and younger son of Jean-Frédéric, First Baron Bartholdi. Amedée Bartholdi was the French minister to the United States, c. 1875–78, and minister to the Netherlands, c. 1878–79. He was a member of the French Committee, Franco-American Union. He was a lifelong bachelor.

Bartholdi Museum (Musée Bartholdi). Museum in the old Bartholdi family house located in the Rue des Marchands, Colmar, Alsace. Dedicated to the sculptor Auguste Bartholdi, the museum was opened with great fanfare on 18 November 1922 by Gabriel Alapetite, the French minister of justice, and Maurice Colrat, the regional commissioner-general. Its exhibits include the household furnishings of the artist and his family, many of his maquettes and other art works, and personal souvenirs and heirlooms. Notable curators have been Jacques Betz, Pierre Burger, and Jean-Marie Schmitt.

Bartholdi streets. Several streets have been named in honor of Auguste Bartholdi, including one in Paris (Rue Auguste Bartholdi), and two are Bartholdi avenues in the New Jersey towns of Jersey City and Butler.

(above) Bartholdi Museum, Colmar, France

(opposite page) Auguste Bartholdi working in his Paris studio

Bartholdi studios. The studios in which Auguste Bartholdi designed and planned the majority of his artistic works were located in Paris. They were in his house at 40 Rue Vavin. Here he resided and maintained three studios suited to a sculptor's calling from about 1854 until 1892. The main studio, giving onto the street, provided Bartholdi with comfort and the agreeable look of an artist's dwelling. The other two studios were set up as workshops. Bartholdi created his most famous works, including *Liberty Enlightening the World* and the *Lion of Belfort,* at the house in Rue Vavin. He resided there for about thirty-eight years. Bartholdi was forced to give up the house when Paris authorities decided to extend the Boulevard Raspail. In December 1892, the artist moved in protest to the Rue d'Assas, with his home at number 82 and his studio at number 84.

Bartholdi un sin Rabmannella (*Bartholdi and His Little Vinegrower*). Play written in Alsatian by Leopold Netter. It was presented at the Théâtre Alsacien in 1934. In 1936, Jean Kemm, in collaboration with Netter and Dupuy-Maznel, filmed a French version, retitled *La Liberté.* It was shown throughout France and in New York during the fiftieth anniversary of the Statue of Liberty's unveiling. The work was a biography of Alsatian sculptor Auguste Bartholdi.

Bartholdi visit of 1871. Auguste Bartholdi made this visit in the company of his assistant sculptor, Monsieur Marie Simon. Their ship, the *Pereire,* left France on 8 June 1871 and arrived in New York harbor and docked at a Hudson River pier on 21 June. During the voyage, the sculptor carefully reflected on how best to embody the monument to America's centennial of independence. Should it recall Delacroix's revolutionary liberty leading the masses through the bloodbath of war and rebellion, or Libertas, the austere and dignified goddess of Roman antiquity who was the first spirit of freedom? At the entrance of New York harbor,

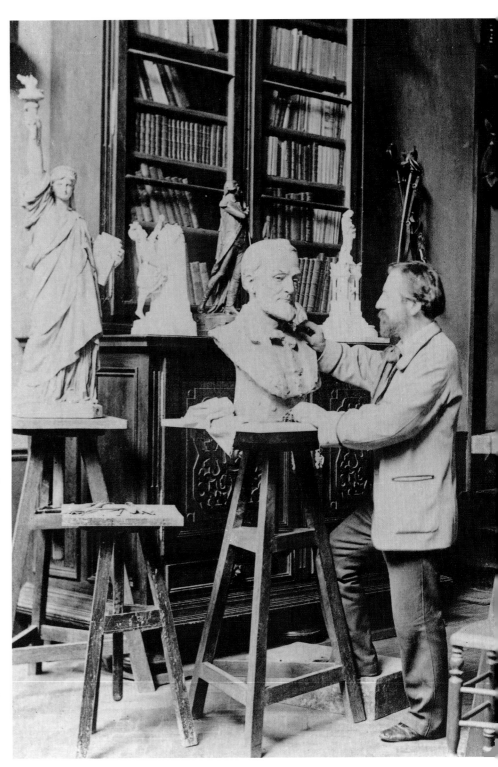

with Simon at his side, Bartholdi spotted the small island where he determined that Liberty must stand. Its commanding visual position in the harbor and its perfect proportions made the island an ideal location. Later he learned its name: Bedloe's Island.

Provided with Edouard de Laboulaye's various letters of introduction, Bartholdi was received by numerous American dignitaries and artists and made an extensive journey across the nation in order to acquaint himself with its character. Following a tour of New York City, he called on President Ulysses S. Grant at his house in the nearby town of Long Branch, New Jersey. They smoked cigars while the Frenchman eagerly explained his ideas. Although polite, Grant impressed Bartholdi as being rather cold. Bartholdi next traveled to Nahant, Massachusetts, where he visited the celebrated poet Henry Wadsworth Longfellow, whom he called "the American Lamartine." Bartholdi had known the poet's son Charles Longfellow in Suez, Egypt. Bartholdi visited Longfellow several times and also talked with Louis Agassiz. The Frenchman spent the Fourth of July with Senator Charles Sumner in Washington, D.C. He also became warm friends with the painter John La Farge. From the capital city, Bartholdi returned to New York, where he composed for Laboulaye a chronicle of his experiences, including information on his discovery of Bedloe's Island.

He continued to acquaint himself with America's most influential citizens. In New York City, he met the woman who translated Professor Laboulaye's books, Mary L. Booth, as well as Laboulaye's old friend Professor Vincenzo Botta of Columbia University and his wife, anthologist Anne Lynch Botta. In Philadelphia, he made friends with newspaper publisher Colonel John Forney—a step that would prove to be fruitful to both men over the years. He then went to Chicago, whose bustle and energy inspired him to dub the place "the most American city." Continuing his American pilgrimage, Bartholdi crossed the Rocky Mountains. At Salt Lake City, he saw Brigham Young, leader of the Mormons. In a written description, Bartholdi noted that he was a "happy husband of sixteen wives, and no less happily the father of forty-nine children." He continued onward to Sacramento and then San Francisco. Here, Bartholdi received a letter from Laboulaye and promptly responded. He described the cordial welcome that he had received from Henry Longfellow and Louis Agassiz. He now took the time to elaborate Longfellow's views: "Monsieur Longfellow, very enthusiastic, charged me to inform you that he will do all that you would like him to do in order to make a success of this demonstration of friendship at the Centennial." While in California, he also visited Sequoia Park and Stockton. On the return journey, he passed through Denver, Saint Louis, Cincinnati, and Pittsburgh. In all of the cities that he visited, he tried to persuade the people to help him with Laboulaye's centennial project by becoming correspondents and committee organizers; he fervently hoped that the project would become a national movement, but in this he was to be disappointed. At long last he was back in Philadelphia and then on to New York, where he embarked for France in October 1871.

Bartholdi visit of 1876–77. The sculptor's second visit to the United States. Edouard de Laboulaye arranged Bartholdi's appointment as the second adjutant secretary in the French delegation to the Philadelphia Centennial Exhibition in May 1876 and as a passenger aboard the ship *L'Amérique*. On the journey, Bartholdi made sketches of his fellow delegates and shipboard scenes. The sketches, accompanied by fellow passenger Louis Simonin's comic verses, were bound and published as a single volume of thirty plates under the title *Album du bord* in 1879. The money raised by the *Album* was donated to the Franco-American Union. In Philadelphia, Bartholdi again met Colonel John Forney, who introduced the sculptor to Philadelphia society. Several of Bartholdi's works were displayed at the Philadelphia Exhibition,

The arm and torch on display at the Philadelphia Centennial Exhibition, 1876

including Liberty's arm and torch, the Bartholdi Fountain (later purchased by Washington, D.C., for $6,000), *The Young Alsatian Vintner,* and his paintings of old and new California. Bartholdi next went to New York City for the unveiling of his statue of Lafayette in Union Square. Funds still had to be raised to build a pedestal for it. This was undertaken by the French Committee of New York, whose members included Frédéric Coudert (president), Charles Villa (secretary), Amédée Vatable (treasurer), Adolphe Salmon, Louis Delmonico, Louis de Bebian, and Henri de Stucklé (who also designed the pedestal). Before the pedestal could be finished, the Lafayette statue was unveiled in elaborate ceremonies on 6 September 1876, in the presence of French and U.S. troops, representatives of Masonic lodges, French societies, and thousands of spectators. On 8 September, Bartholdi and a small group of people, including Henri de Stucklé, Nathan Appleton, Jr., and several military officers, inspected Bedloe's Island, the prospective site of the Statue of Liberty. In celebration of the successful Lafayette statue unveiling, Stucklé arranged for a banquet to be given in Bartholdi's honor at the Lotos Club on 16 September. Bartholdi was similarly honored at the Palette Club on 12 October and attended several dinners at Delmonico's Restaurant at Madison Square. In September, the sculptor had overseen the installation of Liberty's arm and torch at the Philadelphia Centennial Exhibition. Bartholdi in the meantime was courting Jeanne-Emilie Baheux, and the couple were married in a religious ceremony at Newport, Rhode Island, on 20 December 1876. Bartholdi also continued the task charged to him by Edouard de Laboulaye: to set up American fund-raising committees for the Statue of Liberty. The French Committee for the Lafayette Statue project agreed to transform itself into the French Committee of New York, a branch of the Franco-American Union. Next, Bartholdi met with New York Union League Club members led by William M. Evarts at the Century Club on 2 January 1877 to plan the formation of the American Committee of the Franco-American Union. This last action was a triumph for Laboulaye and Bartholdi, for it committed the Americans to raise funds for the colossal statue's pedestal. Bartholdi and his new wife embarked for France on 26 January 1877.

Bartholdi visit of 1885. Bartholdi made this visit to ensure that the Statue of Liberty, which had been taken apart in Paris and shipped to New York, would be reassembled correctly. Accompanied by the painter Carrier Belleuse, Senator Edouard Millaud, and a journalist from *Figaro,* he boarded the steamer *Amérique,* on 24 October 1885. He was determined to advise and counsel chief engineer Charles Stone and others responsible for the work to ensure nothing would go wrong. He received many tributes during the visit. One was an elaborate dinner banquet at the Union League Club on 21 November, which included such guests as former president Chester Alan Arthur, Andrew Carnegie, Daniel F. Appleton, Noah Davis, Francis Lecompte, and members of the American Committee. Greatly reassured, he departed New York on 25 November 1885 aboard the *Normandie,* accompanied by such friends as Fritz Brauer, Vincente Hurtado (a friend of Georges Glaenzer), Captain Krebs (the aeronaut), A. Koechlin of Lille, theatrical producer E. L. Poy, and the singer Mademoiselle Spader.

Bartholdi visit of 1886. Auguste Bartholdi and his wife came to New York to participate in the inauguration of the Statue of Liberty on Bedloe's Island. They boarded the steamship *La Bretagne* at Le Havre on 17 October 1886 for an eight-day voyage, in the company of Viscount Ferdinand de Lesseps, Admiral Benjamin Jaurès, General Philippe-Xavier Pélissier, National Assembly deputies Eugène Spuller and Frédéric Desmons, geographer Napoléon Ney, journalist Charles Bigot, diplomat Baron Albert Salvador, and many others. The delegation was given a reception by the French colony of New York on 26 October. On the following day, Mayor William R. Grace presented Auguste Bartholdi with the key to the city. Bartholdi was also feted by the Colmarian Society of New York and the Alsatian Union of New York. On seeing the statue the sculptor said, "When I first came to America I dreamed of this. I said to myself: 'What a great thing it would be for this enormous statue to be placed in the midst of such a scene of life and liberty!' My dream has been realized. I can only say that I am enchanted. This thing will live to eternity, when we shall have passed away and everything living with us has moldered away." On 28 October, Bartholdi attended the inauguration parade in Manhattan and went to Bedloe's Island for the dedication speeches and unveiling. Bartholdi went to the crown of the statue and unveiled the French flag from Liberty's face at a signal from below. He was uneasy during the trip because of the delicate health of his mother. On 12 November, he announced he would have to cut short his visit to return to her bedside. As a result of the triumphant unveiling of the Statue of Liberty, the French government elevated Bartholdi to the grade of commander of the Legion of Honor on 30 December 1886.

Bartholdi visit of 1893. Bartholdi's fifth and final visit. He arrived in New York harbor aboard *La Champagne* with his wife on 3 September 1893. The Bartholdis were booked into the Hotel Martin, University Place. His intention was to investigate the condition of the Statue of Liberty, after having heard various complaints concerning its lighting failures and its worsening condition due to neglect. On the morning after his arrival, he had an interview with a reporter from the *New York Times* at the hotel. He gently criticized the care provided for the Goddess of Liberty by the Americans. The reporter asked the sculptor, "How did your statue impress you as you came up the bay?" Bartholdi replied, "Well, as you know, we arrived last night just fifteen minutes too late to be inspected by Quarantine officials. This gave me an opportunity of seeing from Quarantine the effect of the lighting of the statue. I must confess I was somewhat disappointed at the effect. The lights do not show up well at all. For appearance's sake in the daytime I should prefer to have the statue left as it is. But to make it show off the light better, I think it ought to be gilded.

Gilding is the very best background for either stationary, flash, or revolving lights. For the best possible results of the lighting, the statue is at present far too dark. Then, again, I hear that it is wearing away somewhat rapidly. Now the gilding would preserve the statue wonderfully. But, at any rate, it should be varnished at intervals to keep it in a good state of preservation. You have plenty of rich men here, and if they would only . . ." Bartholdi also went on to Chicago for a two-week visit to see the World's Columbian Exhibition.

Bartlett, Paul Wayland (*b.* 24 January 1865, New Haven, Connecticut; *d.* 20 September 1925, Paris, France). Sculptor and painter whose equestrian statue of the marquis de Lafayette was America's reciprocal gift to France for the Statue of Liberty. Fund raising for this monument was begun in 1898. Children contributed pennies and nickels until $50,000 had been raised. Bartlett was commissioned to undertake the work, completed in 1908. It is displayed in a garden of the Louvre in Paris.

Battery Park. Area in Lower Manhattan named for its former use as a land battery for harbor defense. The Battery has long been a gateway to the various islands of New York harbor, particularly Staten, Governor's, Ellis, and Bedloe's, as well as being an entry point for foreigners in the past. Today tourists coming to the Statue of Liberty and Ellis Island buy their tickets at the Circle Line office in Castle Clinton, a tourist attraction in its own right.

Beaux-Arts. Rich classical style of architecture taught in the nineteenth century at the Ecole des Beaux-Arts, founded in Paris in 1807. In 1830, the school's premises were relocated on the Left Bank of the River Seine and began to attract an international set of students. An example of its influence is seen in Charles Garnier's Paris Opera house (1861–75) and Joseph Poelaert's Palace of Justice in Brussels, Belgium. Its influence on American students was pro-

found; architects Richard Morris Hunt, Henry Hobson Richardson, and Charles McKim received their instruction there.

Bedloe, Isaac [also Isaack or Isaacq Bedloo, Bidloo or Bethloo] (*b.* c. 1620, Calais, France; *d.* February 1673, New York, New York). Dutch colonist and owner of Bedloe's Island, which he obtained in a colonial land grant in 1667. He served as an alderman and collector of customs. Captain Bedloe emigrated from Calais (France) and became a leading merchant in colonial Nieuw Amsterdam. The earliest colonial record of him dates from 1653, when he was haled before the colonial Court of Burgermeesters en Schepens on a charge of slander. In 1660, he was described in Dutch colonial records as a burger, or "select townsman," residing in the fashionable Hoogh Straat. The English conquest of New Netherland opened fresh opportunities for Bedloe. English authorities, anxious to appease the Dutch, rewarded those who cooperated with them, and Bedloe reaped great advantage from the new regime. The colonial court, or Worsh, appointed him a legal officer empowered to argue and examine cases, make decisions, and reconcile parties. The court twice appointed him an executor and caretaker of residuary estates in the Dutch community. The English conquest also removed certain trade barriers, and Bedloe invested in the tobacco trade with the English colony of Virginia. He purchased enormous casks of the plant to sell in New York. He also bought a three-quarters interest in the trading vessel *Jaen* and another one-quarter interest in another ship on the same day. In 1668, Bedloe (now an alderman) found perhaps an even better friend and patron in the new colonial governor, Colonel Francis Lovelace. In 1669, Bedloe was appointed captain of foot soldiers charged with laying a road that would connect New York with Harlem. The completion of this project strengthened Bedloe's prestige in the colony. Around this time, Bedloe began making improvements on one of the oyster islands off the New Jersey coast. Governor

Lovelace confirmed his ownership of the island on condition that it be named Love Island and that it also serve as a sanctuary for persons facing civil charges. Bedloe died suddenly in 1673; shortly after, Lovelace was overthrown by the Dutch navy, and Love Island was renamed Bedloe's Island.

On 16 May 1653, Isaac Bedloe married Elisabeth de Potter (also known as Lysbeth Potters), who had been born in 1636 in Batavia, Dutch East Indies (now Jakarta, Indonesia). Their children were Isaac Bedloe, Sarah (wife of Claes Burger), Catherine (wife of Thomas Harvardern), and Mary (wife of Joseph Smith). The

Widow Bedloe married on 22 April 1680 to Pieter de Lanoy, who later served as mayor of New York City (1689–90). By December 1693, Elisabeth de Potter may have been deceased, as her children equally divided their parents' estate among themselves, including Bedloe's Island.

Bedloe's Island (formerly anglicized as "Bedlow's Island"). The site of the Statue of Liberty, now officially known as Liberty Island, in deference to the sculptor's wishes. The name comes from Isaac Bedloe, an early colonial proprietor. Auguste Bartholdi spied Bedloe's Island for the first time on 21 June 1871 from the deck of the ship *Pereire*. Certain that it was the most suitable place to build the monument, he reported to Edouard de Laboulaye in a letter sent from New York in July 1871: "I have found an admirable site and have made a sketch of it; it is Bedloe's Island, in the middle of the bay. It belongs to the Government; [thus] is the common property of all the States, facing the narrows . . . the gateway of America." A visit to the island made him fully aware of the extent of the military base. He wrote, "Unfortunately there is a fort and, consequently, a conflict with the army, but I think this will be solved after the work has received approval."

Bedloe's Island was a military post from 1807 until 1937, Fort Wood being completed in 1811. It was used as an army garrison almost continuously between 1811 and 1904. In 1877, Fort Wood was last used for military purposes, but the rest of Bedloe's Island was kept for army use. In 1904, the troops were pulled out and replaced by the Army Signal Corps, which built a telegraph and wireless station on the island in 1905 and 1906. In 1923, the Signal Corps were withdrawn and replaced by the U.S. Military Police, which maintained a brig or prison for disorderly soldiers. The Military Police left on 30 September 1937, and Bedloe's Island came under the complete jurisdiction and management of the National Park Service, with one minor exception: the Park Service permitted the Army Signal Corps to continue operating their radio station. The station was at last removed to Governor's Island in 1941. The island was enlarged by landfill from approximately 10.7 acres to 12.7 acres from the 1920s through 1952. The island's name was changed to Liberty Island by a joint resolution of Congress, and signed into law by President Dwight D. Eisenhower on 3 August 1956. Despite its new name, many people still call it Bedloe's Island. *See also* Army; Bedloe, Isaac; Congressional Joint Resolution of 1877; Fort Wood; Governor's Island; Landscape and vegetation; Liberty Island.

Bell, Clark (*b.* 12 March 1832, Whitesville, New York; *d.* 22 February 1918, New York, New York). Lawyer and member of the American Committee, Franco-American Union, 1877–86; he served on the Press and Legislation subcommittees. In addition, he was a member of the La Pallette Club and was instrumental in arranging a banquet there in honor of Liberty's sculptor, Auguste Bartholdi, in 1877. Bell was an attorney for the Union Pacific Railroad in the 1860s and later for the Rock Island Railroad and the Pacific Mail Steamship Company. An expert in medico-jurisprudence, he founded and became the editor of the *Medico-Legal Journal* in 1884. He founded the American Congress of Tuberculosis in 1900. His many books included *Judicial History of the Supreme Court of the United States and Provinces of North America* (1895) and *Spiritism, Telepathy and Hypnotism* (1902).

Belly, Léon-Adolphe (*b.* 1827, Saint-Omer, France; *d.* 1877, Paris, France). Painter. Belly was a leader in the orientalist art movement and traveled with Narcisse Berchère, Auguste Bartholdi, Léon Gérome, and Edouard Imer in Egypt in 1855–56. This was actually his third trip to the Near East; he had already visited Lebanon, Palestine, and lower Egypt in 1850–51 with a scientific expedition led by the cartographer L. F. Caignart de Saulcy and the writer Edouard Delissot. A highly successful orientalist painter, he received a first-class medal for his *Les Pelerins se rendant à la Mecque* at the Paris Salon of 1851. He also achieved prominence in the ranks of the Barbizon school (roughly 1830–78), whose practitioners specialized in rustic and landscape scenes of the forests of Fontainebleau and the surroundings of the village of Barbizon, where they resided. Fellow Barbizon artists were François Millet, Camille Corot, Narcisse Díaz, William Morris Hunt, and César de Cock.

Bennett, James Gordon, Jr. (*b.* 10 May 1841, New York, New York; *d.* 14 May 1918, Beaulieu, France). Publisher of the *New York Herald,*

Aerial view of Bedloe's Island, c. 1950

for which Herald Square is named and where stands the world-famous Bennett Clock, named in his honor. When Bennett inherited the newspaper from his father in 1872, he continued his father's tradition of aggressive journalism. Bennett resided in Paris, where he maintained friendly relations with members of the Franco-American Union. He was characterized as Joseph Pulitzer's rival in the 1949 Broadway musical *Miss Liberty,* written by Robert Sherwood and Irving Berlin. Bennett was also a famous yachtsman.

Berchère, Narcisse (*b.* 1819, Etampes, France; *d.* 1891). Painter. Traveled with Auguste Bartholdi, Léon Belly, Léon Gérome, and Edouard Imer to Egypt in 1855–56. Berchère made his artistic debut at the Paris Salon of 1843. He began looking abroad for new inspiration and in 1847 traveled to the Balearic Islands and parts of Spain. His wanderings took him to Syria and lower and upper Egypt in 1848, where he made fine drawings that later served as the foundation for many of his paintings. He concluded his tour in the Greek islands and Venice in 1849–50. His return to Egypt with Bartholdi added to his collection of drawings. Several of his paintings won prizes at the expositions of 1859, 1861, and 1864. In 1860, Ferdinand de Lesseps chose him as painter-in-ordinary for the Suez Canal Company. In this post, he painted scenes of the new canal. Berchère, Belly, and Bartholdi were reunited in Egypt during the opening of the Suez Canal in 1869. Berchère has been ranked among the greatest orientalist painters of his time and was especially admired for his talent in expressing the solitary grandeur and mystery of Egypt. Among his exemplary works are *Vue du Nil près Rosette* (1853), *Environs du Caire* (1855), *Colosses de Memnon* (1859), *Caravane passant la mer Rouge* (1861), and *Le Désert de Suez, cinq mois dans l'isthme* (1863).

Beysser, Simon (*b.* 1762, Ribeauvillé, Alsace, France; *d.* 1829, Colmar, Alsace, France). Merchant and maternal grandfather of Auguste Bartholdi. Beysser was an innkeeper and supplier of all sorts of goods. He was mayor of the village of Ribeauvillé, 1810–14. He married a young Colmarian named Marguerite Graf, widow of Abraham Mattio. In 1829, their daughter, Charlotte, married Charles Bartholdi of Colmar. Beysser was distantly related to General Jean-Michel Beysser, a French Revolution hero who fought in the Vendée and was executed in 1794. *See also* Bartholdi, Charlotte; Bartholdi Genealogy.

Bigelow, John (*b.* 25 November 1817, Malden-on-Hudson, New York; *d.* 19 December 1911, New York, New York). Author, editor, and diplomat. Bigelow came to know Edouard de Laboulaye during the American Civil War after having read his pro-Union writings; he then wrote to the scholar, offering to copy and distribute the writings to French legislators, diplomatists, and all of the principal journals of Europe. He praised Laboulaye to Secretary of State William Seward and forwarded the writings to the United States, where translated versions soon appeared in such newspapers as the *Boston Daily Advertiser.* After this, Seward corresponded with Laboulaye with Bigelow as intermediary. In one 1865 letter, Laboulaye strongly urged Seward to ensure that America's freed slaves would be given voting rights. Following his return to the United States, Bigelow wrote to Laboulaye, "You enjoy here a more endurable fame than any of your country's people now living, permit me to add that I think it well deserved." Following Laboulaye's death in 1883, Bigelow delivered a eulogy in his memory before the Union League Club of New York.

Although Bigelow began his career as an attorney, he soon was drawn to journalism and then diplomacy. He was editor of the *New York Evening Post* (1850–61); he was appointed U.S. consul general in Paris in 1861 and then minister to France, 1865–66. During the U.S. Civil War, he helped to persuade Emperor Napoleon III not to grant diplomatic recognition to the

Confederacy. While still in Paris, Bigelow discovered the previously lost manuscript *Autobiography of Benjamin Franklin,* which he edited and published. He described the amazing events that led to his finding the lost Franklin manuscript in the book *Some Recollections of the Late Edouard Laboulaye* (1888) and credited Laboulaye with having helped him. Bigelow was also a founder of the New York Public Library.

Bigot, Charles (*b.* 14 September 1840, Brussels, Belgium; *d.* 15 April 1893, Paris, France). Journalist and historian. Bigot was the official representative of the Paris press at the inauguration of the Statue of Liberty in 1886. Originally a schoolmaster, Bigot became increasingly preoccupied with political education and social questions. He gave up teaching to become a full-time political journalist in 1871, making his mark in such periodicals as *La Siècle, La République française,* and *Revue des Deux Mondes.* His extensive foreign travels provided him a wealth of material to draw on for his many books and articles. His works include *Les Classes dirigeantes* (1875), *La Fin de l'Anarchie* (1878), and *De Paris au Niagara* (1887).

Black Tom explosion. Early on the morning of 30 July 1916, a disastrous explosion at the Lehigh Valley Railroad terminal on Black Tom Island, New Jersey, occurred. Barges and railway cars loaded with munitions and dynamite destined for France and England exploded, killing seven people, and causing a severe fire. The financial loss was estimated at $15 million. Military engineers inspected the Statue of Liberty the next day and found only minor damage. The Bedloe's Island Signal Corps post commander, Captain A.T. Clifton, announced that roughly one hundred rivets had popped loose from their fittings, chiefly in the right arm. Shrapnel and debris from the barges were found to have nicked Liberty's copper skin. Some buildings on Bedloe's Island were also damaged. For the next ten days, the statue was closed for repairs, and visitors' access to the torch was permanently ended on the ground of public safety. The total cost for repairs was estimated at $100,000. In 1939, after many years of speculation, the responsibility for the explosion was finally placed on German saboteurs. *See also* Borglum, Gutzon.

Bliss, Cornelius Newton (*b.* 26 January 1833, Fall River, Massachusetts; *d.* 9 October 1911, New York, New York). Wealthy dry goods merchant and politician. Bliss was a prominent Republican and a friend of Richard Butler. He was also a member of the American Committee and, with Butler and few others, managed affairs on Bedloe's Island after the Statue of Liberty was completed. After Butler's death in 1902, he was the last surviving active member of the American Committee. Bliss served as President William McKinley's secretary of the interior, 1897–99. He also served as president of the American Protective Tariff League.

Boller, Alfred Pancoast (*b.* 23 February 1840, Philadelphia, Pennsylvania; *d.* 9 December 1912, New York, New York). Civil engineer. Boller was the consulting engineer for construction of the foundation of the Statue of Liberty's pedestal in 1883. He advised General Charles Stone, contractor F. Hopkinson Smith, and subcontractors Alexander McGaw and John Drake. Boller's engineering credits include the Thames River Bridge (New London, Connecticut) and the Central Bridge, which crosses the Harlem River in New York City. He was the author of *Practical Treatise on the Construction of Iron Highway Bridges* (1876).

Booth, Mary Louise (*b.* 19 April 1831, Long Island, New York; *d.* 5 March 1889, New York, New York). Translator, author, and editor. Booth was the translator of Edouard de Laboulaye's *Paris en Amerique* (1863), published by Charles Scribner's Sons. She was also the translator of many of his liberal abolitionist friends. Booth introduced American readers to such books as Count Agénor de Gasparin's

LIBERTY STATUE STANDS TEST.

Only a Few Bolts Ripped Off—Loss on Island, $100,000.

After the United States Army engineers had surveyed the Statue of Liberty and the buildings on Bedlow's Island yesterday Captain A. T. Clifton, the commandant of the Signal Corps which is stationed there, said the repairs there would cost about $100,000.

It would take about ten days to make the temporary repairs, such as fitting the casings of the windows in the houses and the doors which had been blown off by the explosion, he said, and during that period the public would be excluded from the island.

Captain Clifton went on to say that the buildings were not damaged, with the exception of the western storehouse, a corrugated iron structure, which had been ripped to pieces by the concussion. The main structure of the Statue of Liberty practically escaped uninjured, as well as the power plant which provides the light. About 100 iron bolts in the inner shell of the statue had been ripped off and the base and outer envelope of the statue had been chipped a little with the shrapnel from the barges at Black Tom Island.

Captain Clifton stated that the officers' houses now had no windows, frames or doors, and were being blocked up with tarred paper until the proper materials could be obtained. Several of the shells found on Bedlow's Island had time fuses in them, the Captain said. Boxes of smokeless powder, with a quantity of wreckage of all kinds, were washed ashore yesterday.

The Uprising of a Great People (1861), *America Before Europe* (1862), and Auguste Cochin's *The Results of Slavery* (1863) and *The Results of Emancipation* (1863). Laboulaye sent her a short piece by Francis Lieber for translation into English, and the two became great correspondents. In 1868, so taken was Booth by Laboulaye's sincere devotion to reform that she urged him to become active in American politics. In 1871, Laboulaye gave Bartholdi a letter of introduction to Booth, ensuring that the sculptor could meet her in New York. In 1880, Booth received a sad letter from Laboulaye to tell her that he did not think he would live to see the statue of the Goddess of Liberty erected. Mary Booth was also the translator of *The Marble Workers' Manual* (1856) and the author of the highly successful *The History of the City of New York* (1859), which went through several printings.

Borglum, John Gutzon (*b.* 25 March 1867, Great Bear Lake, near Idaho Territory; *d.* 6 March 1941, Chicago, Illinois). Sculptor and painter, son of a Danish Mormon immigrant. Directly following the Black Tom munitions explosion of 1916, which slightly damaged the Statue of Liberty, Borglum was asked to inspect the torch and find a way to improve its illumination. His solution was to cut away portions of the copper and replace it with some 250 panes of amber glass. In the upper half, he cut the grid out of the original copper. He installed new copper in the lower half, which had been altered in 1892 when portholes and a glass belt were installed in a vain attempt to improve the torch's illumination. Borglum's work made the statue's interior vulnerable to water seepage and was the cause of the severe corrosion that Liberty would suffer in years to come. Borglum is world famous for his colossal sculpture of the American presidents George Washington, Thomas Jefferson, Abraham Lincoln, and Theodore Roosevelt on Mount Rushmore.

Borie, Victor (*b.* 1811, Tulle, France; *d.* 1880, Paris, France). Economist and journalist. Victor Borie, a friend of Edouard de Laboulaye, served as a member of the French Committee, Franco-American Union, 1875–80. He attended the gala inaugural banquet given at the Hotel du Louvre. Borie, a freemason of the La Justice lodge, was an ardent defender of freedom of the press and edited numerous liberal journals, which usually ran afoul of the government. His courage was often tested, as he was imprisoned and fled into exile more than once in defense of liberty. His periodicals included *Eclaireur de l'Indre* (1842–47); *Cause du Peuple* (1848, with his friend novelist George Sand); and *Le Travailleur* (1849). He supported the Charter of 1830 and in 1844, issued his own defiant views in *Liberté de la presse*. Although a politically controversial figure, his contributions in economics and agriculture were more influential. His many books include *L'Agriculture et la liberté* (1866) and *Etude sur le crédit agricole et le crédit foncier* (1877).

Boston. Capital city of the Commonwealth of Massachusetts. In 1882, Boston made a bid for the Statue of Liberty, in response to the slowness of the pedestal campaign in New York City. A jealous *New-York Times* editorial of 3 October 1882 commented: "She proposes to take our neglected statue of Liberty and warm it over for her own use and glory. Boston has probably again overestimated her powers. This statue is dear to us, though we have never looked upon it, and no third rate town is going to step in and take it from us. Philadelphia tried to do that in 1876, and failed. Let Boston be warned . . . that she can't have our Liberty . . . that great light-house statue will be smashed into . . . fragments before it shall be stuck up in Boston Harbor. If we are to lose the statue it shall go to some worthier and more modest place—Painted Post, for instance, or Glover, Vt." *See also* American Committee.

Botta, Vincenzo (*b.* 11 November 1818, Piedmont, Italy; *d.* 5 October 1894, New York, New York). Educator. Professor Botta was a longtime friend of Edouard de Laboulaye. In arranging Auguste Bartholdi's social itinerary in

A *New York Times* report on the Black Tom explosion

1871, Laboulaye ensured that the artist would meet Botta and his wife in New York. He would remain a steadfast friend of the Statue of Liberty project and live to see its unveiling. Botta was educated at the University of Turin (Ph.D., 1846) and served one term as a deputy in the Sardinian Parliament, 1849–50, before coming to the United States in 1853 to study its educational system. He decided to remain and became a U.S. citizen. He was professor of Italian literature at the University of the City of New York (now New York University), 1854–90. During the Civil War he was an ardent supporter of the Union cause. His publications included *Public Instruction in Sardinia* (1858), *Discourse on the Life of Count Cavour* (1862), *Dante as a Philosopher, Patriot and Poet* (1867), and *Introduction to the Study of Dante* (1886). He was made a commander of the Order of the Crown of Italy.

Boutmy, Emile (*b.* 13 April 1835, Paris, France; *d.* 25 January 1906, Paris, France). Philosopher and sociologist and teacher of constitutional law. One of Edouard de Laboulaye's students, Boutmy was deeply influenced by his professor's ideas of higher education in France. Thus encouraged, he founded the Ecole Libre des Sciences Politiques in 1872 to train elite French civil servants. Boutmy's school was endorsed by Laboulaye's political allies: François Guizot, Hippolyte Taine, Louis Wolowski, and Edmond Scherer. Their assistance helped it to overcome political opposition and receive a license to open. Laboulaye delivered a gracious address at its inaugural ceremony and agreed to serve as an adviser and to lecture occasionally. The school prospered and remained in existence until 1939, just prior to the collapse of the Third Republic. Boutmy was the author of *Etudes du droit constitutionnel* (1885).

Bozérian, Jean-François "Jeannotte" (*b.* 28 October 1825, Paris, France; *d.* 9 March 1893, Paris, France). Lawyer and politician. A friend and political ally of Edouard de Laboulaye,

Bozérian served as vice president of the French Committee, Franco-American Union, 1875–86, and was chairman of the Statue of Liberty Lottery Commission in 1879. It was Bozérian who famously revealed that the model of the Statue of Liberty was the sculptor's mother, Madame Charlotte Bartholdi, a story he recounted at many public events and dinner parties.

Bozérian began his legal career as a barrister in the Paris courts in 1851 and by 1860 rose to the position of prosecuting attorney for the Council of State and the Court of Cassation. Additionally, he was recognized as an expert in commercial law. In 1871, he was elected to the National Assembly and in 1876 was elected a senator, a position he would hold for the remainder of his life. Like his colleague Edouard de Laboulaye, Bozérian was politically a moderate republican. When he died in 1893, former Premier Jules Ferry eulogized him in the Senate chamber with these words: "As you know, he had many friends here and not a single enemy; he charmed by his loyalty, his good grace, his good humour. He shall be greatly missed." *See also* Bartholdi, Charlotte.

Broglie, Third Duke of (Prince Victor de Broglie) (*b.* 28 November 1785, Paris, France; *d.* 25 January 1870, Paris, France). Statesman and liberal politician. Served as prime minister and foreign secretary, 1835–36. A leading advocate for the abolition of slavery, he joined his son, Prince Albert, as a member of the French Emancipation Society founded by Edouard de Laboulaye in 1865. In 1855, the duke of Broglie was inducted into the French Academy. He wrote *Ecrits et discours* (1863) and issued his *Souvenirs* in 1866.

Broglie, Fourth Duke of (Prince Albert de Broglie) (*b.* 13 June 1821, Paris, France; *d.* 19 January 1901, Paris, France). Statesman and historian. Inspired by his father, the third Duke of Broglie, he assumed the mantle of leadership in the French antislavery movement; his considerable social influence was particularly valuable. He

was titular head of Laboulaye's French Emancipation Society, formed in 1865, and also presided over the International Emancipation Congress of 1867. He succeeded his father to the dukedom in 1870. After the fall of the Second Empire in 1871, he served as ambassador to Great Britain and was twice appointed prime minister in the 1870s. Among his numerous publications was *L'Eglise et l'Empire romain au IVe siècle* (1856).

Richard Butler

Butler, Richard (*b.* 9 August 1831, Birmingham, Ohio; *d.* 12 November 1902, New York, New York). Manufacturer and art collector. Secretary of the American Committee, Franco-American Union, 1877–1902. Butler came to New York City as an orphan in 1845. He rose to the position of president of the Butler Hard Rubber Company, which manufactured Ace combs, bowling balls, pipe stems, syringes, and surgical appliances at a plant in what is now Butler, New Jersey. His executive office was at 33 Mercer Street in Manhattan. Butler was one of Auguste Bartholdi's most steadfast and loyal American friends, throughout both the Liberty project and into the sculptor's later years, during which the two men kept up a close correspondence. Perhaps for Bartholdi's sake, Butler remained a dedicated member of the American Committee even after its numbers steadily evaporated in the years following Liberty's inauguration. Butler was a founder of New York City's Metropolitan Museum of Art and was a prominent member of the Union League Club and the Century Association. He was buried in Greenwood Cemetery, Brooklyn, New York.

C

Cameron, Simon (*b.* 8 March 1799, Lancaster County, Pennsylvania; *d.* 26 June 1889, Lancaster County, Pennsylvania). Politician, publisher, and banker. Senator Simon Cameron of Pennsylvania (1845–49, 1857–61, and 1867–77) was the author of the 1877 joint resolution of Congress that accepted France's offer to the United States of the *Statue of Liberty Enlightening the World*. Senator Cameron argued convincingly that a vote in favor of the resolution would cost the U.S. government nothing. The resolution passed both houses of Congress and was signed into law by President Ulysses S. Grant on 3 March 1877.

Cameron began his career as a journeyman printer and rose to the post of printer of the Commonwealth of Pennsylvania, 1825–27. Afterward, he became a banker and financier and grew rich and influential through many successful investments. But his true talent lay in politics, where his almost unrivaled ability made him one of the most successful machine politicians of his era. For a time, he was an important adviser to President Abraham Lincoln, serving as secretary of war, 1861–62, and minister to Russia, 1862–63. *See also* Congressional Joint Resolution of 1877.

Camp, Oswald Edward, civil servant. Oswald Camp served as superintendent of the Statue of Liberty National Monument, 1935–37. His predecessor was George Palmer (1934–35). Although he developed some early interpretive programs, Camp's administration was marked by major national events that took place on the island, especially the Statue of Liberty's Golden Jubilee (fiftieth anniversary), celebrated on 28 October 1936. This event attracted even greater media attention than anticipated since President Franklin Delano Roosevelt came to Bedloe's Island and presided over the festivities in person. He was accompanied by a motorcade entourage that included French ambassador André de Laboulaye, Interior Secretary Harold Ickes, and American military and naval officers. President Roosevelt arranged a naval parade in New York harbor led by the *U.S.S. Indianapolis.* He then delivered a ringing speech warning the world to preserve democracy in spite of the dark clouds gathering in Europe.

In September 1937, Superintendent Oswald Camp arranged the celebration of the 150th anniversary of the U.S. Constitution, in which an altar of liberty was constructed, after the manner of ancient Roman religion. This reminded visitors of the statue's origins as Libertas, the goddess of liberty. Camp was also deeply inter-

Oswald Camp on the torch with NBC journalist John B. Kennedy, 1936

ested in the history and symbolism of the monument; some of his findings were included in his manuscript, "A Brief Pictorial History of the Statue of Liberty and Its Interesting Surroundings and Approaches" (1937). *See also* Anniversaries; Liberty Altar; National Park Service; Palmer, George; Roosevelt, Franklin D.; Superintendents.

Cap of Liberty. *See Pileus libertatis.*

Castle Clinton National Monument (formerly Castle Garden, 1823–1950). Located in Battery Park, New York City, this structure was originally built as a military fortification (1807–11) and named West Battery; in 1815 it was renamed

Castle Clinton in honor of Governor George Clinton of New York. In 1823, it was demilitarized and given to the city by the War Department; entrepreneurs were allowed to take it over and gave it yet another name, Castle Garden. It now functioned as one of New York City's major locations for entertainment and public receptions. Many spectacular events occurred there, including the start of the thirty-mile balloon flight of aeronaut Charles Durant in 1830, and it was the site of the American debut of singer Jenny Lind, the Swedish Nightingale, in 1850. The Castle Garden Theatre existed there from 1839 to 1855. Beginning on 3 August 1855, Castle Garden was used by the New York state government as an immigration depot; over 7 million

Aerial view of Castle Clinton and Battery Park

immigrants were processed there, largely Germans, Irish, English, Scottish, Scandinavians, and French. During its heyday, the depot was run by a board of commissioners, a superintendent, and over 100 employees; its detention facility was on Ward's Island in the East River, which was available by steamboat, shuttling between the two places. Due to corruption, scandals, and the maltreatment of aliens, the Castle Garden immigration establishment was closed in April 1890. From 1896 to 1941, Castle Garden served as the New York City Aquarium. Thereafter it was abandoned and nearly demolished by city authorities before President Harry S. Truman intervened in 1950, declaring it a national monument; he also restored the old name, Castle Clinton. The castle was restored in the 1970s and has since housed the ticket booths for the Statue of Liberty and Ellis Island ferry service.

Castle Garden. *See* Castle Clinton National Monument.

Century Association. Exclusive art society, commonly called the Century Club. The Century Association was the site of the first meeting of what became the American Committee, which was charged with building the pedestal of the Statue of Liberty. The meeting was held on 2 January 1877, with William M. Evarts presiding. The club was founded in 1846 by William Cullen Bryant and others to promote interest in literature and the fine arts. Its membership included prominent artists, amateurs, and society men, all of whom were included in New York's prestigious Social Register.

Ceracchi, Giuseppe (*b.* 1760, Corsica, Italy [later ceded to France]; *d.* 1802, Paris, France). Sculptor. In 1791, this neoclassical artist came to the United States to persuade the U.S. Congress to pay him a $30,000 commission to sculpt a colossal monument to the goddess of liberty, whose torch symbolically scatters the fog of error and illuminates the universe. It was planned as a group of figures 100 feet in height. The proposal

rejected, Ceracchi returned to France. In 1793, he tried in vain to win a commission from the radical National Convention to sculpt a colossal female figure representing *Le Peuple Français* with the word *lumière* on her forehead. He later sought to obtain a commission to build a monument to fellow Corsican Napoleon Bonaparte, who had gained absolute power in France. When Bonaparte pointedly ignored him, Ceracchi joined in a conspiracy against his life. However, the plot was discovered, and Ceracchi and three of his fellow conspirators were executed.

Channing, William Ellery (*b.* 7 April 1780, Newport, Rhode Island; *d.* 2 October 1842, Bennington, Vermont). Clergyman best known for his leadership of the Unitarian church. Channing's writings, distinguished by a high moral tone and a fervor and solemnity of expression, greatly influenced the thinking of Edouard de Laboulaye. They were much in the manner of his sermons. Laboulaye was impressed by Channing's ideas about the goodness of God, the essential virtuousness and perfectibility of man, and the freedom of the human will and its responsibility for action. Channing's writings also drew Laboulaye's thoughts to the vital question of human slavery in Christian society: "Every man is a rational and moral being and must be recognised by all as a Person, not as a 'thing' merely. He can never be an instrument for the purposes of others. He may not be deprived of his prerogative of personality. ALL MEN . . . ARE EQUAL." One of his best-known books was *On the Evils of the Spirit of Conquest and on Slavery* (1837).

Chase, William Merritt (*b.* 1 November 1849, Franklin, Indiana; *d.* 25 October 1916, New York, New York). Painter and organizer of the Pedestal Art Loan exhibition in 1883. The success of the exhibit was largely achieved through Chase's extensive personal contacts in Europe. Chase was prominent in art circles as painter, teacher, and guide. He was also a president of the Society of American Artists. His most noted works are his still lifes.

Chenoweth, Alexander Crawford (*b.* 5 June 1849, Baltimore, Maryland; *d.* 13 April 1922, New York, New York). Contract engineer. In 1883, Chenoweth and his workmen, many of whom were Italians, carried out the necessary excavations and subsoil engineering in preparation for the construction of the masonry foundation of the Statue of Liberty's pedestal.

Choate, Joseph Hodges (*b.* 24 January 1832, Salem, Massachusetts; *d.* 14 May 1917, New York, New York). Lawyer, diplomat and member of the American Committee, Franco-American Union. Choate owed the advancement of his career to his friend and law partner William M. Evarts. Their firm was Evarts, Choate, Sherman & Léon. A popular after-dinner speaker, Choate was also a prominent member of the Union League Club, the Century Association, and the Harvard Club. He served as U.S. ambassador to Great Britain, 1899–1905.

Circle Line. Ferryboat sightseeing company. Founded in April 1945, the original partners were Frank Clair, Joseph Moran, Francis J. Barry and the brothers Gerald O'Driscoll and Jeremiah T. Driscoll. In 1947, Jeremiah Driscoll left to form his own sightseeing boat service and was replaced by a new partner, George Sanders. Operating around New York harbor, the original Circle Line fleet was composed of former yachts, the most famous of which was *Sightseer*. In the 1950s, the company began to enlarge by acquiring former infantry landing craft naval vessels that had transported thousands of battle-ready troops to Europe and North Africa during World War II. Circle Line converted them into attractive sightseeing boats under the names *New Yorker* (1952) and *Circle Line* (1953).

(below) Circle Line ferry docked at Liberty Island

(opposite page) Army garrison quarters at Bedloe's Island, 1864

Garrison Quarters Bedlows Island 1864

In 1981, Circle Line ceded control to new investors, while the original owners continued to operate the Circle Line–Statue of Liberty ferry, now known as the Statue of Liberty–Ellis Island Ferry, Inc.

Civil War. At the time of its completion in October 1886, twenty-one years after the end of the Civil War, the Statue of Liberty was widely regarded as a symbol of the preservation of the Union. Members of the Union League Club saw *Liberty Enlightening the World* as a monument to the northern victory. At the inaugural ceremony, at least two significant references to the Civil War were made. Senator William Evarts of New York clearly saw France's gift as a celebration of the defeat of the Confederacy: "The liberty loving people of France hailed the triumph with an immense and vivid enthusiasm. Nor was this . . . to be satisfied but by some

adequate and permanent expression of their sympathy in our fiery trial." French consul Albert W. Lefaivre spoke directly of the "momentous war which . . . ended in the emancipation of five millions of human brethren. This religious faith [in the goddess Libertas] was perfectly justified . . . and . . . it entrusted to Liberty the task of healing the wounds caused by the war."

Edouard de Laboulaye, ideological father of the statue, was himself a president of the French Anti-Slavery Society and an honorary member of the Union League Club. As the great American war unfolded, Laboulaye published several important pieces on the question in the *Journal des Débats.* The first was *La guerre civile aux Etats-Unis,* in which he wrote, "To intervene in this struggle on the side of slavery would be to deny our past. In America as everywhere else, France can only be allied to liberty."

Laboulaye's influence over the editorial board caused the *Journal des Débats* to remove Confederate sympathizer Michel Chevalier from his post of chief commentator on American affairs and confine his writings to economic matters. Laboulaye's literary contributions to the Union League's Loyal Publication Society were also especially valuable to the Union cause. These efforts brought him many honors, including honorary membership in the Massachusetts Historical Society and an honorary doctorate from Harvard University (1864); the Union League Club of Philadelphia enthroned a bronze bust of Laboulaye in its lobby, and the Union League Club of New York had his portrait painted and hung in the club.

Cleveland, (Stephen) Grover (*b.* 18 March 1837, Caldwell, New Jersey; *d.* 24 June 1908, Princeton, New Jersey). Statesman and politician. Governor of New York, 1883–85; president of the United States, 1885–89, 1893–97. Cleveland was drawn into the affairs of the Statue of Liberty in 1884 when the American Committee, having run out of funds to complete the statue's pedestal, arranged for the passage of a measure in the New York State legislature that billed the state $50,000 to help complete the structure. Governor Cleveland promptly vetoed the measure and denounced it as an unconstitutional use of state funds. This was a great disappointment to the fund raisers.

Cleveland's election to the presidency in the autumn of 1884 vouchsafed yet three further roles for him during the unfolding months when the statue was transferred from French to American jurisdiction. In 1886, he was confronted by a congressional appropriation to pay for repairs and improvements on Bedloe's Island and the installation of electric lighting for the statue, and to fund the inaugural ceremonies. But Senator William Evarts, president of the American Committee, was able to overcome any presidential misgivings through the evidence of the committee's having successfully raised over $300,000 and by arguing that the 1877 resolution warranted a legal obligation of the federal government to cover these final costs. By 1886, Cleveland was "most happy to cooperate" and formally asked Congress to appropriate the necessary funds; $56,500 was duly appropriated that August.

Cleveland's next task was to decide whether to preside at the statue's inaugural ceremonies to take place on the 28th of October. Initially he designated General John Schofield to stand in for him, but perhaps realizing the importance of the occasion and seeing its effect on New York and the rest of the nation, as well as its international implications, he altered his plans and left Washington by train with several cabinet members. The president presided over the ticker-tape parade from his reviewing stand at Madison Square. Greatly impressed by the popular adulation conferred on Liberty's sculptor, Auguste Bartholdi, Cleveland looked at Bartholdi and exclaimed, "You are the greatest man in America today!" The presidential party sailed to Bedloe's Island aboard the *Dispatch,* where Cleveland officially accepted the statue on behalf of the people of the United States, in these words:

> The people of the United States accept with gratitude from their brethren of the French Republic the grand and completed work of art we here inaugurate. This token of the affection and consideration of the people of France demonstrates the kinship of republics, and conveys to us the assurance that in our efforts to commend to mankind the excellence of a government resting upon popular will, we still have beyond the American continent a steadfast ally.

> We are not here today to bow before the representation of a fierce warlike god, filled with wrath and vengeance, but we joyously contemplate instead our own deity keeping watch and ward before the open gates of America, and greater than all that have been celebrated in ancient song. Instead of grasping in her hand thunderbolts of terror and of death she holds aloft the light which illuminates the way to men's enfranchisement.

> We will not forget that Liberty has here made her home, nor shall her chosen altar be neglected. Willing votaries will constantly keep alive its fires and these shall gleam upon the shores of our sister republic thence, and joined with answering rays a stream of light shall pierce the darkness of ignorance and man's oppression, until Liberty enlightens the world.

In November, President Cleveland assigned the care and maintenance of the statue of *Liberty Enlightening the World* to the Light-House Board, an agency of the U.S. Department of the Treasury. *See also* Dedication; Inauguration; Jurisdiction; Pedestal Campaign.

Cochin, Pierre-Suzanne Augustin (*b.* 11 December 1823, Paris, France; *d.* 15 March 1872, Paris, France). Social scientist, politician, and abolitionist. Secretary of the French Anti-Slavery Society. Augustin Cochin dedicated his life to helping the disadvantaged members of French society. His interest in improving conditions in Paris drew him into municipal politics; he held the offices of deputy mayor of the Tenth Arrondissement, 1850–53, and mayor, 1853–58. He rose to municipal councilor, 1858–59, but resigned in opposition to French action in the Italian war of unification and utterly withdrew from politics. He then turned his attention to writing and produced his *L'Abolition de l'esclavage* (Abolition of Slavery) (1861), which was acclaimed by the French Academy and translated into English. This indisputably established his reputation as a leading light on the topic. His other books included *De la Condition des ouvriers français* (1862), *Paris, sa population, ses industries* (1864), *La Manufacture de glaces de Saint-Gobain de 1665–1865* (1865), *La Service de santé avant et pendant le siège de Paris* (1871), and *Etudes sociales et économiques* (1880, edited by the duke of Broglie). With the fall of the Second Empire, Cochin returned to politics, serving as prefect of the Seine-et-Oise department before his death. He was elected a member of the Academy of Moral Sciences in 1864.

Coinage. Widely used on ancient Roman coinage, Libertas, goddess of liberty, was revived in various forms for use on French, American, and Mexican coinage in modern times. In 1792, she was brought to U.S. coinage in the classic form of Libertas; in the twentieth century, she was transformed into the modern world's most recognized interpretation of liberty. The ancient goddess was adopted as a symbol of the state on French medallions and seals, and occasionally

Grover Cleveland

coinage, in France's five republican governments, the images appearing on the Seal of the Second Republic (Jean-Jacques Barre, 1848) and the medallion of the Second Republic (Eugène-André Oudiné, 1848). The Statue of Liberty sculpture was adapted from them, probably under the influence of Edouard de Laboulaye. In 1865, a memorial gold medal was struck in France by Laboulaye's political circle as a gift for Mary Todd Lincoln, widow of President Abraham Lincoln.

Colmar. Located in Upper Alsace, France, near the foothills of the Vosges mountains, this town was the birthplace of the sculptor Auguste Bartholdi (1834) and the residence of his family for generations. Many of Bartholdi's artistic works can be seen there, including a handsome statue of General Rapp (1856), located in Rapp Square; a bronze statue of Baron Lazare Schwendi (1897) in the Old Customs Square; a statue, *Alsatian Cooper* (1902), atop the Maison des Têtes; the Admiral Armand Bruat statue (1863) in the Champs de Mars; and the Jean Roesselmann statue and fountain (1888) in the Place des Six Montagnes Noires. Near the River Lauch is the fountain and bronze statue *Le Petit vigneron* ("Little Vine-Grower," 1869). Fellow Alsatian sculptor Louis Noël executed an imposing statue of Bartholdi that stands in one of Colmar's lovely parks. The Bartholdi family house, 30 Rue des Marchands, contains the Bartholdi Museum, which opened to the public in 1922.

Colossus of Rhodes (Latin: *colossus solis;* Greek: Χολοσσός ἡλίου). Monument dedicated to Helios, the Greek god of the sun, and erected in thanksgiving to him. Although the worship of the sun was almost universal throughout the ancient world, it became particularly popular on the Greek island of Rhodes, where the people adopted Helios as their patron deity. The devotion to the god reached its zenith in the fourth century B.C. when the giant bronze "Colossus of the Sun," 110 feet high, bearing a

torch of freedom, was constructed. This astonishing piece of religious sculpture was one of the seven wonders of the ancient world.

Congressional Joint Resolution of 1877. The Statue of Liberty was formally accepted by the United States in a joint resolution of Congress. After President Ulysses Grant sent a letter expressing his support of such an action, Congressman Abram Hewitt of New York introduced the legislation on 22 February 1877 (H.R. 196); by a unanimous order of the House Foreign Affairs Committee, it was sent to the floor of the House of Representatives. It was read three times without objection and passed. It went next to the Senate, where it was approved by the Foreign Relations Committee and sent to the floor of the Senate, where it was

Sketch of the Colossus of Rhodes

introduced by its sponsor, Senator Simon Cameron of Pennsylvania. It was passed on 27 February and signed into law by President Grant on 3 March 1877, his last day in office. The resolution states:

> Whereas the President has communicated to Congress the information that citizens of the French Republic propose to commemorate the one hundredth anniversary of our independence by erecting, at their own cost, a colossal bronze statue of "Liberty Enlightening the World" upon a pedestal of suitable proportions, to be built by private subscription upon one of the islands belonging to the United States in the harbor of New York;
>
> And, whereas it is proper to provide for the care and preservation of this grand monument of art and of the abiding friendship of an ancient ally:
>
> Therefore,
>
> Be it resolved by the Senate and the House of Representatives of the United States in Congress Assembled, That the President of the United States be hereby authorized and directed to accept the colossal statue of "Liberty Enlightening the World" when presented by citizens of the French Republic, and to designate and set apart for the erection therefore a suitable site upon either Governor's or Bedloe's Island, in the harbor of New York; and upon completion thereof shall cause the same to be inaugurated with such ceremonies as will serve to testify the gratitude of our people for this expressive and felicitous memorial of the sympathy of our sister republic; and he is hereby authorized to cause suitable regulations to be made for its future maintenance as a beacon, and for the permanent care and preservation thereof as a monument of art and of the continued good will of the great nation which aided us in our struggle for freedom.

Construction (France). Auguste Bartholdi's final clay model for the Statue of Liberty, the *modèle d'étude,* was approved by Edouard de Laboulaye and his associates of the Franco-American Union in 1875 and was unveiled at their opening fund-raising banquet held at the Hôtel du Louvre in November 1875. Bartholdi and Eugène Viollet-le-Duc, who were responsible for the successful construction of the monument, reached an agreement with Honoré Monduit, principal of the respected Monduit and Béchet foundry, 25 Rue de Chazelles, Paris, to undertake the construction work. Viollet-le-Duc was responsible for choosing both copper as the medium and repoussé as the method, as well as selecting the Monduit foundry (a firm that he had used for other projects since 1861). Laboulaye originally intended the monument to be given to the United States in time for that nation's centennial; however, the work required was too great to expect an early completion. Therefore, it was decided to build a portion of the giant goddess as an example of what was to follow. The arm and torch were constructed in time for display at the Philadelphia Centennial Exhibition in August 1876. The second portion of the statue to be constructed, its head, was also fabricated at Monduit's (on this occasion, his younger partners, Gaget and Gauthier, probably played an equal role). The completed head, with nimbus spikes, was unveiled at the Paris Universal Exposition of 1878. Viollet-le-Duc made plans for the repoussé copper body's internal structure in this way: "In place of masonry there will be inferior coffers rising to about the level of the hips; these shall be filled with sand. Were an accident to happen, stonework would have to be dismantled; [but] with the coffers, simply open the flap valve affixed to the inner surface of each one and the sand will run out by itself." However, he died before his plans were realized, and Bartholdi had to seek guidance elsewhere.

The brilliant engineer Gustave Eiffel was chosen to succeed Viollet-le-Duc. Eiffel designed an entirely new structural support system for the statue, one similar to the railroad bridges for which he was so famous. In about

1880, he designed a powerful iron tower or pylon. Rising 96 feet, 11 inches high (29.54 meters), it is composed of four iron posts, which bear the statue's weight. From the pylon, there is a secondary body of trusswork and flat bars that the copper skin or sheets hang upon, and also a single projecting beam (the arm) extending vertically a full 40 feet, 7 inches (12.38 meters). While Eiffel was engaged in these activities, Bartholdi and his trusted assistant sculptor, Marie Simon, were not idle. They supervised work on the statue's body parts at Gaget and Gauthier's (Monduit had retired in 1878). Using the approved *modèle d'étude* (1.25 meter, about 4 feet tall, clay *maquette*) the foundry staff and artisans were prepared to begin their work.

In building a giant Liberty, three enlargements were made from wood and plaster; then solid wood impressions were taken from them and laminated together. The first enlargement stood a bit over 9 feet (2.85 meters); the next, four times higher, about 36 feet (10.97 meters). This structure was studied in every detail to avoid any mistake. Then it was divided into many sections, and each of these was copied at four times their size. Each new enlargement (each section required 9,000 separate measurements) created could now be joined together through lamination to form the completed, colossal statue. The final enlargement stood 111 feet (33.9 meters) high (with the arm and torch added, it reached 151 feet, or 46 meters).

The next step was to prepare the copper for the repoussé sculpturing work. (The metal had been donated to the Franco-American Union by industrialist Pierre-Eugène Secretan.) Heated by a soft flame, the copper was ready for hammering into the wooden molds. In this repoussé process, the copper grew thinner (3/32 of an inch, or 2.5 millimeters, in thickness). Thus the sculpture was shaped: its drapery, left arm, tablet, feet, and shackle. Now came mounting the sculptured copper onto the iron pylon that stood in the foundry yard, where it had been erected in 1881; workers stood on a scaffold that

(opposite page, clockwise from top left) Liberty's pylon, designed by Gustave Eiffel (Paris, 1881); Liberty under construction (Paris, 1882); entrance through Liberty's foot (Paris, 1882); Liberty nearing completion (Paris, late 1883)

(below) Honoré Monduit

surrounded it, and the metal pieces were screwed into Eiffel's pylon. The statue, completed by January 1884, became a popular tourist attraction. On 4 July 1884, it was formally presented to the American minister to France, L. P. Morton. Months later, it was disassembled, each piece meticulously coded, and then carefully packed in 214 numbered and labeled cases for shipment to the United States, aboard the *Isère*. The voyage lasted from 21 May until 17 June 1885. *See also* Anchorage; Construction (United States); Pedestal; Repoussé.

Construction (United States). The Statue of Liberty was transported to the United States aboard the French frigate *Isère* and arrived in New York harbor on 17 June 1885. The 214 cases of varying sizes that contained the statue's

body parts were unloaded at Bedloe's Island to await unpacking when the statue's pedestal was complete (April 1886). From May through August 1886, the statue's iron pylon and its secondary and tertiary extensions were assembled. The copper body pieces were taken out of cases (some required repair) and then riveted together. Soon the skeleton of Liberty appeared atop the pedestal, held in place by General Charles P. Stone's effective steel anchorage system. In attaching the first copper sheet to the skeleton, the first two rivets driven in were christened "Bartholdi" and "Pulitzer." Due to the pedestal beneath, a scaffold could not be erected for the workers, so the men had to carry out their jobs by hanging as best they could from the armature (there were no casualties). The huge, thin copper sheets (3/32 inches, or 2.5

(below) A group of the Liberty construction crew, Bedloe's Island, 1886

(opposite page, left) Reassembly of Liberty atop pedestal, Bedloe's Island, 1886

(opposite page, right) Calvin Coolidge

millimeters, thick) were riveted on the skeleton horizontally. By early October 1886, only the head was still missing, but it was soon attached. Landscape gardener Frederick Law Olmsted supervised a clean-up of Bedloe's Island in time for the statue's inauguration and dedication on 28 October 1886. *See also* Anchorage; Construction (France); Foundation; Pedestal.

Coolidge, Calvin (*b.* 4 July 1872, Plymouth, Vermont; *d.* 5 January 1933, Northampton, Massachusetts). President of the United States, 1923–29. President Coolidge was confronted with a curious anomaly in 1924 when he learned that the War Department had named the Statue of Liberty a national monument (in its Bulletin 27), without legal authority, in 1915. The department had assumed that the Antiquities Act

of 1906 (the legislation that controlled the matter of national monuments) could be enacted by the secretary of war without approval of the president. This was an enormous blunder, for the act explicitly empowers the president alone to proclaim and set aside federal property and artifacts as national monuments. The Statue of Liberty's listing as a national monument by the War Department was noticed by National Park Service director Arno Cammerer in March 1923. He at once sent a query about the legality of the status, declaring, "I cannot understand under what authority other than the President's a monument can be created under the Antiquities Act of 1906." The War Department, after some bureaucratic delay and considerable embarrassment, rescinded Bulletin 27. On 15 October 1924, President Coolidge resolved the matter by legally proclaiming the statue, pedestal, and Fort Wood the Statue of Liberty National Monument. *See also* Antiquities Act.

Copper. Two hundred thousand pounds (100 tonnes) of copper were used in the construction of the Statue of Liberty. The donation of 128,000 pounds (64 tonnes) of copper came from industrialist Pierre-Eugène Secrétan. It is not certain if the remainder also came from him or from another source. It is believed that Secrétan obtained the copper from his interests in the Franco-Belgian–controlled mine of Vigsnes, Karmøy, Norway. Copper from this mine was exceptionally pure.

On the Periodic Table of the Elements, copper has the atomic number 29, the symbol Cu, and the atomic weight of 63.546. The metal is malleable (it can be bent and shaped without cracking, when either hot or cold), ductile (it can be drawn into a thin wire), and an excellent conductor of both heat and electricity. In a pure state, copper is noncorrosive (it cannot rust); it also protects itself from dampness by forming a naturally green film as a physical coating. This patina halts further corrosion. *See also* Corrosion; Patina.

Copyrights and patents. The Statue of Liberty and its pedestal received copyright and patent protection under U.S. law from the Library of Congress and the U.S. Patent Office. "Augustus F. Bartholdi and Henry de Stuckle of New York" received copyright 9939G on 31 August 1876 for the "Statue of American Independence," accompanied by a photograph of a model of the Statue of Liberty and a painting or sketch of it. On the same day, he received copyrights 9940 for the "Statue of General Lafayette" and 9941 for his decorative fountain (now known as the Bartholdi Fountain). As "August Bartholdi, sculptor of Paris," he received patent 10,893 on 5 November 1878 for "a bust of a female figure symbolizing Liberty and Enlightenment." An illustration was included, and "Geo A. Glaenzer and Robt. M. Hooper" were

witnesses. On 18 February 1879, "Auguste Bartholdi of Paris" received patent 11,023 for his original design of a monument statue representing "Liberty Enlightening the World, being a commemorative monument of independence of the United States." Attached was a full-figure drawing of the Statue of Liberty. Architect Richard Morris Hunt received copyrights 8762Q and 8763Q for his "Statue of Liberty Pedestal." He received patent 16,167 on 14 July 1885 for design of a "Pedestal or Stand for a Statue" (Statue of Liberty pedestal). A. R. Spofford, the librarian of Congress, signed all of the copyrights; each patent was signed by two witnesses and attested by two Patent Office clerks. *See also* Pedestal patent and copyright; Spofford, A. R.

Cornell, John Black (*b.* 7 February 1821, Rockaway, Long Island, New York; *d.* 26 October 1887, Lakewood, New Jersey). Iron manufacturer, and philanthropist. Cornell's firm supplied iron and steel used in the anchorage system of the Statue of Liberty in 1885. In addition, Cornell was a member of the Union League Club.

Corrosion. General corrosion of metals such as copper is caused by electrochemical reactions that occur uniformly over the whole of a metal's surface. A gradual thinning of the copper damaged the Statue of Liberty, and the salt-bearing sea air of New York harbor caused further damage. Liberty also suffered from the effects of galvanic corrosion, caused by a reaction of the iron armature bars against the copper plates, saddles, and rivets. Corrosion was especially bad in sections where the armature bars were secured by copper saddles. During the 1982–86 restoration, the corroded iron bars were replaced with bars made of steel, and entire sections of corroded copper were replaced by new copper of verdigris hue. *See also* Patina; Restoration of 1982–86; Torch.

Coudert, Frédéric René (*b.* 1 March 1832, New York, New York; *d.* 20 December 1903, New York, New York). International corporate

(opposite page, top) Copper fragment of Liberty, showing original color.

(opposite page, bottom) Interior corrosion of Liberty, 1980s

FRAGMENT
DE LA STATUE COLOSSALE DE LA LIBERTÉ
PRÉSENTÉ
À L'ILLUSTRE APÔTRE
DE LA PAIX, DE LA LIBERTÉ, DU PROGRÈS
VICTOR HUGO
LE JOUR OU IL A HONORÉ DE SA VISITE
L'ŒUVRE
DE L'UNION FRANCO-AMÉRICAINE
29 NOVEMBRE 1884

COURRIER DES ÉTATS-UNIS

Organe des Populations de Langue Française

FONDÉ EN 1828

109e ANNÉE. — No. 69.

NEW YORK, SAMEDI 31 OCTOBRE 1936

Membre de l'Associated Press

LE NUMÉRO: 5 CENTS

Temps probable pour aujourd'hui dans la région de New York: Beau.

Copyright 1936 by Courrier des Etats-Unis Corporation

Lire en page 4:
Les Accords Monétaires
Par FRÉDÉRIC JENNY

La Célébration du Cinquantenaire de la Statue de la Liberté a Lieu en Présence de MM. Roosevelt, de Tessan et de Laboulaye

Le président Lebrun envoie à la nation américaine un message de fervente amitié de la part du peuple français. Le président Roosevelt rappelle qu'en acceptant le don de la France, le président Cleveland a déclaré que l'Amérique n'oublierait pas que la liberté a élu domicile parmi nous. Les Etats-Unis ne séparent pas la paix de la liberté

La France et les Etats-Unis, dit M. de Tessan, restent fidèles au principe de liberté bien que certaines nations se soient tournées vers le despotisme et les formes autocratiques de gouvernement. M. de Laboulaye explique comment son grand-père eut l'idée de faire un don à l'Amérique à l'occasion du centième anniversaire de l'Indépendance américaine

Vingt-huit octobre 1936. Date qui doit compter dans l'histoire de la France et des Etats-Unis. La plupart d'entre nous n'ont pas vu cette émotionnante cérémonie de l'inauguration de la Statue de la Liberté, il y a cinquante ans. Combien, parmi nous, assisteront aux cérémonies de son centenaire? Car il y aura un centenaire, nous en sommes sûrs. D'ici cinquante ans, la liberté, apanage de nos deux nations, existera toujours.

M. André Lefebvre de Laboulaye, ambassadeur de France à Washington

L'île Bedloe s'est parée dans l'attente de ses visiteurs d'aujourd'hui. Les couleurs françaises et américaines décorent l'œuvre de Bartholdi, des navires de guerre américains, pavoisés, attendent l'arrivée du président des Etats-Unis. Le ciel s'enorgueillit de quelques nuages qui, balayés par le vent, font mieux ressortir les glorieux rayons du soleil. Des avions survolent l'île, tournent autour d'elle, comme pour la protéger..

Midi quarante. La foule, qui arrive en masse depuis la fin de la matinée, s'assied. Au premier rang, symbole de la continuité entre le passé et le présent, se trouve M. de Drambour, qui en qualité d'officier de *L'Isère*, foula du pied la passerelle de ce navire qui apporta en pièces détachées la statue qui maintenant nous domine de toute sa sereine puissance.

De grands paquebots, se dirigeant vers l'Europe, passent devant nous.

Une heure. L'estrade s'anime. M. Barclay, des Boy Scouts of America, préside à la cérémonie préliminaire de la présentation des prix qui vont être décernés aux gagnantes des deux concours qui furent organisés à l'occasion du cinquantenaire. Il donne la parole à Mme Charles Cyrus Marshall, qui, en termes émus, fait résonner la note de toutes les cérémonies de l'après-midi: patriotisme sain et bonne volonté entre nations. La présidente de la National Life Conservation Society remet à Mlle Sheila Jane Crooke la médaille frappée à l'occasion, et qui lui est offerte en reconnaissance de son poème, classé premier dans le concours.

Le commandant en chef des Veterans of Foreign Wars of the United States, M. B. W. Kearney, ainsi que Mme Winifred D. Toussaint, ancienne présidente des Ladies Auxiliary de la même organisation, présentent une médaille ainsi qu'un chèque de cent dollars à Mlle Edna Falk, lauréate du concours de composition dont le sujet était également l'immortelle statue. Avec un sérieux qui n'arrive pas à assombrir la grâce de son âge, Mlle Falk remercie; puis M. Barclay présente M. Maurice G. Roux, distingué président de la *Fédération des Vétérans Français* de la Grande Guerre, qui offre à la gagnante un voyage en France.

Discours de M. Maurice G. Roux

Chère Edna,

Avant que le jury du concours du meilleur essai sur la Statue de la Liberté ait rendu sa décision, j'avais eu l'occasion de lire les trois copies qui avaient survécu à l'élimination de milliers d'autres; je pensais que la vôtre était de beaucoup la meilleure, et je formais des vœux pour que vous soyiez déclarée lauréate du concours. Plus tard, j'ai appris que les jurés, d'accord avec moi sans le savoir, avaient choisi votre essai; je me réjouis de leur décision et à la pensée qu'ils étaient en vérité de très, très bons juges.

J'aime votre composition parce que vous avez eu conscience la signification exacte qu'a prise la statue de la Liberté dans le cœur des hommes de la nation française qui l'ont offerte à l'Amé-

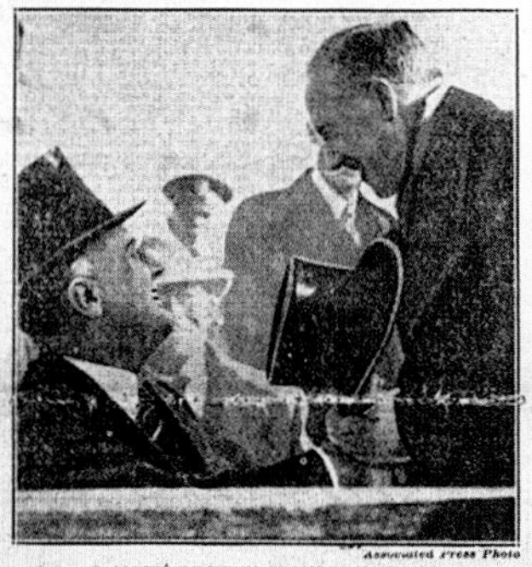

Associated Press Photo

L'AMITIÉ DE DEUX GRANDES NATIONS

Le président Roosevelt souhaite la bienvenue à M. François de Tessan, sous-secrétaire à la présidence du Conseil, au pied de la Statue de la Liberté à la cérémonie du cinquantième anniversaire du monument

rique, et pour l'idéal des Américains qui son devenus ses gardiens, car cette statue de la Liberté n'est, en aucune façon, une statue ordinaire: c'est une déesse, symbole de la liberté de pensée et du droit de s'exprimer, un droit plus précieux encore aujourd'hui, parce qu'il est plus rare que vous ne pouvez le croire à cette époque d'éducation avancée. Vous avez la chance de vivre dans cette grande nation libre, et je suis heureux de vous inviter à visiter cet autre grand pays, la France, où la liberté est aussi considérée le bien le plus précieux de l'homme.

Vous comprendrez facilement la France; parce que votre essai montre la qualité de votre cœur, vous qui, de tous les élèves de toutes les écoles supérieures des Etats-Unis, et sans l'avoir jamais vue, avez le mieux senti le véritable sens de la Statue de la Liberté.

Au bon vieux temps, votre grand'mère aurait dit qu'une jolie fée était venue vous apportant sa baguette magique, mais vous, très moderne vous-même, avez seulement pris pour votre fée la plus grande statue du monde, cette déesse née de la main des hommes, et fait de votre essai votre talisman. Alors les choses se passèrent comme dans les vieux contes; toute votre petite ville est venue vous voir partir pour les terres lointaines, le tapis magique des temps présents vous a amenée à travers l'espace jusqu'à la plus grande cité du monde, et vous voilà ici maintenant, reçue par le président de votre grand pays, et par l'ambassadeur d'une autre grande nation, aimée et fêtée par tous; demain vous continuerez votre merveilleux voyage par delà l'océan que jamais encore vous n'avez vu, à bord du plus beau et du plus grand des navires, pour être accueillie et fêtée par les ministres du peuple de France.

Vous avez très bien mérité ces honneurs, Edna, et je suis fort heureux de vous offrir ce voyage en France, au nom de la Fédération des Vétérans Français de la Guerre aux Etats-Unis, et j'espère que chaque minute de votre séjour en France vous sera une joie toujours renouvelée. Vous ne verrez pas seulement Paris, notre superbe capitale, et notre vieille cité de Colmar, où le maire, ici présent, a exprimé le désir de vous accueillir, mais aussi et surtout les Français, et j'espère que vous les aimerez autant que je suis certain qu'ils vous aimeront.

Associated Press Photo

Le président Roosevelt, face à la statue, prononce un discours devant la foule venue dans la petite île de Bedloe pour assister au cinquantenaire

Après les remerciements émus de Mlle Falk, M. Barclay présente M. Peter Dudan, des Boys of America, qui présente à M. Oswald E. Camp, conservateur de la statue, une médaille frappée dans le même métal que celui qui servit à construire l'œuvre de Bartholdi, et que M. Dudan avait reçu de Mme Victor Hugo, descendante du grand poète, lors du voyage qu'il fit l'été dernier en France comme

Le président Lebrun

"Good Will Representative" de son organisation. La musique de la police new yorkaise et celle du 18e régiment d'infanterie jouent. Une salve retentit dans le grand port. Le président a mis le pied sur l'île de Liberté.

Arrivée du président

Le Très Révérend William T. Manning, évêque du diocèse épiscopal de New York, élève la voix pour invoquer la clémence de Dieu sur le président et sur les deux pays, ainsi qu'en faveur de la paix, puis récite un *pater noster* ému. M. La Guardia, maire de New York, préside. Soudain, les notes du *Star Spangled Banner* résonnent dans l'air, et voici M. Franklin D. Roosevelt, habillé d'une jaquette et d'un pantalon gris, coiffé d'un haut de forme, qui s'avance vers le fauteuil d'honneur qui lui est réservé. Il se découvre. La foule applaudit frénétiquement. Sur l'estrade, nous remarquons M. François de Tessan, sous-secrétaire d'Etat à la présidence du Conseil de la République française, venu pour représenter notre pays aux cérémonies. M. de Tessan est assis à la droite du président. M. La Guardia présente alors M. Harold L. Ickes, secrétaire de l'Intérieur, qui fait l'éloge de l'esprit symbolisé par la statue et la cérémonie, puis le maire de New York présente M. André Lefebvre de Laboulaye, ambassadeur de France aux Etats-Unis.

Discours de M. André de Laboulaye

M. le Président
M. le Maire,
Mesdames et Messieurs,

C'est un grand jour, en vérité, que celui-ci pour les amis de la liberté, et il convient de remercier le gouvernement américain et tout spécialement le président des Etats-Unis, d'avoir tenu à célébrer solennellement le cinquantième anniversaire de l'inauguration de ce monument.

Liberté! Ce mot a dans tous les temps couvert dans l'esprit des hommes de vastes et heureux horizons. Il correspond en effet à une aspiration inhérente à la nature humaine. Mais ce don magnifique qui confère à l'homme sa haute dignité est aussi un don redoutable. De l'usage qu'il en fait dépend son infortune ou sa félicité.

Il en est pour les sociétés comme pour les individus et l'abus de la liberté peut leur être parfois aussi funeste que la privation de ses bienfaits.

L'histoire nous montre que les institutions libérales ne peuvent être pratiquées avec fruit que quand la majorité d'un peuple se maintient à un niveau de moralité, de savoir et de raison suffisamment élevé pour lui permettre de tirer profit de la liberté sans la laisser dégénérer en abus.

Les bouleversements économiques et sociaux que suivent d'ordinaire les grandes catastrophes telles que la guerre, constituent par l'ébranlement des mœurs et la succession précipitée de périodes de prospérité et de crise, un grand danger pour les institutions politiques fondées sur la liberté.

C'est ainsi que nous avons vu depuis la fin de la Grande Guerre sombrer l'un après l'autre nombre de régimes démocratiques et plusieurs nations soumises à des formes de gouvernement que l'on pouvait croire appartenir au passé.

Heureusement, la contagion n'a pas gagné le monde civilisé tout entier et trois des plus grands pays tiennent toujours haut et ferme l'étendard de la liberté: les liens cordiaux qui unissent leurs gouvernements et leurs populations augmentent encore la confiance que l'on peut avoir légitimement dans le maintien de leurs institutions libérales et démocratiques pour leur bien propre et pour l'honneur de l'humanité.

L'occasion qui nous réunit aujourd'hui évoque un événement unique, je crois, dans les annales de l'histoire: le don d'un peuple à un autre peuple en vue de symboliser un commun idéal.

Bien qu'en raison des liens de famille étroits qui m'unissent à lui, je sois un peu embarrassé pour citer le nom de l'homme qui eut l'idée de ce don du peuple français au peuple des Etats-Unis, je suis obligé de dire que c'est à Edouard de Laboulaye, mon grand-père, que revient cet honneur. Ce qui m'excuse d'agir ainsi c'est non seulement le souci de la vérité, mais encore la forme particulièrement gracieuse que M. le Secrétaire de l'Intérieur a bien voulu donner à son invitation, en marquant que ma participation à cette cérémonie était spécialement souhaitée pour la raison que j'étais le petit-fils d'Edouard de Laboulaye.

Professeur de législation comparée au Collège de France, membre de l'Institut, député puis sénateur, mon grand-père avait toujours été un admirateur convaincu et passionné des institutions américaines et un ardent défenseur de la liberté dans son propre pays.

Lorsque approcha la date de l'anniversaire de l'Indépendance des Etats-Unis, dès 1865, dans ses discours et ses écrits, il soutint l'opinion que la France ne pouvait pas laisser passer un événement de cette importance et auquel elle avait été étroitement mêlée, sans manifester son attachement et sa sympathie à l'Amérique. Au cours d'entretiens qu'il eut avec ses amis, Henri Martin, Remusat, Gasparin, etc., et auxquels assista le jeune sculpteur Bartholdi, aussi épris de liberté que lui-même et brûlant de mettre son talent au service de nobles causes, s'ébaucha peu à peu le projet définitif de la statue qui s'élève aujourd'hui à Bedloe Island.

Mais les circonstances rendaient la réalisation pratique du projet difficile et de longs et persistants efforts durent être entrepris pour l'assurer.

A la suite de la guerre franco-allemande et de l'écroulement du régime impérial, les Français, désireux de donner à leur pays des institutions libres, reprirent courage et le grain qu'avaient semé dans les esprits Tocqueville, puis Laboulaye lui-même et bien d'autres en vantant les bienfaits de la démocratie pratiquée en Amérique, porta son fruit.

En 1875, "l'Union Franco-Américaine" se constitue à Paris sous la présidence d'Edouard de Laboulaye et la vice-présidence d'Henri Martin, en vue d'ériger un monument commémoratif du centième anniversaire de l'Indépendance américaine, tandis qu'un comité correspondant s'organisera à New York afin de trouver les fonds nécessaires à la construction du monument qui servira de piédestal à la statue.

Le comité de Paris adresse aussitôt un vibrant appel au peuple français et est autorisé à ouvrir une souscription nationale pour recueillir des fonds.

Les termes de cet appel définissent parfaitement l'esprit et l'objet de l'entreprise.

"Il s'agit d'élever, en souvenir du glorieux anniversaire, un monument exceptionnel. Au milieu de la rade de New York, sur un îlot qui appartient à l'Union des Etats, en face de Long Island, où fut versé le premier sang pour l'Indépendance, se dresserait une statue colossale, se dessinant sur l'espace, encadrée à l'horizon par les grandes cités américaines de New York, Jersey City et Brooklyn. Au seuil de ce vaste continent plein d'une vie nouvelle, où arrivent tous les navires de l'univers, elle surgira du sein des flots; elle représentera: "La Liberté éclairant le Monde." La nuit, une auréole lumineuse, partant de son front, rayonnera au loin sur la mer immense.

"Ce monument sera exécuté en commun par les deux peuples, associés dans cette cause fraternelle, comme ils le furent jadis pour fonder l'Indépendance. Nous ferons hommage de la statue à nos amis d'Amérique. Ils se joindront à nous pour subvenir aux frais de l'exécution et de l'érection du monument qui servira de piédestal.

"Nous affirmerons ainsi par un souvenir impérissable l'amitié que le sang versé par nos pères avait scellée jadis entre les deux nations."

Cet appel fut entendu et le 6 novembre 1875 on put célébrer par un banquet la naissance de la statue.

A ce banquet, qui réunissait des hommes de toutes opinions, les principaux ministres, des députés, des généraux américains et français, des académiciens, des littérateurs, des savants, des journalistes représentant toutes les variétés et les nuances politiques, Edouard de Laboulaye déclara:

"Dans un siècle, on célébrera encore le centenaire de l'Indépendance. Nous ne serons plus alors qu'une poussière oubliée; l'Amérique, qui aura plus de cent millions d'habitants, ignorera nos noms, mais cette statue restera; elle sera le souvenir de cette fête, la preuve visible de notre affection. Symbole d'une amitié qui brave les orages du temps, elle sera là, inébranlable au milieu des vents qui gronderont autour de sa tête et des flots qui briseront leur fureur à ses pieds."

Comme le prouve la cérémonie de ce jour, la première partie de cette prédiction a été dementie par les faits. Avant même que soit célébré le second centenaire de leur Indépendance, les Etats-Unis ont plus de 100 millions d'habitants et les noms des hommes qui ont eu l'idée de la Statue de la Liberté et l'ont réalisée ne sont pas oubliés du peuple américain.

Mais s'il est vrai que, suivant cette même prédiction, la liberté devra affronter maints orages, nous pouvons cependant avoir pleine confiance dans la lumière qui rayonne de cette statue, car elle représente la vraie liberté, la seule contre laquelle ni vents ni marées ne prévaudront jamais et qui continuera, tant qu'il y aura sur cette terre des hommes à l'esprit élevé et au cœur bien placé, à éclairer le monde et à maintenir étroit les liens d'amitié qui unissent les peuples américain et français.

L'ambassadeur de France présente ensuite M. François de Tessan, qui interrompit son discours afin de permettre au président Roosevelt de parler avant que l'on entendît le discours du président de la République française.

Discours de M. François de Tessan

La France républicaine a voulu s'associer avec ferveur à cette fête de la Liberté qui, dans les circonstance présentes, revêt pour elle un caractère particulièrement symbolique.

La présence du grand président des Etats-Unis à cette cérémonie en souligne la haute portée. Elle sera chaleureusement appréciée de toute la nation française. Qu'il me soit permis de dire à M. Franklin Roosevelt tout le plaisir que j'éprouve de le remercier au nom de notre gouvernement pour son geste si amical.

Aussi bien, non seulement le chef de l'Etat, M. Albert Lebrun, a tenu à adresser un message de chaleureuse amitié au peuple américain, mais encore, le gouvernement démocratique de mon pays m'a délégué ici pour affirmer, avec force, sa fidélité aux principes d'indépendance, d'émancipation humaine et de paix, qui sont à la base constitutionnelle de nos deux Républiques.

Il y a cinquante ans exactement — pour l'inauguration de ce monument dû à un fils d'Alsace aujourd'hui réintégré à la France — le président Cleveland se félicitait de l'heureuse rencontre de la volonté populaire américaine et de la volonté populaire française.

Dans son allocution, il célébrait la déité sereine montant la garde aux portes ouvertes de l'Amérique, plus grande que toutes les autres déités chantées par les poètes: "Au lieu de tenir dans la main, disait-il, les foudres qui portent la terreur et la mort, elle soutient le flambeau qui guide les hommes dans la voie de l'affranchissement." Et le chef de l'exécutif américain annonçait que de fidèles adorateurs entretiendraient, dans les temps à venir: "les feux destinés à percer l'ignorance jusqu'à ce que la Liberté éclaire le monde".

En vérité, si le programme n'a pas été entièrement rempli et si la liberté ne projette pas ses lueurs sur toutes les parties de l'Univers, les Etats-Unis — pas plus, d'ailleurs, que la France — n'ont rien à se reprocher. En toute occasion, ils ont montré, dans leurs relations, leur générosité politique, leur dévouement à la cause de la liberté. Ils n'ont pas hésité, lorsque de graves menaces [illegible] le monde et quand ils ont vu en danger les fondements d'une civilisation issue de la liberté, à se porter à son secours. Nous nous sommes ainsi retrouvés — Américains et Français — fraternellement unis sur les champs de bataille de la Marne et de l'Argonne, pour le triomphe d'un même idéal.

Nous aurions souhaité n'user toujours que d'armes pacifiques. Dans la victoire nous sommes demeurés modérés et humains. Notre ambition, après avoir dégagé les minorités opprimées et rappelé à la vie des nations injustement rayées de la carte politique, eût été de voir tous les peuples en venir au méthodes de sagesse, de conciliation, de coopération, en laissant à chacun d'eux le soin de développer chez lui les institutions propres à fortifier la compréhension mutuelle.

Ce n'est point la faute de la France — qui a consenti tant de concessions et qui a fait preuve de tant de patience — si toutes les nations d'Europe n'ont pas profité des possibilités qui leur étaient offertes et si, au lieu de saisir les chances de liberté qui leur étaient fournies, elles se sont laissées entraîner à la dictature ou bien si elles ont préféré des régimes autoritaires contrastant avec les règles que nous appliquons à notre propre vie nationale aussi bien en France qu'en Amérique.

Mais quelles que soient les évolutions politiques de tels ou tels Etats, les glissements vers un nouveau despotisme, les barrages dressés devant les grands courants démocratiques qui ont été déterminés par la déclaration d'indépendance des Etats-Unis et par les principes révolutionnaires de 1789, nous conservons le culte de la liberté.

Nous estimons que nous sommes toujours dans la saine doctrine en proclamant que les individus naissent libres et égaux en droits, que le perfectionnement du citoyen à l'intérieur de l'Etat doit amener l'Etat lui-même à une discipline large, souple et créatrice, que les divers Etats, tout en conservant leurs originalités spirituelles, doivent à leur tour comprendre leurs responsabilités envers la vaste association humaine dont ils font partie.

C'est une telle conception de la liberté et de l'égalité qui guide nos esprits dans l'actuel gouvernement français. L'organisation démocratique de la paix repose sur la conscience des obligations des citoyens d'un même pays entre eux et de leurs obligations loyales envers les autres pays. Notre République, en dépit des difficultés au milieu desquelles se débat le vieux monde, du trouble des esprits, des expériences politiques inspirées ailleurs par une mentalité très différente, poursuit opiniâtrement son œuvre de perfectionnement.

Toutes ses interventions ont pour but de ranimer le sentiment de la communauté et d'exalter les vertus propres à faire régner plus de justice et plus de fraternité dans le monde.

Elle est certaine — en agissant ainsi — de se trouver d'accord avec les démocraties qui restent fermement attachées au progrès et à l'accomplissement d'un désarmement progressif matériel et moral.

La France démocratique sait, surtout, qu'elle est d'accord sur ces points capitaux avec la démocratie américaine.

C'est ce qu'elle est venue dire aujourd'hui, par ma voix, en assurant le peuple des Etats-Unis de son constant désir de travailler avec lui à tout ce qui peut rassembler les hommes de bonne volonté, en lui répétant devant l'œuvre immortelle de Bartholdi qu'elle demeure un des vivants piliers de la liberté. Elle y ajoute sa gratitude pour tout ce que l'Amérique a fait dans le récent passé. Fière d'être à ses côtés, elle lève l'étendard de l'espérance pour que le monde, grâce à des clartés nouvelles, retrouve son équilibre, sa sécurité et sa prospérité.

Le président des Etats-Unis prit la parole...

Discours du président Roosevelt

Les principaux points du discours du président Roosevelt sont les suivants:

Il y a cinquante ans, notre vieil ami et voisin d'outre-mer nous a donné ce monument pour être érigé à l'entrée principale du Nouveau Monde à l'Est. Grover Cleveland, président des Etats-Unis, accepta ce don avec l'engagement que "nous n'oublierons pas que la liberté a élu son domicile parmi nous et les préceptes qu'elle nous enseigne ne seront pas négligés".

Pendant ces cinquante années, cet accord entre nous-mêmes et nos convictions les plus chères n'a jamais été rompu.

Pendant plus de trois siècles, un courant continu d'hommes, de femmes et

(Suite en page 2)

Divisions du Budget de 1937

Les dépenses ordinaires et extraordinaires s'élèveront à 74 milliards

Service de l'Agence Havas

Paris, 29 octobre. — D'après la proposition faite à la commission des finances de la Chambre des députés par M. Vincent Auriol, ministre des Finances, le budget se diviserait en deux parties: dépenses ordinaires de 48 milliards, balancé par les revenus de l'impôt, et dépenses extraordinaires pour une somme de 26 milliards, que le gouvernement se procurerait par des mesures financières spéciales. Cette dernière partie couvrirait les dépenses afférentes à la motorisation de l'armée et à la réorganisation de l'aviation.

Service de l'Agence Havas

Paris, 29 octobre. — Le Conseil des ministres a décidé d'intensifier son programme de réarmement et voté un budget spécial pour la défense nationale s'élevant à 4.700 millions et des budgets spéciaux pour la marine et l'aviation dont le montant n'a pas été publié.

Les propositions pour des budgets d'armements spéciaux ont été soumises par M. Vincent Auriol au Conseil de cabinet, en addition aux articles du budget de 1937 qui prévoient des dépenses s'élevant à 47.250 millions, avec un déficit de 1.500 millions.

Le Parlement a été convoqué en session régulière pour le 5 novembre, date à laquelle les Commissions des deux Chambres auront vraisemblablement accepté le projet de budget.

M. Vincent Auriol a déclaré que les crédits spéciaux pour la marine et l'aviation permettraient non seulement d'accroître les forces navales et aériennes de la France, mais la construction de nouveaux aérodromes et l'augmentation des stocks d'essence et d'huile nécessaires.

Le budget est considéré comme étant le plus important des projets gouvernementaux qui ont été examinés par le dernier Conseil des ministres, présidé par M. Albert Lebrun.

Les ministres ont à l'unanimité décidé de s'en tenir à la politique de non-intervention en Espagne et ont discuté la nouvelle politique de la Belgique et des répercussions probables sur la sécurité de la France.

Le ministre de la Défense nationale, M. Edouard Daladier, fit l'examen de la situation en ce qui concerne la sécurité. On croit que M. Daladier, accompagné du chef d'état-major, après les conversations qu'il a eues avec le ministre de l'Intérieur, M. Roger Salengro, et le ministre du Travail, M. Jean Lebas, ira visiter les fortifications de la frontière du Nord, afin d'y étudier la question des nouvelles mesures de protection à y apporter. Le budget ordinaire prévoyait déjà des dépenses pour l'extension vers le Nord des fortifications de la frontière de l'Est.

Parmi les questions discutées au cours du Conseil des ministres fut celle du réglement des dépenses afférentes à la nationalisation de plusieurs industries de guerre et des décrets du ministre du Travail établissant la semaine de 40 heures. Ces derniers furent signés par le président Lebrun.

Le ministre des Finances déclara que la situation de la Trésorerie s'était améliorée depuis la signature de l'accord monétaire dont le résultat fut le réalignement du franc avec le dollar et la livre.

Le rendement des impôts pour le second semestre et les souscriptions aux bons du Trésor, qui ont repris normalement depuis l'adoption du nouveau programme monétaire, ont grandement contribué à l'amélioration de la situation de la Trésorerie.

M. Auriol a fait remarquer que l'un des devoirs principaux du gouvernement était d'établir un budget reposant sur des bases saines. D'accord avec M. Léon Blum, il a fait ressortir la nécessité d'atteindre un équilibre stable sans avoir à rendre plus lourd le fardeau des impôts dont souffre déjà le commerce en général.

Parmi les réformes considérées, on pense à la suppression de certaines taxes sur le chiffre d'affaires qui ont une répercussion directe sur les prix de détail. Ces différentes cédules seront remplacées par un nouvel impôt touchant les produits avant la distribution au détail. Ces taxes s'élèveront probablement à six pour cent. On pense de même à accroître le taux de l'impôt sur le revenu à un maximum de 35% pour les revenus supérieurs à 70.000 francs.

Rejet d'une Plainte Contre le Gouvernement

Service de l'Agence Havas

Paris, 29 octobre. — Le juge d'instruction Roussel a annoncé qu'il ne pouvait légalement donner suite au procès intenté par l'Association nationale des contribuables à M. Léon Blum, président du Conseil, et M. Vincent Auriol, ministre des Finances, sous prétexte que ces derniers avaient émis un emprunt à un moment où ils préparaient secrètement la dévaluation du franc.

M. Roussel explique sa décision en spécifiant que cette prétendue violation de la loi était du ressort de la juridiction des "actes du gouvernement" plutôt que de la juridiction ordinaire civile et commerciale, puisque ces actes soi-disant illégaux n'ont pas un caractère personnel, mais impliquent les pouvoirs souverains de l'Etat.

M. Lemaigre Dubreuil, président de l'Association, a l'intention d'interjeter appel.

Degrelle a été en Allemagne

Le chef rexiste a conféré avec M. Goebbels, ministre du Reich

Service de l'Agence Havas

Bruxelles, 30 octobre. — Le journal *Le Matin*, d'Anvers, accuse le chef rexiste Léon Degrelle d'avoir promis aux autorités allemandes de rendre à l'Allemagne le territoire qui lui avait été enlevé par le traité de Versailles dès qu'il aurait pris le pouvoir en Belgique.

Dans les dépêches reçues de leurs correspondants à Berlin, *Le Matin* et *Midi-Journal* annoncent que le récent voyage de Léon Degrelle à Berlin avait pour but de conférer avec les autorités allemandes sur la campagne anticommuniste menée par son parti, campagne subventionnée par les nazis, et pour recevoir toutes sortes d'encouragements.

Au cours d'une réunion avec le ministre de la Propagande du Reich, M. Goebbels, Degrelle aurait promis que l'un de ses premiers actes de gouvernement serait de redresser le tort fait à l'Allemagne en ce qui concerne Eupen et Malmédy.

Le correspondant du journal assure comme venant d'une source allemande certaine que M. Goebbels aurait conseillé le chef rexiste sur les moyens à employer en Belgique pour s'emparer du pouvoir. Le ministre du Reich aurait suggéré une campagne destinée à terroriser le peuple en décrivant les horreurs de la menace communiste et, de cette façon, obtenir les votes aux élections. M. Goebbels aurait de plus remis à Degrelle un certain nombre d'enveloppes mystérieuses que celui-ci aurait rapportées en Belgique.

Midi-Journal et *Le Matin* annoncent que Degrelle voulait tenir son voyage à Berlin secret et qu'il avait informé ses amis allemands qu'il ne se rendrait à Berlin que s'il avait l'assurance qu'il n'y serait pas reconnu.

Le chef rexiste a été reçu à Berlin par quatre nazis importants, dont Goebbels. Les agents de la Gestapo allemande chercheraient à déterminer l'identité des personnes qui ont dévoilé la nature du voyage de Degrelle en Allemagne.

Bruxelles, 30 octobre (*AP*). — La nouvelle politique étrangère belge "d'indépendance sans neutralité d'avant-guerre" a été approuvée par la Chambre des députés par 126 voix contre 42. Ont voté contre le groupe rexiste, les nationalistes flamands et les communistes.

La Croix Rouge obtient des otages en Espagne

Genève, 29 octobre (*Havas*). — La Croix Rouge annonce qu'elle a obtenu du gouvernement autonome des provinces basques et du haut commandement fasciste la libération immédiate des femmes et des enfants retenus comme otages.

Les négociations continuent en vue d'obtenir l'extension de l'accord aux personnes âgées de plus de 60 ans et de moins de 18 ans, ainsi qu'aux enfants, aux médecins et aux infirmes.

En attendant, les femmes et les enfants d'origine basque pourront passer librement en territoire insurgé et les femmes et enfants affiliés avec les rebelles auront la permission de traverser les trois provinces basques.

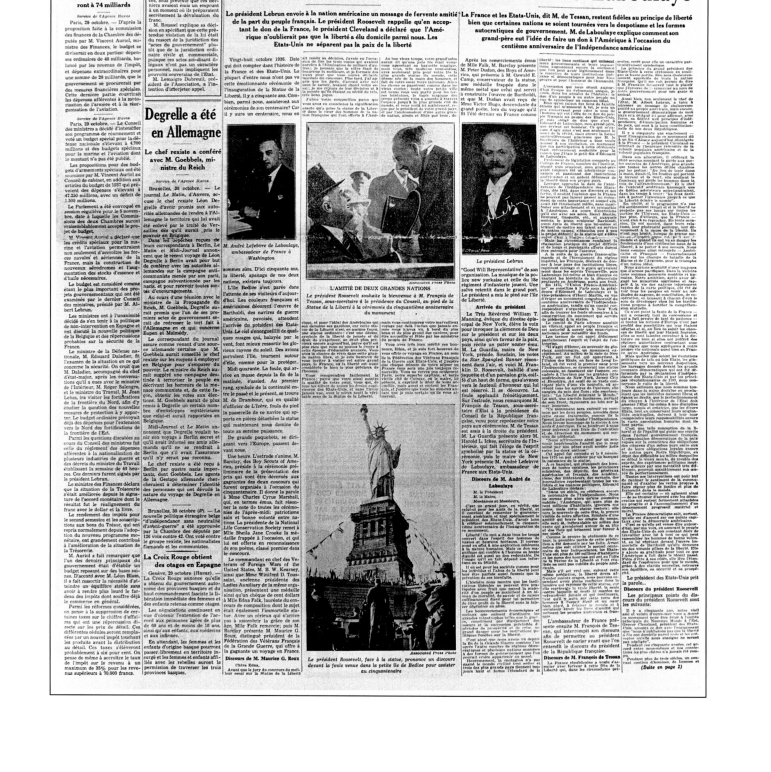

lawyer. Widely regarded as spokesman of the French ethnic community in Manhattan, Coudert was active in ensuring the success of the Statue of Liberty project. His fluency in the French language and his social influence with prominent New Yorkers eased occasional difficulties. Coudert's parents were French immigrants. With his brothers, he founded the famous law firm of Coudert Brothers in 1854. He served as president of the New York City bar association. In politics, he aligned himself with the liberal Democrats and enjoyed close ties with manufacturer Peter Cooper and Cooper's son-in-law, Congressman Abram Hewitt. *See also* French Committe of New York.

Courrier des Etats-Unis. Leading French-language newspaper published in New York City, 1828–1937. The newspaper was quite predictably enthusiastic about the Franco-American Union's statue project and described it in glowing terms. One of its journalists, Charles Viele, attended the dinner banquet given in Auguste Bartholdi's honor at the Lotos Club in 1876. The owner of the *Courrier,* Léon Meunier, was himself a member of the French Committee of New York until his retirement to Paris in 1883. He returned for the inauguration of Liberty three years later. The *Courrier des Etats-Unis* was a daily from 1851 to 1932. The French newspaper *Le Figaro* continues the publication of the paper under the name *France-Amérique.*

Crown. Diadem forming the upper part of the head of the Statue of Liberty. At 260 feet above sea level, this is the highest point open to public visitation in the monument (the torch has been closed since 1916). It is accessible by a helical or circular staircase that rises through the statue's body. Holding approximately thirty people, the crown platform's twenty-five windows afford an exceptional view of New York harbor, New Jersey, and the surrounding area within a radius of twenty miles on a clear day. The seven spikes emanating from the statue's head represent a nimbus. *See also* Dimensions; Manhattan skyline; Nimbus; Observation balcony; Visitation.

Curtis, George W. (*b.* 24 February 1824, New York, New York; *d.* 31 August 1892, New York, New York). Journalist, editor, author. Associate of the American Committee, Franco-American Union. Curtis was an influential New York City reformer and writer whose works appeared in such leading publications as *Putnam's Monthly, Harper's Monthly Magazine,* and *Harper's Bazaar.* He advocated low tariffs and women's suffrage, and served as president of the National Civil Service Reform League, 1881–92.

Courrier des Etats-Unis, 31 October 1936

THE DAILY GRAPHIC

AN ILLUSTRATED EVENING NEWSPAPER.

39 & 41 PARK PLACE.

VOL. XLI | NEW YORK, MONDAY, OCTOBER 18, 1886 | NO. 4215

THE GREAT STATUE—SKETCHES OF THE INTERIOR.

D

Daily Graphic. Newspaper, 1873–89. This was New York City's most grandly illustrated daily of the period. It produced many splendid illustrations of *Liberty Enlightening the World.* Its political tendencies were Republican.

Dedication. A key part of the inauguration of the Statue of Liberty was the dedication ceremony that took place on Bedloe's Island and was reserved for special guests. It began at 3:15 on the afternoon of 28 October 1886 and was marked by dedicatory speeches delivered within the walls of Fort Wood on a dais set up against the pedestal, with over two thousand dignitaries and guests below. Music was provided by P. S. Gilmore's Band. The ceremony was opened with a prayer led by Reverend Richard S. Storrs. Then Viscount Ferdinand de Lesseps made the first speech in his capacity as president of the Franco-American Union and successor to the late Edouard de Laboulaye, who had conceived the idea, commissioned Auguste Bartholdi as Liberty's sculptor, enlisted American support, and organized the fund raising in France. The next remarks came from American Committee chairman William Evarts, who delivered the presentation address, and during a brief pause, a signal was given to Bartholdi (who was in the statue's crown) that prematurely unveiled the French flag from the goddess's face. After the excitement died down, President Grover Cleveland delivered the acceptance address for the people of the United States, promising that the American people would care for the Goddess of Liberty, who had "here made her altar." At this point, Bartholdi was spotted near the dais, and a cheering throng demanded a speech from him. However, he politely declined, and the program continued with words from France's consul general, Albert Lefaivre. Next came a long address from the skilled orator Chauncey Mitchell Depew. Speaking in the grand style reminiscent of England's Lord Macaulay, Depew made a historical summary of French and American achievements in founding modern democratic institutions of the republican type. This was followed by the Doxology, sung to the tune of the "Old Hundred." The assembly was dismissed with a benediction given by Bishop Henry C. Potter and reembarked on steamers that returned to the piers of Manhattan. *See also* Cleveland, (Stephen) Grover; Inauguration.

Delacroix, (Ferdinand Victor) Eugène (*b.* 26 April 1798, Saint Maurice, Val-de-Marne, France; *d.* 13 August 1863, Paris, France). Painter and son of a prominent cabinet minister. Best known for creating the controversial painting *Liberty Guiding the People* (1831), which greatly influenced artistic considerations and political thought in the nineteenth century. Certainly the image of the goddess of liberty as a vigorous female revolutionary gave rise to much comment, including Edouard de Laboulaye's deprecating observations about it in his 1876 fund-raising speech for *Liberty Enlightening the World*. Once considered a rebel, Delacroix later came to be regarded as one of the most ingenious painters of his age. His other notable works include *The Prisoner of Chillon* (1835), *The Capture of Constantinople by the Crusaders* (1841), and *Algerian Women* (1849).

DeLeo, Charles (*b.* 1948, New York, New York). National Park Service maintenance mechanic, popularly known as the "Keeper of the Flame," from 1972 through 1999. DeLeo was responsible for maintaining the lighting in the Statue of Liberty's torch and cleaning the flame and other upper areas of the statue, including the interior. He began his career in the U.S. Marines and fought in the Vietnam War, 1967–70; he was awarded the Purple Heart. Much inspired by "Lady Liberty," he has devoted his life to her. In the 1980s, he wrote much poetry in tribute to the statue, the best known of which is *This Lady Prays*.

Demonstrations. The use of the Statue of Liberty in advertising, propaganda, and public iconography has made her image universally popular and thus has drawn a wide range of demonstrators, legal and illegal, to New York harbor. Perhaps the first of these were women's rights activists who strongly identified the goddess of liberty with women's issues. On 28 October 1886, the day of her inauguration, a group hired a boat and sailed near Liberty to protest the ongoing denial of women's right to vote and, further, that few women had been permitted to attend the ceremony on Bedloe's Island. In July 1915, another group of suffragettes, this time under the leadership of Carrie Chapman

Catt, came to Bedloe's Island and made their voting rights demand at the base of the monument. One of the demonstrators delighted the throng by donning a palla and striking Liberty's classic pose. In August 1970, women's rights demonstrators returned to the island. On this occasion, they mounted a huge banner across the top of the pedestal, under Liberty's feet, which read, "Women of the World Unite!" In December 1971, Vietnam Veterans Against the War occupied Liberty Island for two days.

Statue of Liberty deputy superintendent Frank W. Mills recalls four or five illegal takeovers of the monument during his tenure as chief of protection in the 1980s. Three were responses to the unfolding Iranian Revolution, in which Shah Reza Pahlavi was dethroned by Muslim clerics led by the Ayatollah Khomeini. In a dramatic anti-shah takeover, demonstrators hung a banner from Liberty's crown. There was also an enthusiastic pro-shah takeover of the monument. In 1982, demonstrators opposing the U.S. military intervention in Grenada staged a dramatic takeover by chaining themselves to the support structure of the crown. Another disruption of normal park operation occurred when antiabortion demonstrators briefly took over the sixth floor of the pedestal. In the 1981 New York City mayoral campaign, one candidate climbed on the Statue of Liberty's head. From 1981 to 1984, there were more sinister threats to the monument: thirty-five bomb threats. In contrast, legal demonstrations have included the annual Captive Baltic Nations rally and the first Gay Pride Parade rally, which drew nine thousand demonstrators to Liberty Island. *See also* National Park Service.

Depew, Chauncey Mitchell (*b.* 23 April 1834, Peekskill, New York; *d.* 5 April 1928, New York, New York). Prominent American statesman known for his oratory and wit. On 28 October 1886, Depew, president of the Union League Club, gave a learned discourse at the in-

auguration and dedication ceremonies of the Statue of Liberty at Bedloe's Island that was recalled for years after. A descendant of French Huguenot colonists, Depew distinguished himself as a corporate attorney and became a Republican party leader. He was New York's secretary of state during the Civil War and afterward served briefly as U.S. minister to Japan. In 1866, he was appointed attorney of the New York Central Railroad by Cornelius Vanderbilt; he served as vice president of the railroad (1882), president (1885–99), and chairman of the board of directors (1899–1920s). Depew was a Republican U.S. senator for New York (1899–1905). In 1916, he attended a banquet at the Waldorf Astoria Hotel with President Woodrow Wilson and French ambassador Jules Jusserand to celebrate the Statue of Liberty's thirtieth anniversary on 28 October 1916. He was a member of the Sons of the American Revolution and both the Holland and the Huguenot societies. His autobiography, *My Memories of Eighty Years,* was published in 1922.

Desmons, Frédéric (*b.* 14 October 1832, Brignon, France; *d.* 4 January 1910, Paris, France). Politician and Protestant clergyman. Desmons was the official delegate of the French Chamber of Deputies (National Assembly) at the inauguration of the Statue of Liberty in 1886. He became a freemason in 1860 and by 1873 had attained the position of grand master. His prominence in the Masonic order made him an influential figure in French liberal circles. He was also an avid scholar of Mormonism and visited Salt Lake City, Utah, during his 1886–87 trip to the United States. Desmons served as a National Assembly deputy, 1881–94, and as a senator, 1894–1910.

Detmold, Christian Edward (*b.* 2 February 1810, Hanover, Germany; *d.* 2 July 1887, New York, New York). Civil engineer and surveyor. Detmold emigrated to the United States in

Puerto Rican nationalists draped the island's flag across Liberty's forehead in an illegal demonstration, c. 1980

1826. He gained experience in surveying for railroad companies. In 1833–34, he worked for the U.S. War Department supervising the construction of Fort Sumter in South Carolina. Although he returned to railroad surveying and engineering, his greatest achievement was the construction of the Crystal Palace in London for the 1853 World's Fair Exhibition of All Nations. The engineer, one of Auguste Bartholdi's earliest supporters, wrote the American Committee regular reports about the progress of the statue's construction in Paris. Detmold was the translator of *The Historical, Political and Diplomatic Writings of Niccolò Machiavelli* (1882), from the Italian. In later life, he divided his time between Europe and New York City.

Dietz-Monnin, Charles-Frédéric (*b.* 1826, Bas-Rhin, Alsace, France; *d.* 1896, Paris, France). Iron manufacturer and politician. Vice president of the French Committee, Franco-American Union, 1875–86. A conservative republican (*centre gauche*) supporter of the policies of Premier Adolphe Thiers, he was elected to the National Assembly in 1871. He also represented the Sixteenth Arrondissement as a Paris municipal councilor, 1874–78. He was appointed a senator for life in 1882. A leading proponent of the international expositions, he directed the French section at the world's fairs of 1876, 1878, and 1889. Dietz-Monnin was a cousin of Auguste Bartholdi.

Dimensions.

Height of Statue of Liberty from base to torch, 151 feet, 1 inch (46 meters)

Height of pedestal base to Liberty's torch, 305 feet, 1 inch (93 meters)

Height from Liberty's heel to top of head, 111 feet, 1 inch (33.9 meters)

Height of torch, 21 feet (6.4 meters)

Height of pedestal, 89 feet (27.1 meters)

Height of foundation, 65 feet (19.8 meters)

Height of pedestal and foundation, 154 feet (46.9 meters)

Height of pedestal's cavernous space, 126 feet, 7 inches (38.6 meters)

Height of pedestal's stairway, 126 feet, 7 inches (38.6 meters)

Breadth of each separate eye, 2 feet, 6 inches (0.76 meter)

Breadth of the waist at the thickest section, 35 feet (10.7 meters)

Width of head from ear to ear, 10 feet (3 meters)

Width of tablet, 13 feet, 7 inches (4 meters)

Width of mouth, 3 feet (0.9 meter)

Width of nail, 1 foot, 6 inches (0.46 meter)

Thickness of tablet, 2 feet (0.6 meter)

Thickness of right arm at broadest point, 12 feet (3.7 meters)

Length of right arm, 42 feet (12.8 meters)

Length of right arm and torch, 45 feet (14 meters)

Length of head from neck to diadem, 28 feet (8.5 meters)

Length of hand, 16 feet, 5 inches (5 meters)

Length of index finger, 8 feet (2.4 meters)

Length of nose, 3 feet, 8 inches (1.1 meters)

Length of longest ray in crown, 11 feet, 6 inches (c. 3.50 meters)

Size of index fingernail, 13 x 10 inches (33 centimeters x 25 centimeters)

Circumference of index finger at second joint, 4 feet, 8 inches (1.4 meters)

Distance that hydraulic elevator rises in pedestal, 95 feet, 2 inches (29 meters)

Distance that small emergency elevator rises to the crown, 210 feet, 2 inches (64 meters)

Material, 310 riveted copper plates, approximately 3/32 inch thick.

Number of armature bars, 1,830

Number of saddles, approximately 2,000

Number of armature rivets, approximately 12,000

Number of flat bars (springs), 325

Number of steps: total, 354; spiral, 162

Number of new rest platforms, 5

Number of dunnage beams in pedestal, 4 in each of 2 sets

Liberty's drapery

Number of anchor bars in pedestal, 16 in groups of 4

Weight, 560,000 pounds (254,000 kilograms), of which 179,200 pounds (81,300 kilograms) are copper.

Old torch, 250 panes of amber glass and 19 lamps powered by 13,000 watts of electricity; the lantern skylight consists of red and yellow glass

Crown, consists of 25 windows

See also Torch.

Drapery. Liberty is clothed in much the same fashion as other statues of classical Roman female deities. She wears a *palla,* a cloak that is fastened on her left shoulder by a clasp. Underneath is a *stola,* which falls in many folds to her sandaled feet. Early modern European engravings often show the goddess Liberty wearing the stola only. In later Roman times, goddesses and matrons were also shown wearing togas, which had previously been restricted to gods and male Roman citizens.

Drexel, Joseph William (*b.* 24 January 1833, Philadelphia, Pennsylvania; *d.* 25 March 1888, New York, New York). Banker and philanthropist. Drexel was an active member of the American Committee, Franco-American Union, from 1881 to 1886, eventually serving as chairman of its executive board. In 1886, he sent a letter informing the U.S. secretary of state of the Franco-American monument's imminent completion and brought up the question of financing the inaugural ceremonies and other expenses. His efforts resulted in a congressional appropriation of $56,500.

Throughout his career in finance, Drexel sat on the boards of eleven banks. He was a collector of music and paintings, some of which he donated to New York City's Lenox Library and the Metropolitan Museum of Art. He was a director of the latter institution. In addition, he held the presidency of the Philharmonic Society of New York. Drexel was also the owner of

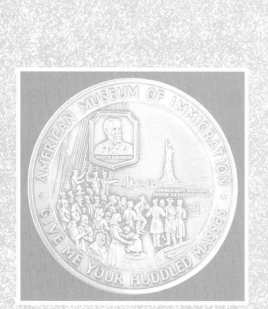

Edward Moran's famous painting of the 1886 unveiling of the Statue of Liberty Enlightening the World. He was a prominent member of the Union League Club. Drexel married Lucy Wharton in 1865.

Du Pont, Pierre Samuel III (*b.* 1 January 1911, Wilmington, Delaware; *d.* 9 April 1988, Rockland, Delaware). Industrialist and philanthropist. Du Pont was one of the founders of the American Museum of Immigration, which was located in the base of the pedestal of the Statue of Liberty from 1972 until 1991. Du Pont, with General Ulysses Grant III, became fund-raising co-chairman for the museum project in 1954. In that year, he led a delegation to the White House, where he obtained an endorsement from President Dwight Eisenhower. Du Pont served as president of the American Museum of Immigration from 1972 until his death.

(opposite) Pierre S. Du Pont III

E

Egypt Carrying the Light to Asia (*L'Egypte apportant la lumière à l'Asie*). Auguste Bartholdi's unrealized colossal monument intended for Egypt. Bartholdi first proposed the idea to Egypt's ruler, the khedive Isma'il Pasha, during the latter's visit to Paris in 1867. Two years later, at the time of the opening of the Suez Canal, Bartholdi went to Egypt with a drawing and a terracotta statuette to show the khedive. The monument, intended as a lighthouse, was to be constructed at the entrance to the Suez Canal. Its proposed form was that of a veiled Egyptian *fellah* (peasant woman) in native dress, holding aloft a lantern. Originally the source of its light was to be in the lantern, but Bartholdi instead determined to install it in the figure's diademed head. This diminished the lantern's importance and allowed powerful rays, which Bartholdi compared to the light that shone from the forehead of Moses, to issue from the diadem. At one point, perhaps in sly jest, the khedive suggested that the lantern be carried on the statue's head as was the custom of peasant women; Bartholdi responded politely: "It would be easier that way, but it would not look so well." The statue was to stand nearly 48 feet from head to toe, 86½ feet from the toe to the lantern's top. Her pedestal was to be over 46 feet high. The statue and pedestal combined were to rise 133 feet, only 18 feet shorter than the Statue of Liberty. The khedive rejected the proposal as too expensive. Bartholdi then tried to interest the khedive in another proposal. This was to build a monumental mausoleum for the ruler. Bartholdi's sketch for it pictured a circular Grecian tomb with minor Egyptian architectural features, surmounted by a colossal figure of Isma'il Pasha reclining against a lion. It was also rejected.

Eiffel, (Alexandre) Gustave (*b.* 15 December 1832, Dijon, France; *d.* 28 December 1923, Paris, France). Engineer. Designer of the Statue of Liberty's internal skeletal support system in 1880, for which he was paid a commission by the Franco-American Union. The primary structure of this system, the iron pylon, 96 feet (29.54 meters) high, was adapted from his previous work on bridges. This massive tower serves as the central attachment point for a complex asymmetrical girder of lightweight trusswork that forms the statue's body (the base structure of Liberty's arm alone rises 65 feet, or 19.81 meters). Thin, flat metal bars are bolted at one end to the pylon tower and at the other to the interior of the statue's skin, forming a flexible suspension against which the sculpted plates adhere. This elasticity allows the skin of the statue to adjust to expansions and contractions caused by tempera-

(opposite, left to right)
A clay model or maquette of *Egypt Carrying the Light to Asia,* dated 1869; Gustave Eiffel

ture changes and to resist the force of winds. The design has been judged by critics as a work of stunning originality—indeed, of genius. But perhaps conscious of the framework's invisibility, Gustave Eiffel seldom numbered it among his triumphs. His most acclaimed work is the Eiffel Tower, approximately 985 feet (280 meters) high, which he designed in 1885 for the Paris World's Fair of 1889. The metal structure held the record as the world's highest building until 1931. In addition, he was renowned for his elegant yet serviceable railway bridges, in particular, the Pia Maria Bridge over the River Douro in Oporto, Portugal (1877) and the Garabit Viaduct Bridge in the Auvergne mountains of France (1884). He also designed railway stations and department stores. Maurice Koechlin and Emile Noguier were perhaps his most trusted and talented assistant engineers. In 1893, Eiffel fell into disgrace with Viscount Ferdinand de Lesseps over the failed French Panama Canal scheme. Eiffel was convicted of breach of trust and condemned to prison for two years.

Eisenhower, Dwight David (*b.* 14 October 1890, Denison, Texas; *d.* 28 March 1969, Washington, D.C.). President of the United States, 1953–61. In August 1954, Pierre DuPont and Ulysses Grant III received President Eisenhower's approval of their plan to launch a private fund-raising campaign to found the American Museum of Immigration at the

Statue of Liberty National Monument. In 1956, the president approved a congressional resolution that changed the name of Bedloe's Island to Liberty Island, a public relations proposal strongly supported by the fund raisers.

Ellis Island. Island located near Liberty Island in New York harbor and named for its colonial proprietor, Samuel Ellis. It was known to Native Americans as *kioshk* (Gull Island) and originally measured 3½ acres. The island became federal property in 1808, and in 1890 Secretary of the Treasury William Windom chose it as the site of America's first federally operated immigrant inspection station. The choice was quickly confirmed by a congressional resolution and approved by President Benjamin Harrison that April. In the next year, Congress and President Harrison debated and approved an extensive new immigration act that created the Bureau of Immigration (now known as the Immigration and Naturalization Service, the INS) to operate Ellis Island and other stations (such as those later opened in Philadelphia, Boston, San Francisco, and Los Angeles) and barred the admission of various types of aliens such as persons likely to become a public charge, those suffering from a loathsome or contagious disease, convicts, lunatics, idiots, contract laborers, and immoral persons; it also extended the Chinese exclusion law for another ten years (this was finally repealed in 1943). Subsequent measures have barred anarchists and radicals (1903) and Asians and illiterates (1917). Despite these laws, over 12 million immigrants were admitted through Ellis Island. Predominant nationalities were the Italians, Eastern European Jews, Germans, Poles, Hungarians, Irish, English, Scandinavians, Scots, Greeks, Austrians, West Indians, Dutch, Portuguese, Spaniards, Armenians, Romanians, and Arabs. The first immigration inspection buildings (made of pinewood) were completed in time for the island's opening day, 1 January 1892; the first immigrant was Miss Annie Moore of Ireland. In 1897, the buildings were destroyed in a fire, and

construction of fireproof brick and limestone buildings was completed for Ellis Island's reopening on 17 December 1900. Over the years, the island was enlarged by landfill until it reached its current size, 27 1/2 acres, in 1935.

The INS's work at such seaport stations as Ellis Island was changed due to the passage of the restrictive Immigration Acts in 1921 and 1924, which effectively ended mass migration to the United States. The INS kept Ellis Island open for use as a national detention and deportation station for undocumented aliens, immigrant criminals, refugees, wartime enemy aliens, and suspected communists. In November 1954, it was closed by President Dwight Eisenhower on the recommendation of Attorney General Herbert Brownell and General Joseph Swing, an INS commissioner. The popularity of the Statue of Liberty among immigrants was due to the millions who passed by it on their way to Manhattan docks and the often inescapable forced ferry ride to Ellis Island for observation and questioning. To them, the goddess of liberty offered hope. Immigrants who passed through Ellis Island and gained distinction in later life include Cardinal Timothy Manning of Los Angeles, cosmetologist Max Factor, painter Arshile Gorky, Israeli politician Golda Meir, the Von Trapp family singers, journalist James Reston, actress Claudette Colbert, social reformer Father Edward Flanagan of Boys' Town, novelist Ole Rölvaag, singer Arthur Tracy, comedian Bob Hope, poet Kahlil Gibran, actor Rudolph Valentino, musician Xavier Cugat, and bodybuilder Charles Atlas. *See also* Ellis Island Immigration Museum; Ellis Island Oral History Project; Immigrants.

Ellis Island Immigration Museum. Inaugurated by Vice President J. Danforth Quayle on 10 September 1990, this museum is housed in the main building on Ellis Island. Its exhibitions were designed by MetaForm, Inc., and financed through a public fund-raising campaign led by the Statue of Liberty–Ellis Island Foundation. The main building was restored to

Aerial view of Ellis Island in the 1930s

its 1918–24 appearance. The Registry Room (Great Hall), the most historically significant space within the building, contains such early features as Catalan tiles, three elegant chandeliers, and some twenty long benches where immigrants awaited inspection. The tiles were installed on the floor and vaulted ceiling by the firm of Spanish immigrant Rafael Guastavino in 1916. There are historic photographs of the immigration experience throughout the museum's galleries. Immigrant memorabilia on permanent exhibit can be seen in the Baggage and Treasures from Home exhibits. In addition, there are on display numerous Immigration Service and Public Health Service artifacts left behind or discarded after Ellis Island was closed and later found by Park Service staff and other restorers. These include benches, a fan, detention signage, a piano, and furniture; items not on public display include a large German safe, dishes, silverware, mattresses, and detention record cabinets. Other exhibit galleries tell Ellis Island's origins, the history of the Immigration and Naturalization Service (INS), and that agency's varied law enforcement activities on the island. Daily programs include tours led by park rangers and a presentation of a half-hour-long film documentary, *Island of Hope, Island of Tears,* in the museum's two cinemas. Seasonal programs include theatrical dramatizations of the Ellis Island immigration experience, National Archives genealogy seminars, and occasional lectures. Further, the museum houses a reference library containing such materials as books, manuscripts, and pictures on migration studies, immigration law and policies, ethnic studies, and the history of the Statue of Liberty. More than 1 million tourists visit the museum each year.

Ellis Island Oral History Project. National Park Service program primarily designed to capture the recollections of Ellis Island immigrants and former Immigration Service employees on audiotape, although military, medical, and other personnel of Ellis Island and the Statue of Liberty are also included within the scope of the project.

Approximately two thousand persons have been interviewed since the founding of the program in 1973. Each immigrant interview includes such topics as everyday life in the country of origin, social and cultural background, family or personal motivations for emigrating, the journey to the port of embarkation, the sea voyage, arrival and experiences at Ellis Island, and life in America. The oral history interviews are available to the public at computer stations in a special listening room that adjoins the park's reference Library. On 15 February 1995, an invaluable addition was made to the collection when National Park Service personnel interviewed the legendary vaudeville and radio star Arthur Tracy (1899–1997), known also as "The Street Singer." Eighty-nine years before, Tracy had arrived at Ellis Island as a poor, frightened Russian refugee named Abba Tracavutsky. The National Park Service is still seeking people to interview. *See also* Statue of Liberty Oral History Program.

Emancipation Movement. Worldwide nineteenth-century campaign to abolish slavery. Although its origin lay primarily in France, pioneered by the secular *philosophes* of the Enlightenment, its practical application was carried out in England by such Christians as Quakers and Methodists. Notable organizations were the Clapham Sect and the British Emancipation Society. Leaders included William Wilberforce, Thomas Clarkson, and Zachary Macaulay. As a result, Great Britain abolished the slave trade during the reign of George III (1807) and slavery itself during the reign of William IV (1833). In the same year, William Lloyd Garrison founded the American Anti-Slavery Society. In the 1830s, an abolitionist society was organized in France and, through the uncompromising persistence of Victor Schoelcher, secured the liberation of slaves in the French colonies in 1848.

In 1865, Edouard de Laboulaye, Count Agénor de Gasparin, and others decided to carry the fight a step further when they formed the French Anti-Slavery Society, which called on all nations to abolish slavery. The society sent charitable assistance to the newly freed Africans and mulattoes in the United States. With their assistance, a former Spanish prime minister, Don Salustiano de Olózaga, founded the Spanish Emancipation Society in 1866. Knowing that there would be many attractions in Paris at the Universal Exposition of 1867, Laboulaye invited all abolitionist organizations to convene there for the world's first International Emancipation Congress. The congress was officially presided over by the popular Prince Albert de Broglie, who was regarded as the doyen of the European emancipationists. Laboulaye was chairman and host. *See also* Civil War; French Anti-Slavery Society; Laboulaye, E. R.; Shackle; Slavery.

Enabling authorization. Federal legislation governing jurisdiction of national parks. The Statue of Liberty National Monument exists by virtue of the Antiquities Act of 1906, which allows a president to proclaim federal property deemed to be of historic or archaeological value as national monuments. The *Statue of Liberty Enlightening the World* and Fort Wood became a national monument by the proclamation of President Calvin Coolidge on 15 October 1924. In 1933, by executive orders 6166 and 6228, President Franklin Roosevelt transferred the

Entertainer Arthur Tracy discusses his immigrant past at Ellis Island with Paul Sigrist and Barry Moreno (center)

Statue of Liberty National Monument from the War Department to the Interior Department (National Park Service). On 7 September 1937, President Roosevelt transferred all of Bedloe's Island to the jurisdiction of the National Park Service. On 11 May 1965, President Lyndon Johnson issued a proclamation decreeing Ellis Island to be a part of the Statue of Liberty National Monument.

Enlightenment. Touchstone of European political philosophy and masonic thought. The choice of *Liberty Enlightening the World* as the Statue of Liberty's full name reveals the extent of the influence that liberal and progressive philosophy had on the sculpture's intellectual creator, Edouard de Laboulaye. The torch, its flame, and the shining seven rays that emanate as a nimbus from Liberty's crown are potent expressions of her symbolic duty as enlightener. Although Laboulaye's dominant influence is evident in the ideology of this symbol, as in most others, Auguste Bartholdi's plans for the Statue of Liberty and the unrealized statue of *Egypt Carrying the Light to Asia* as lighthouses are also significant.

Etex, Antoine (*b.* 20 March 1808, Paris, France; *d.* 14 July 1888, Chaville, France). Sculptor, painter, architect, and engraver. Although Auguste Bartholdi studied under Etex in Paris only briefly (1847–48), he gleaned from him an appreciation for colossal statuary that would later become an obsession. Etex had distinguished himself at the Paris Salon of 1833 when he presented his colossal statuary group, *Caïn et sa race, maudite de Dieu*. In the following year, he began his two high reliefs for the Arc de Triomphe in the Place de l'Etoile: *La Résistance de la France* and *La Paix*. Bartholdi had already been deeply moved by the ornamental reliefs and might have pursued this further had Etex not suddenly closed his studio and left Paris, abruptly ending Bartholdi's studies. Etex went on to write several books, such as *Cours élémentaire de dessin* (1853), *Beaux-Arts: Cours public fait*

à l'association polytechnique pour les élèves des écoles et pour les ouvriers (1861), and *Les Souvenirs d'un artiste* (1878).

Evarts, William Maxwell (*b.* 6 February 1818, Boston, Massachusetts; *d.* 28 February 1901, New York, New York). Statesman and lawyer. Chairman of the American Committee, Franco-American Union, 1877–86. Evarts was the key figure in ensuring the success of the fund-raising campaign for the pedestal of the Statue of Liberty. Although the support of newspaper publisher Joseph Pulitzer in 1886 brought welcome financial relief in completing the project, it was Evarts's many years of commitment to the project and his willingness to exert his social and political influence that were decisive in legitimizing the campaign before the public and the press and bringing it to a successful conclusion. Edouard de Laboulaye asked his fellow Union League Club member William Evarts for assistance in founding an American committee to raise funds for the pedestal. Sculptor Auguste Bartholdi was an effective representative of Laboulaye at the first meeting of the American Committee organized by Evarts early in 1877. Evarts's group included such prominent New Yorkers as John Jay, Theodore Roosevelt, and Edwin D. Morgan. That spring, Evarts's political influence was felt in Congress with the quick passage of a joint resolution in which the United States formally accepted the French gift. Powerful New York Republicans such as George Jones, publisher of the *New York Times,* Chauncey Depew of the New York Central Railroad, and trial lawyer Joseph Hodges Choate jumped aboard the Liberty pedestal campaign. Evarts later enlisted the assistance of Cornelius Vanderbilt, Montague Marks, Constance Cary Harrison, and Emma Lazarus with such successful ventures as the Pedestal Art Loan Exhibit of 1883. With his French counterpart, Viscount Ferdinand de Lesseps (Laboulaye's successor), Evarts presented the Statue of Liberty to President Grover Cleveland and the people of the United States at inaugural and dedication ceremonies at Bedloe's Island on 28 October 1886.

The senior partner of the law firm of Evarts, Choate, Sherman, and Léon, Evarts was also a founder and the first president of the New York City Bar Association. He successfully defended President Andrew Johnson in his impeachment trial before the Senate in 1868. In addition, he represented the United States at the Geneva arbitration in 1871–72 for its claims against Great Britain for having plundered the ship *Alabama* during the Civil War, and he was also legal counsel for the Republican party in the disputed presidential election of 1876. Evarts served as U.S. attorney general, 1868–69; U.S. secretary of state, 1877–81; and U.S. senator (Republican, New York), 1885–91, where he was responsible for the passage of the Evarts Act of 1891, which created the federal court of appeals.

William Maxwell Evarts

F

Feet. The folds of a long *stola* surround Liberty's sandaled feet, front and back. Her right foot is raised, as if in movement, while the left foot is planted, all five toes easily observable. Beside each foot lie the pieces of Liberty's broken shackle.

Ferry, Jules François Camille (*b.* 5 April 1832, Saint Dié, Vosges, France; *d.* 17 March 1893, Paris, France). Politician and statesman. Ferry began his career as a lawyer and journalist in Paris and eventually became an outspoken detractor of the government of Emperor Napoleon III. Elected to the imperial legislative body in 1869, he voted against the declaration of war with Prussia. He demonstrated his leadership ability while serving as mayor of Paris when the city was under Prussian siege (1870–71). During his term as minister of education and beaux-arts, 1879–80, he brought about the expulsion of the Jesuits from the French education system. Ferry was prime minister, 1880–81, 1883–85; his last ministry collapsed over his aggressive policy of attempting to force colonialism on Madagascar and Indochina. Ferry was enthusiastic over the Statue of Liberty project and in 1885 provided free transport of the statue to New York aboard the French naval frigate *Isère*.

Ferry service. The War Department received the first request for a ferry and wharf landing license at Bedloe's Island in 1885. After the statue's inauguration the following year, a regular ferry service for tourists from the battery in lower Manhattan was set up and maintained by the American Committee. The landing stage for visitors was the East Pier, which had been built of timber between 1839 and 1842; it continued to be used for this purpose until 1951. By the 1890s, visits to Bedloe's Island and the great statue of *Liberty Enlightening the World* had become quite the fashion. However, tourists soon became conscious of Fort Wood's neglected appearance and that the copper goddess was turning green.

The army took control of the statue in 1902 and continued to provide ferry service to the island. Two years later, the army noted that daily visitation ran into the hundreds on summer days and that most of the visitors were not only strangers to the city but were foreigners. When the National Park Service became responsible for the monument in 1933, a complaint was raised that "visitors must pay the cost of Army transportation." A 1939 Park Service report noted that the Statue of Liberty received thousands of visitors each day, nine-tenths of whom were not residents of New York City.

The West Pier became the principal dock for

(clockwise, from top) Liberty's foot and heel, 1936; Sutton Line ferries docked at Bedloe's Island, 1938

arriving ferries after it was rebuilt in the late 1940s and came into use late in September 1951. Until that time, the ferries were coal-burning boats. The Sutton Line had operated ferry service to the monument since army days, but was replaced by Benjamin B. Wills under a ten-year contract in 1943; his tourist boat to the island was called *Liberty.* But due to a fairly regular breakdown of equipment, Wills often had trouble maintaining the daily boat schedule and providing a night boat. In addition, his operating costs continued to rise due to the spiraling inflation that characterized the postwar Truman years. In order to cope with the problem, the government allowed him to increase the boat fare for tourists; between 1944 and 1951, an adult return ticket rose from fifty-eight to seventy-five cents. But it was a labor problem that would eventually cause Wills to lose his concession. Crew members repeatedly demanded a wage increase, but Wills steadfastly resisted. For seven years the crew threatened a strike, which finally occurred in June 1953, effectively blocking visitor access to Bedloe's Island; only service for the staff was provided. Although the strike ended after only two days (Wills's negotiators gave in to most of the union's demands), a month later Secretary of the Interior Douglas McKay arranged a new ferry contract with Circle Line. Circle Line first used its tourist boat *Sightseer,* but in February 1954 it bought and overhauled Wills's *Liberty.* In June 1954, the new ferry *Miss Liberty,* which could hold 750 passengers, made its inaugural run. Park Service employees traveled to work aboard the tourist ferryboats until the government acquired a small boat and christened it *Liberty II,* after Wills's old ferry *Liberty.* A final shift occurred in the summer of 1952 when the Manhattan ferry dock was moved from the inadequate Pier A on the Hudson River to the newly built sea wall at Battery Park. The Circle Line continues to hold the ferry concession for the Statue of

(left) Actress Mae West as the Statue of Liberty in an advertisement for the film *Myra Breckenridge* (1970)

(opposite page) The fingers of Liberty's right hand

Liberty, and in 1990 service to Ellis Island was included as well. *See also* Circle Line; Statue of Liberty–Ellis Island Ferry, Inc.; Visitation.

Films. The Statue of Liberty has been featured in numerous motion pictures and film documentaries. An early production was the 1936 French film *La Liberté,* which was based on a 1934 stage play; these were tributes to the goddess on the occasion of her golden jubilee. Although occasionally seen in films of the silent era and the early sound period, it was not until 1942 that Liberty made a dramatic impact in the genre. This was in Sir Alfred Hitchcock's classic espionage thriller, *Saboteur,* in which a hero played by actor Robert Cummings pursues the Nazi saboteur to Bedloe's Island. There, the enemy alien met a frightful end by falling to his death from the torch of the Statue of Liberty. The effect suggested a goddess aroused to fury by an unholy figure within her sacred precincts. Liberty appears in a far more favorable light in the delightful musical *On the Town* (1949), which starred Gene Kelly, Frank Sinatra, and Jules Munshin, all of whom visited Bedloe's Island. Liberty was also used effectively in *Planet of the Apes* (1968) when its partly buried remains testify that human civilization has been destroyed. In *Escape from New York* (1981), the Statue of Liberty and her island are used as the prison warden's headquarters of the penal colony of Manhattan. Liberty has also appeared in *Funny Girl* (1968) with Barbra Streisand, and *Mame* (1974) with Lucille Ball. Imitations of the Statue of Liberty can be seen in a range of films, including *Yankee Doodle Dandy* (1942), which starred James Cagney. Demonstrating her identification with late 19th-century America, film star Mae West (1892–1980) posed twice as the Statue of Liberty, once in 1934 and again in 1970. Film documentaries have included the Discovery Channel's *On the Inside: The Statue of Liberty* (1999).

Fingers. The five fingers of Liberty's right hand can easily be seen as she grasps the torch, while the fingers on her left hand are equally

evident as she holds her tablet. The artistic construction of them is wonderfully lifelike. The fingers, hand, and torch were fabricated in 1876 at the Monduit and Béchet foundry in Paris.

Flame *(flambeau)*. Symbolically burning in the torch, the fiery flares represent the sacred enlightening force of liberty. It was originally constructed of copper. Lieutenant John Millis in October–November 1886 designed its original electric lighting system. He had two rows of circular openings cut into the copper flame and electric lamps installed inside. The weak effect led to the creation of a new system in 1892. One row of circular openings was eliminated and replaced with larger windows, sometimes referred to as a skydome. In 1916, stained glass was installed in the windows while the upper half of the flame was also replaced by stained glass. The old flame and torch were replaced by a new one between 1984 and 1986. The new flame's internal armature is made of flat bars of stainless steel riveted to the flame with copper saddles and insulated by Teflon tape. In October 1985, Fabrice

Gohard and his craftsmen gilded the new flame with 5,000 sheets of heavy gold leaf (33 grains per 1,000 sheets). The process took three weeks to complete. *See also* Gold leaf; Torch.

Forney, John Wein (*b.* 30 September 1817, Lancaster County, Pennsylvania; *d.* 9 December 1881, Philadelphia, Pennsylvania). Newspaper publisher and journalist. Colonel Forney was an antislavery Democrat and founder and publisher of the *Philadelphia Press,* 1857–77. He also was editor and publisher of the *Washington Chronicle* during the Civil War. Forney served as clerk of the U.S. House of Representatives, 1851–56, 1860–61; and secretary of the U.S. Senate, 1861–68. From 1874 to 1876, he traveled through Great Britain and Europe as chief of the Philadelphia Centennial commission to drum up interest in the Philadelphia Centennial Exhibition of 1876. The colonel's grace and charm persuaded many European nations to participate in the exhibition. He also introduced Auguste Bartholdi to Philadelphia social circles. In 1876, he founded the American Committee

(below) Old flame

(opposite page) New flame

of Philadelphia and tried to obtain the Statue of Liberty for that city.

Fort Wood. Fortress on Liberty Island and base of the foundation of the Statue of Liberty; artistically, it forms the third element in the composition of the monument, after Liberty and the pedestal. The Army Corps of Engineers began constructing the fort—which takes the shape of an 11-pointed star—in 1807 and finished in 1811. Cannons were mounted in time for the outbreak of America's second armed conflict with Great Britain, the War of 1812. The fort was part of a chain of land batteries capable of defending New York harbor against possible attack by sea. Other batteries included Castle Williams on Governor's Island, Castle Clinton in Manhattan, and Fort Gibson on Ellis Island. It was originally known only as the "works on Bedloe's Island" until Colonel Eleazer Wood died a hero in the Battle of Lake Erie near the war's end. Governor Daniel D. Tompkins of New York christened the works Fort Eleazer D. Wood in his memory on 9 November 1814.

The fort was in military use almost continually until 1823. But in the years that followed, it was seldom used, and decay set in. In 1844, the War Department reconstructed the 1811 fort with large, heavy, rusticated blocks of granite; the old drawbridge was replaced in the 1850s. During the Civil War, Fort Wood saw service as an army recruiting station. After the Union victory it resumed garrison duty.

In 1877, General William T. Sherman, at the request of President Rutherford B. Hayes, selected it as the permanent site of the French Statue of Liberty. The garrison promptly vacated the fort and its buildings, although an ordnance post supervised by a sergeant was authorized to continue on a temporary basis. After the completion of the statue in 1886, a lighthouse keeper was posted to the island to maintain Liberty as a beacon, and the American Committee opened Fort Wood to tourists. In 1907, new repairs were begun, and by 1912 the army had filled in the old parade ground. Around 1930, the parapet's granite coping was

replaced, and pointing work was done on the parapet and the rampart walls. In the 1950s, designs and plans were drawn for the American Museum of Immigration, which was to be installed within Fort Wood's walls, at the base of the Statue of Liberty. Work began in 1960 when Fort Wood's rampart, main gate, interior passageways, and rooms were demolished. The museum area was constructed with difficulty from 1961 through 1965. President Nixon formally opened its exhibits to the public in 1972.

Fort Wood received a new set of double entrance doors as part of the 1986 restoration. Known as the Centennial Doors, they were cast in bronze, with ten decorative panels designed by Jordan Steckyl. The left side door's five individual panels represent, one by one, copper repoussé, scaffolding, mechanical tools, armature, and stonework; the five on the right, in their turn, stand for craft tools, the refurbished circular staircase, shoulder repair, the new pedestal elevator, and the tools of the architect, engineer, and surveyor. *See also* Army; Bedloe's Island; Visitation; Williams, Jonathan; Wood, E. D.

Foundation. The foundation of the Statue of Liberty and its pedestal is a massive pyramidal concrete structure that was laid within the walls of Fort Wood from 9 October 1883 to 17 May 1884, following the ground-breaking ceremony of April 1883. It was designed by General Charles P. Stone. The majority of laborers were Italian immigrants who lived on the island throughout the winter. Their work consisted largely of building platforms, unloading construction materials and supplies (which were moved by railway cars driven on high wooden trestles), and mixing and pouring concrete. The design and laying of the 11,680-cubic-yard concrete foundation was planned and supervised by

(left) Masonry foundation of the pedestal, 1884

(opposite page) Franco-American Union fund-raising appeal, 1875

General Charles P. Stone. The firm supplying materials and laborers was Smith, Magan & Drake. Its senior partner, F. Hopkinson Smith, went to Bedloe's Island regularly to ensure the successful completion of the biggest contract of his career. Two barrels of cement, two barrels of sand, three barrels of stones, and four barrels of slightly larger stones were required for the 13 feet of concrete foundation that lies beneath the earth's surface; two barrels of cement, five barrels of sand, and six barrels of stones were required to build the 52 feet, 10 inch mass of concrete that rises above it. The cement was carefully tested, and the concrete was then laid and rammed in course by course, with 200 to 250 barrels of cement used each day. The surface breadth of the concrete foundation is 91 feet square at the bottom and 65 feet square at the top. The long, hollow interior is 10 feet broad. *See also* Pedestal.

France. *See* Second Empire; Second Republic; Third Republic.

Franco-American Union (Union Franco-Américaine, UFA). Central fund-raising organization founded at Paris in 1875 by Edouard de Laboulaye to finance the construction of the Statue of Liberty and its pedestal. The Union was the official name of the unified French Committee in Paris and the American Committees in New York City, Philadelphia, and Boston. Laboulaye was both president of the Franco-American Union and chairman of the French Committee, the governing board for the whole organization. Members of honor were the marquis de Rochambeau, the marquis de Noailles, Elihu Washburne, Amédée Bartholdi, and John W. Forney. Vice presidents were senators Henri Martin (d. 1883) and C. F. Dietz-Monnin. Jean-François Bozérian was chairman of the Statue of Liberty Lottery Commission, and Count Sérurier served as the director of administration (Bozérian and Sérurier were promoted to vice president c. 1883). Other key members were Oscar de Lafayette, Jules de Lasteyrie, Paul de

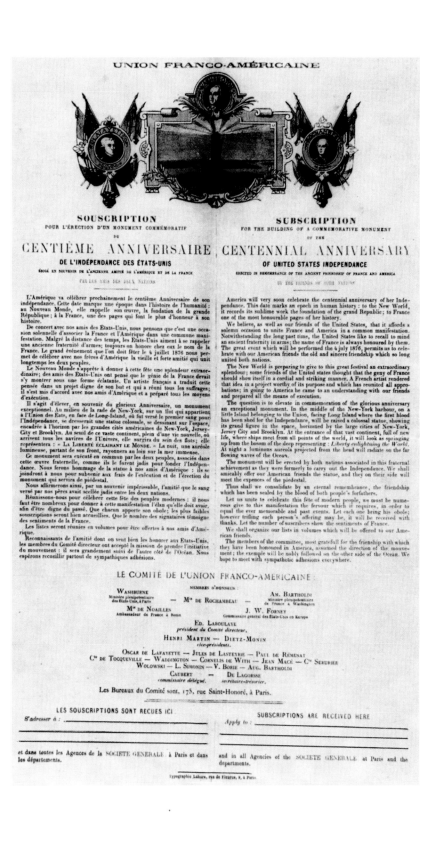

Rémusat, Count Hippolyte de Tocqueville, W. H. Waddington, Cornélis de Witt, Jean Macé, Louis Wolowski, Louis-Laurent Simonin, Victor Borie, and Auguste Bartholdi. Also included on executive rosters were Maître A. Caubert of Rouen. J. de Castro and Georges A. Glaenzer shared the office of secretary, while Pierre de la Gorce was treasurer. Upon Laboulaye's death in May 1883, the Union selected Viscount Ferdinand de Lesseps to fill the presidency.

The American Committee in New York bore the responsibility for the entire national fund-raising campaign in the United States. William M. Evarts chaired it. The Philadelphia Committee was formed separately by Colonel John W. Forney and others in the autumn of 1876; however, its members lost interest after it became clear that the Statue of Liberty could not be built in their city. The Boston Committee was a successful fund-raiser, due to Nathan Appleton, Joseph Iasigi, and others. *See also* American Committee; Boston; French Committee; Fundraising campaign; Lottery; Pedestal campaign.

Franklin, Benjamin (*b.* 17 January 1706, Boston, Massachusetts; *d.* 17 February 1790, Philadelphia, Pennsylvania). Statesman, diplomat, author, and inventor. Franklin's views on the importance of moral virtue and duty influenced Edouard de Laboulaye's views on democracy and his opinions of the United States. It was one of many American influences that affected his thoughts and was one of the indirect causes for his campaign to build and donate the Statue of Liberty to the United States. Laboulaye translated, edited, and annotated several books by Franklin (beginning each volume with an introductory essay to assist the French reader). The books Laboulaye issued included a partial text of *The Autobiography of Benjamin Franklin* (1865), *Poor Richard's Almanack* (1872), and *Essais de morale et d'économie politique.*

Freemasonry (Order of Free and Accepted Masons). An international secret society consist-

ing of persons united in fraternity. In Europe and America in the eighteenth and nineteenth centuries, freemasonry was associated with political and social enlightenment. Its influence on the Statue of Liberty project in the 1870s and 1880s can be seen in the membership of the Franco-American Union and the cornerstone laying ceremony of the pedestal. The most obvious Masonic symbolic element of the Statue of Liberty is perhaps her role of enlightenment seen in her official name, *Liberty Enlightening the World.* Prominent freemasons in the Statue of Liberty's beginnings included the sculptor Auguste Bartholdi, Henri Martin, C. F. Dietz-Monnin, Jean Macé, Victor Borie, and Richard Morris Hunt. *See also* Pedestal.

French-American Committee for the Restoration of the Statue of Liberty. In existence from January 1981 until 1986. The committee's team of French engineers and architects issued a study of the condition of the Statue of Liberty that was released to the media in July 1983. It was also involved in restoration fund raising. Its members included Jacques de Broissia, Philippe Vallery-Radot, Roger d'Amecourt, Paul Windels, Jr., Susan L. Snyder, Albert Swanke, and Philippe Grandjean.

French Anti-Slavery Society (Comité française pour l'émancipation des esclaves). Founded in 1865 and disbanded around 1870. Edouard de Laboulaye was president. The duke of Broglie and François Guizot were *présidents d'honneur;* advisory council members were Prince Albert de Broglie, Henri Martin, Count Agénor de Gasparin, Edmond de Pressené, and others. The secretary of the society, Eugène Yung, editor of the *Revue des cours littéraires de la France et de l'étranger,* ensured that the review published the society's proceedings. Its initial aim was to raise funds in France to help feed and clothe freed slaves in the United States. Laboulaye's wife, Micheline de Laboulaye, led a women's group that had been established at about the same time to make clothes for the freed slaves. By 1866, the society's interests expanded to include the abolition of slavery in Brazil, as well as in such Spanish colonies as Cuba. Relations with the British Emancipation Society were quickly established, and efforts made toward founding an abolitionist society in Spain were led by Don Salustiano de Olózaga. In 1867, an international congress of abolitionist societies met in Paris in conjunction with the Universal Exposition. Representatives included Prince Albert de Broglie presiding for France; Joseph Cooper, William Allen, and L. A. Chamerovzow for the British Emancipation Society; William Lloyd Garrison of the American Anti-Slavery Society; and Congressman John Gorham Palfrey. Other nations represented were Brazil, Haiti, Venezuela, and for the continent of Africa, M. Rainy. The sessions were presided over by Laboulaye. The congress passed a resolution of congratulations for the nations that already abolished slavery: Great Britain, France, Sweden, Denmark, the Netherlands, the United States, Mexico, the Central American republics, and Tunisia. A second resolution called on the following nations to end their systems of slavery: Spain, Portugal, Brazil,

the Ottoman Empire, and Egypt. At the first session, Laboulaye addressed the assemblage on the history of the abolitionist movement and cited the contributions of William Penn, Baron Charles de Montesquieu, Benjamin Franklin, John Jay, Thomas Clarkson, William Wilberforce, Thomas Fowler Buxton, Elizabeth Fry, Joseph Sturge, William Ellery Channing, Horace Mann, William Lloyd Garrison, and Senator Charles Sumner. He credited each of them in contributing to the fall of slavery in the United States. His paramount hope was that slavery would end everywhere in the world. *See also* Slavery.

French Committee (Comité français). French governing board of the Franco-American Union established by Edouard de Laboulaye to build the Statue of Liberty. Laboulaye set up the Comité of the Union Franco-Américaine on 26 September 1875 from among his fellow progressive deputies in the National Assembly, including some prominent freemasons. The French committee had Laboulaye as president and as vice presidents, Henri Martin and C. F. Dietz-Monnin. Prominent members were Count Sérurier, Louis Simonin, J. de Castro (secretary), Pierre de la Gorce (treasurer), Maître Caubert, Jean Macé, William H. Waddington, Cornélis de Witt, Victor Borie, Louis Wolowski, Eugène Viollet-le-Duc, Jean-François Bozérian, Auguste Bartholdi, Joseph Cazot, Adolphe Goupil, Honoré Monduit, Emile Gaget, Nathan Appleton, Thomas G. Appleton, Georges A. Glaenzer, and Viscount Ferdinand de Lesseps. The honorary members included Elihu Washburne, Amédée Bartholdi, Colonel John W. Forney, the marquis de Rochambeau, the marquis de Noailles, Oscar de Lafayette, Edmond de Lafayette, Jules de Lasteyrie, Paul de Rémusat, and Count Hippolyte de Tocqueville. *See also* Franco-American Union; Fund-raising campaign (France).

French Committee of New York (Comité français de New-York). The French commu-

Pedestal cornerstone-laying ceremony conducted by the Freemasons, 1884

nity of New York City formed this fund-raising committee for the Statue of Liberty on 18 October 1876. It was the successor of the Lafayette Committee (1871–76), which had raised funds for Auguste Bartholdi's statue of the marquis. But once the Lafayette monument stood gracefully on Henri de Stucklé's pedestal in Union Square, the committee no longer had a purpose. It was preparing to dissolve itself when a letter arrived from Paris from no less a person than Senator Edouard de Laboulaye. Noting the success the committee had had in erecting the Lafayette statue, he asked the committee to continue, but this time as the American arm of his Franco-American Union. After debates, at which Auguste Bartholdi was present, the committee was enlarged and reconstituted as the Comité français de New-York. Its officers were Frédéric Coudert (president); Adolphe Salmon, Henri de Stucklé, and E. Charlier (vice-presidents); Amédée Vatable (treasurer); and Charles Villa (secretary). Other members included Léon Meunier, W. B. McClellan, and Charles Renauld. In 1879, the Franco-American Union asked the committee to sell Statue of Liberty lottery tickets to French citizens living in the United States. The plan was derailed once it was concluded that such an activity might violate New York State law. The French Committee of New York concentrated its efforts on raising funds by giving theatrical performances.

French delegation (October 1886). Official French delegation for the inauguration of the Statue of Liberty, 28 October 1886. The delegates, passengers aboard the *S.S. Bretagne,* arrived in New York on 25 October 1886. The members were Viscount Ferdinand de Lesseps and Ferdinande "Tototte" de Lesseps (his daughter); Monsieur and Madame Auguste Bartholdi; Admiral Benjamin Jaurès and General Xavier Pelissier of the French Senate; Eugène Spuller and Frédéric Desmons of the Chamber of Deputies; Baron Albert Salvador; Lieutenant Villegente of the Ministry of Ma-

rine; Colonel Bureau de Pusy of the Ministry of War; Colonel Laussédat, director of the Ecole des Arts et Métiers; Léon Robert of the Ministry of Education; Charles Bigot, of the Paris press; Napoléon Ney, president of the Société de Géographie Commerciale; and Léon Meunier, former publisher of the *Courrier des Etats-Unis. See also* Dedication; Inauguration

Fund-raising campaign (France). The French fund-raising campaign to build the Statue of Liberty was launched by Edouard de Laboulaye's Franco-American Union, which raised some 400,000 francs. It began with a great banquet given at the Hotel du Louvre on 6 November 1875. This successful event raised 40,000 francs, about one-tenth of the eventual cost of the monument. The next fund-raising affair was a fête given at the Palais de l'Industrie on 19 November 1875. This attracted only a small audience and was a failure. The next event featured the Liberty Cantata by Gounod and Guiard, presented at the Paris Opera on 25 April 1876. Another failure, it raised a mere 8,291 francs. But the campaign continued with renewed vigor. Pierre Petit issued souvenir Liberty photographs, sized according to the generosity of a donor's contribution. The committee also issued a terracotta cast reproduction of Liberty, standing slightly over 3 feet (one meter) in height. To ensure that it would be valued as a collector's item, Auguste Bartholdi produced only one hundred statuettes and then destroyed the molds. Goupil's Galleries in Paris and New York sold them for 1,000 francs each ($300 in New York).

In 1877, Bartholdi created a permanent diorama exhibition, which turned out to be one of the most successful fund-raising schemes of the French campaign. An 11-yard canvas, bearing a painted scene of the harbor of New York, was installed in the Palais de l'Industrie for the length of the summer. Bartholdi's astonishing illusion of perspective gave viewers the uncanny impression of riding aboard a steamer and

The head of the Statue of Liberty used for fund raising, Paris, 1878

viewing "Yankees" in their curious garb, smoking and talking. In the distance, people could be seen standing on a bridge while a boat sailed in the harbor. Then other boats crowded the harbor around the colossal Statue of Liberty on Bedloe's Island, basking beneath her illuminating rays. A sense of the grandeur of New York and the glorious goddess left a lasting impression on the viewer. Count Sérurier, secretary of the Franco-American Union, was delighted with the simple power of the message. So popular was the Liberty diorama that Count Sérurier decided to move it to a more promising neighborhood, where the rich lived and tourists congregated. He settled on the Jardin des Tuileries. All who entered the Liberty Diorama Pavilion were "crowned" by two sheaves of French and American flags, supported on either side by shields bearing the illustrious names of Washington and Lafayette. The charge was 1 franc on working days and 50 centimes on Sundays and holidays. By special invitation, President Jules Grévy visited, and it is estimated that the attraction drew as many as seven thousand visitors in a two-month period. Bartholdi dismantled it in 1879.

In 1878, the Monduit foundry completed Liberty's head, which was to be put on display at the Paris Universal Exposition in the Champs de Mars. Liberty's head was driven to the Champs de Mars on a wagon, and as it passed the cheering throng, its head shook in a friendly way, and the people tipped their hats in return. The head was officially unveiled on 16 July 1878. Passes were sold by the Franco-American Union that permitted exposition visitors to climb the thirty-six steps inside the head to the crown and view the surrounding Champs de Mars. The British writer Rudyard Kipling, in his book, *Souvenirs of France,* recalled visiting the exhibition as an adolescent: "One ascended by a staircase to the dome of the skull and looked out through vacant eyeballs at a bright coloured world beneath. I climbed up there often, and an elderly Frenchman said to me,

'Now you young Englisher, you can say you have looked through the eyes of Liberty Herself.' " The completion of the fund-raising drive was celebrated with a banquet at the Hôtel Continental on 7 July 1880. Senator Edouard de Laboulaye, U.S. minister Edward F. Noyes, U.S. consul general George W. Walker, Oscar de Lafayette, Henri Martin, Jean Bozérian, and former interior minister Charles Lepère delivered speeches. The Franco-American Union had received donations from more than 100,000 subscribers, including 181 municipalities, 10 chambers of commerce, and the majority of French masonic lodges. The cost of the statue was first estimated at 250,000 francs; then it rose to 400,000 francs ($250,000), which is still the official figure. However, some recent scholars have estimated the figure at nearly 600,000 francs ($450,000). All figures reflect the value of French and American money in 1880.

Fund Raising (United States). *See* Pedestal campaign.

(opposite page) Inside the head of the Statue of Liberty

G

Gaget, Emile (*b.* 6 October 1831, Dun-sur-Meuse, France; *d.* 1904, Paris, France). Engineer and founder. Originally a railway engineer, Gaget, with J. B. Gauthier, went into partnership with the well-known founder Honoré Monduit in January 1874. In 1878, they bought out Monduit and took over the foundry at 25 Rue de Chazelles, Paris. The firm specialized in producing decorative sculpture, often using metals such as bronze and copper. The Statue of Liberty, its most celebrated work of art, is made of beaten copper. In October 1886, Gaget came to New York for the inauguration of the Statue of Liberty armed with three large trunks filled with miniature statuettes of Liberty, all of them stamped "Gaget, Gauthier." Americans often confused Gaget's name with the already widely used sailor's slang word *gadget*. Emile Gaget retired from business in 1891.

Gaget, Gauthier et Companie. Fabricators of decorative metalwork, originally Monduit, Béchet & Cie. Emile Gaget and J. B. Gauthier joined Monduit's firm in 1874 and succeeded Monduit as the owners in 1878. It is likely that Eugène Viollet-le-Duc recommended the firm to Auguste Bartholdi, as he had used it for numerous projects of his own as early as 1861. The Statue of Liberty was constructed at the foundry from 1876 through 1884, at 25 Rue de Chazelles, on the outskirts of Paris.

Gasparin, (Count) Agénor de (*b.* 12 July 1810, Orange, France; *d.* 14 May 1871, Geneva, Switzerland). Abolitionist, politician, and author. Count de Gasparin was a devout Protestant who, guided by his religious convictions, wrote and debated extensively against slavery. He had a long parliamentary career, having served in the Chamber of Deputies during the reign of King Louis Philippe and during the Second Republic. He retired to Switzerland during the reign of Emperor Napoléon III and actively aided efforts to abolish slavery worldwide, especially in the United States, Brazil, Haiti, and the Spanish and Portuguese colonies. He returned to France in the 1860s and joined Edouard de Laboulaye and others in founding the French Anti-Slavery Society in 1865.

Gauthier, J. B. French founder. In January 1874, Gauthier, with Emile Gaget, went into partnership with the respected founder Honoré Monduit, and in 1878, Gaget and Gauthier took over the firm. The foundry, at 25 Rue de Chazelles in Paris, specialized in decorative

(clockwise, from top) Inside the Statue of Liberty workshop at the Gaget, Gauthier foundry, Paris; Gaget, Gauthier and Company advertisement; Applying plaster to a wooden frame in the Statue of Liberty workshop, Gaget and Gauthier foundry, Paris

sculpture of all kinds, and it was the site of the fabrication of the Statue of Liberty. Gauthier was the author of *La Plomberie au XIXe Siècle* (1885), which described the construction of the statue. He retired from business in 1889.

Gérôme, Jean-Léon (*b.* 11 May 1824, Vesoul, France; *d.* 10 January 1904, Paris, France). Painter. Léon Gérôme persuaded Auguste Bartholdi to join him and fellow artists Narcisse Berchère, Léon Belly, and Edouard Imer on a trip to the Near East, a historic site of artistic inspiration. Gérôme began exhibiting his works in 1847. He was appointed professor of painting at the Ecole des Beaux-Arts in 1863; his students included Odilon Redon and Thomas Eakins. Gérôme's genres were orientalism and French historic realism. Representative works are *Porte*

Liberty's Chinese alter ego, the Goddess of Democracy, 1989

de la mosquée El-Hacanyn (1866), and *Marché d'esclaves* (1867). He was one of the great painters of the nineteenth century.

Gilder, Rodman (*b.* 8 January 1877, New York, New York; *d.* 30 September 1953, New York, New York). Publisher and author. During World War II, Gilder wrote one of the first commercially published books on the monument, *The Statue of Liberty Enlightening the World* (1943). His other books included *Joan the Maiden* (1933) and *The Battery, New York: A History* (1935). Gilder's father, the well-known poet Richard Watson Gilder, was a friend of Emma Lazarus, author of "The New Colossus."

Gilman, Daniel Coit (*b.* 6 July 1831, Norwich, Connecticut; *d.* 1908, Baltimore, Maryland). Educator and author. Impressed by Edouard de Laboulaye's work in France on behalf of the United States, Gilman invited him to lecture at Johns Hopkins University. Laboulaye declined the offer, citing delicate health. Gilman was the first president of the University of California, 1872–75, and president of Johns Hopkins University, 1875–1901. His books include *James Madison* (1883), *Bluntschli, Lieber and Laboulaye* (1884), and *The Launching of a University* (1906). In addition, he was editor of *The New International Encyclopedia* in 1902.

Give Me Your Tired, Your Poor . . . *See* New Colossus.

Glaenzer, Georges Auguste (*b.* 1848, Paris, France; *d.?*). Interior decorator and painter. Glaenzer was a member and served as secretary of the French Committee, Franco-American Union. Due to his fluency in French and English, he was a vital communications link between Auguste Bartholdi and the American Committee in New York, a role taken after his 1876 marriage to Alice Cary Butler, Richard Butler's daughter. Glaenzer's German father sent him to Stuttgart, where he received his

diploma in architectural design; he eventually set up his practice in Paris. After his marriage, he also set up a home in New York City, where he worked for a time as a commercial traveler for a dealer in fine wines and fancy groceries. At last he established himself as an interior decorator in New York. His best-known commission was his design of rooms in the Vanderbilt Mansion at Hyde Park, New York. His son, Richard Butler Glaenzer (1876–1937), was a journalist and playwright.

Glatigny. Village near Versailles, France, on the outskirts of Paris. Edouard de Laboulaye lived there from about 1850 until his death in 1883. His estate included a house, conservatory, and stables. The street where the buildings stood were later renamed Place Edouard de Laboulaye in his honor.

Goddess of Democracy (Chinese: *minzhu nü-shen*). A 28-foot-high (10 meters) statue made of Styrofoam plastic that was wired together and then covered by plaster, in the form of a young and strong Chinese peasant woman, holding both arms high, bearing a torch. It was a collaborative work in 1989 of fifteen male undergraduate students at the Central Academy of Fine Arts in Beijing. They were anxious that the sculpture not be imitative of other famous works of art, especially the Statue of Liberty, as they wished to avoid even the slightest appearance of creating a work that might be construed as supporting American or Western propaganda. They especially wanted the goddess to be acceptable to the Chinese people in form and meaning. The statue was erected in Tiananmen Square with great enthusiasm and unveiled at noon on 30 May 1989. A statement printed on a banner read, "We . . . have broken the autocracy of the government and now stand welcoming the Democracy Movement of 1989. . . . Democracy, how long it is since we last saw you. . . . You are the hope for which we thirst. . . . You are the symbol of every student in the Square, of the hearts of millions. . . . You are

the soul of the 1989 Democracy Movement. . . . On the day when real democracy and freedom come to China, we must erect another Goddess of Democracy here in the Square, monumental, towering, permanent." For five days it stood inviolate but was finally toppled by a Chinese army tank and utterly destroyed on 4 June 1989. Soldiers quickly cleared the rubble away.

The *Goddess of Democracy* was clearly inspired by French democratic tradition, whose powerful derivative forms are the Statue of Liberty and the ideological heritage of the French Revolution, among other things. In June 1989, Secretary of the Interior Manuel Lujan and Statue of Liberty superintendent Kevin Buckley laid a wreath in front of the Statue of Liberty in commemoration of the *Goddess* and her slain followers of the Tiananmen Square massacre.

Godwin, Parke (*b.* 25 February 1816, Paterson, New Jersey; *d.* 7 January 1904, New York, New York). Lawyer, author, editor. Godwin was a member of the American Committee, and his influence was especially important in appeals for subscriptions for the pedestal. His father-in-law, William Cullen Bryant, assisted him. Godwin was a publisher and editor of the *New York (Evening) Post, Commercial Advertiser,* and *Putnam's Monthly Magazine.* A distinguished writer, he was the author of many works, including *A Popular View of the Doctrines of Charles Fourier* (1844), *Vala: A Mythological Tale* (1851), *Ancient Gaul* (1860), and his *Cyclopaedia of Biography* (1866 and 1878).

Gold Leaf. Gilding technique used for the new torch's flame in October 1985. Distinguished by its luminous quality and beauty, the visual effect was realized by applying very thin sheets of gold onto the surface of the copper flame. The first step was to apply an organic substance or primer coat onto the copper to act as an insulator. Then a resin or varnish was applied on the surface to receive the titled 980 gold leaf (23.6 carats). The gold leaf measures 3.3 by 3.3 inches

(84 by 84 millimeters). It weighs 1.16 ounces (33 grams) per 1,000 leaves (5,000 leaves were used). The process was completed by gently pounding the leaves into place. The work was accomplished by Fabrice Gohard and craftsmen of Etablissement Dauvet, a French firm. Liberty's gold leaf came as a donation.

Gorce, Pierre de la. Historian. Treasurer of the Franco-American Union, 1875–86. De la Gorce was the author of the seven-volume *Histoire du Second Empire* (*1894–1905*), in which he described Edouard de Laboulaye as the embodiment of "pure liberalism."

Gounod, Charles François (*b.* 18 June 1818, Paris, France; *d.* 18 October 1893, Saint Cloud, France). Musical composer. Gounod's most celebrated operas were *Faust* (1859), *Mireille* (1864), and *Roméo et Juliette* (1867). He also composed masses, anthems, and hymns for the Roman Catholic church. In 1876, he lent his musical genius to the fund-raising effort of the Statue of Liberty in composing a cantata. Gounod failed in persuading the revered poet Victor Hugo to write its lyrics and settled for the talent of a young poet named Emile Guiard.

The composition was presented at a "great solemnity of music," performed at the new Paris Opera on 25 April 1876. The event, organized by the Franco-American Union, opened with a speech delivered by Edouard de Laboulaye, followed by the music of Pierre Auber, Gioacchino Rossini, an earlier piece of Gounod, and a musical poem by Paul Déroulède. All of this provided a romantic buildup for Gounod's triumph, *La Liberté éclairant le monde.* Four male choirs performed the cantata under the direction of Gounod himself.

Goupil, Adolphe (*b.* 7 March 1806, Paris, France; *d.* 9 May 1893, Paris, France). Art dealer and member of the Franco-American Union, French Committee, Paris. Goupil was the founder of an international chain of art gal-

Liberty with her new gilded flame, 1986

leries. The first of his Goupil Galleries was opened in Paris in 1827. He specialized in reproductions of paintings in the manner of the old and new masters and in the execution of grand murals to decorate the interiors of the homes of the upper middle class. Goupil invented an astonishing engraving technique that came to be known as *goupillage*. He next expanded his business to embrace photography. In 1889, he gained control over a gallery that distributed the works of the deceased painter Vincent van Gogh. Van Gogh had been an employee of Goupil from 1869 through 1876, working in the art dealer's galleries in the Hague, Paris, and London. At the height of his career, Goupil also operated Goupil's Galleries in Berlin and New York. His family continued the business until 1920. Many of the art works preserved by his heirs are now housed in the Goupil Museum, which was opened in Bordeaux in 1991.

Governor's Island. An island in upper New York harbor, consisting of 175 acres (70 hectares) of land. For a time, this island was considered a potential site for the Statue of Liberty. Castle Williams was thought of as the best location for the monument on Governor's Island. However, Auguste Bartholdi's preference for Bedloe's Island prevailed and was confirmed by President Rutherford B. Hayes and General William T. Sherman. Known as Pagganck by the Canarsee Indians, it was settled by the Dutch in the seventeenth century and renamed Nooten Eylandt ("island of nuts"). In 1698, the colonial legislature gave it to the English king's governors as an official residence. It remained in British posses-

sion until 1783. The fortress known as Castle Williams was built there by Colonel Jonathan Williams, 1807–11. During the Civil War (1861–65), a recruiting depot was set up on the island, and Confederate officers were kept on the island as prisoners. After the war, Governor's Island was transformed into the U.S. Army headquarters for the North Atlantic area. Pioneer aviator Wilbur Wright took off from Governor's Island for his flight over New York harbor, the Statue of Liberty, and Grant's tomb for the Hudson-Fulton celebration in 1909. The island continued as an army base until 1966, when it was turned over to the Coast Guard. In 1996, the Coast Guard closed its base and vacated the island.

Grace, William Russell (*b.* 10 May 1831, Queenstown, Ireland; *d.* 21 March 1904, New York, New York). Shipping executive, merchant, and politician. Mayor Grace represented the city of New York at the inauguration and dedication of the Statue of Liberty on 28 October 1886. In addition, he presented Auguste Bartholdi with an honor known as the "Freedom of the City" on 27 October 1886, given on behalf of the citizens of New York City in "gratitude to the . . . creator of the statue which will forever remain a splendid ornament of their metropolis." Grace founded the firm of W. R. Grace & Company in Liverpool, England, in 1851. He expanded his shipping operations to Peru and gained control of much of the shipping trade in South and Central America. He also acquired silver mines, guano deposits, oil and mineral rights, and railway properties in Peru. He developed his business in New York in 1865, pioneering direct steamship service from New York to the west coast of South America. Grace was the first Roman Catholic to serve as mayor of New York City.

Graffiti. Inscriptions or drawings made on the surface of the Statue of Liberty. Graffiti desecration by visitors has plagued the statue since her earliest years in the United States. During and after World War II, the problem increased

considerably, culminating in the National Park Service's closing the monument for two weeks in December 1947 and intermittently in the first three months of 1948. The vandalized areas, the worst of which were done in lipstick, were steam-cleaned and painted. Wire fences were then installed around the spiral staircase to keep visitors away from the copper surface.

Granite. Material used in the construction of the Statue of Liberty's pedestal. The American Committee originally advertised for various kinds of stone in newspapers throughout the country, especially in New England. Twenty specimens of granite, sandstone, and bluestone were received from Maine, Connecticut, New York, South Carolina, and Kentucky. The granite from Leete's Island, Connecticut, was at last selected, and a large supply was ordered. The entire pedestal was faced with forty-six courses of the Leete's Island granite. However, the top four steps at the second promenade level are faced with granite from Deer Island, Maine. (This extra material may have been among the samples.) The Connecticut granite was transported from Leete's Island aboard an old Hudson River sloop called *The Wasp*. This boat had been built at Lansingburgh, New York, in 1813, for use in the War of 1812. John Beattie, owner of the Leete's Island quarry, purchased it in 1869, and the hull was strengthened to carry 100-ton loads on its decks. It was equipped with a stern hoisting engine and carried four large lintels, with shield, on each trip to avoid any major losses. The last of the granite was swung into place on 22 April 1886, and the jubilant workmen threw silver coins into the mortar. *See also* King, David H.; Leete's Island; Pedestal.

Grant, Ulysses Simpson (*b.* 27 April 1822, Point Pleasant, Ohio; *d.* 23 July 1885, Mount McGregor, New York). Soldier and president of the United States, 1869–77. Ulysses Grant played an important role in the Statue of Liberty's history. His connection with the French liberal intellectual establishment began when Edouard de

Religious graffiti in the Statue of Liberty, now removed

Laboulaye publicly endorsed him for the presidency in 1868; three years later, Laboulaye sent Auguste Bartholdi to meet Grant and open discussions on building a monument to Liberty and American independence. Although polite, Grant struck Bartholdi as being cold to the notion. However, in 1877, Laboulaye's friend William Evarts was successful in obtaining President Grant's support in the passage of a joint congressional resolution accepting the Statue of Liberty: Grant signed it into law on 3 March 1877, his last day in office.

On 21 November 1877, after his retirement from the presidency, he visited the Paris foundry where the statue was being built. Grant then wrote to Laboulaye and expressed hope that the monument would soon be completed. Laboulaye wrote these words in reply: *"Votre visite a été une sorte de consécration du monument qui doit attester aux générations les plus lointaines l'amitié de la France et des Etats-Unis* [Your visit was a kind of consecration of the monument which ought to prove to future generations the friendship of France and the United States]."

Grant, Ulysses Simpson III (*b.* 4 July 1881; *d.* 29 August 1968). Soldier, engineer, and a grandson of President Ulysses S. Grant. He was a founder of the American Museum of Immigration and served as chairman of its National Committee, 1953–68. General Grant began his long military career with the rank of lieutenant in 1903; after numerous promotions, he attained the rank of colonel in the Army Corps of Engineers in 1934. Over the years, his assignments included the Cuban pacification of 1906, the Vera Cruz expedition of 1914, the Mexican expedition of 1916, and both World Wars I and II. His military decorations included the Distinguished Service Medal, the Legion of Merit, and decorations from six foreign countries. After World War II ended, General Grant retired from active duty and accepted the position of vice president at George Washington University, 1946–51. In 1907, Grant married the former

Ulysses S. Grant III

Edith Root, daughter of U.S. Secretary of State Elihu Root. His clubs were the Army & Navy, the Century Association, and the Union League Club. He is buried at Hamilton College Cemetery, Clinton, New York.

Grévy, Jules (*b.* 15 August 1807, Mont-sur-Vaudrey, France; *d.* 9 September 1891, Mont-sur-Vaudrey, France). President of the French Republic, 1879–87. President Grévy visited the statue at the Gaget and Gauthier atelier on 4 March 1884, a visit regarded as an "official consecration." Grévy rose to power through a combination of political flair and an unswerving opposition to monarchy. His succession to the presidency ensured the permanency of the Third Republic.

Guiard, Emile (*b.* 1852, Paris, France; *d.* February 1889, Cannes, France). Poet, dramatist, and librarian. Guiard was the author of the lyrics of Charles Gounod's great cantata, *La Liberté éclairant le monde,* which was presented at the Paris Opera in April 1876 as a fund-raising event for the Statue of Liberty. The young poet received the commission from Gounod after the latter had failed to enlist the help of Victor Hugo. Guiard was a nephew of the acclaimed comic dramatist Emile Augier (1820–89) and,

through the influence of his uncle, began his career in the Ministry of Beaux-Arts, winning appointment as assistant librarian at the Louvre Museum. After the success of his work with Gounod, he went on to write several plays that proved quite popular at the time. They included *Volte-face* (Comédie-Française Théatre, opened 12 October 1877), *La Mouche* (a verse monologue, 1879), the comedy *Mon fils* (Odéon Theatre, opened 3 March 1882), and *Feu de Paille* (Odéon, 30 March 1885). His last play was *Le Ruffian,* which he wrote with R. Palefroi. Guiard's *Poésies* were published in 1889.

Guizot, François (*b.* 4 October 1787, Nîmes, France; *d.* 12 September 1874, Normandy, France). Statesman and historian. Served as an honorary president of the French Anti-Slavery Society (founded by Edouard de Laboulaye), 1865–70. Guizot was a cautious liberal reformer who believed that the 1830 revolution did for France what the Glorious Revolution of 1688 had done for England: ended absolutism. However, he vigorously resisted the reforms advocated by Adolphe Thiers and Alexis de Tocqueville, such as extending voting rights and ending press censorship. Guizot's son-in-law, Cornélis de Witt, was a member of the governing board of the Franco-American Union.

H

Hair. Liberty's hair is thick and wavy and is parted in the front, then pulled back tightly into a bun; at the sides it is pulled over her ears, behind which fall long curls. The diadem acts as a kind of headband for the coiffure. The style, at once elegant and practical, is suggestive of nineteenth century fashion.

Hamilton, Alexander (*b.* 25 January 1903, New York, New York; *d.* 29 May 1970, New York, New York). Secretary-treasurer and a founder of the American Museum of Immigration. He had also served as chairman of the advisory board on National Shrines, New York City, and was president of the American Scenic Historical Preservation Society. He was an army officer during World War II and attained the rank of major. Hamilton was a direct descendant of Alexander Hamilton, one of the founding fathers of the republic, and a grandson of financier J. Pierpont Morgan.

Harrison, Constance Cary (*b.* 25 April 1843, Fairfax County, Virginia; *d.* 21 November 1920, Washington, D.C.). Author and essayist. Constance Cary Harrison was responsible for her friend Emma Lazarus's writing the now-famous sonnet, "The New Colossus." Montague L. Marks, editor of the *Art Amateur,* had persuaded Harrison to organize an auction for the Pedestal Art Loan Exhibit, to be held at the National Academy of Design on 3 December 1883. The grand event was intended to raise money to complete the goddess of liberty's pedestal. While reflecting on what might be done, the idea of a portfolio came suddenly to her. In it were to be creative works, such as paintings and literary manuscripts, all of which would be auctioned at the gala opening. In her memoirs, published twenty-eight years later, Harrison recalled discussing the auction with her neighbor, the esteemed poet Emma Lazarus, who had come to pay a call: "I begged her to write something for my Portfolio. She declared she could think of nothing suitable . . . [then] I reminded her of her visits to . . . the newly arrived immigrants whose sad lot had so often excited her sympathy." Inspired, Miss Lazarus wrote her sonnet, "The New Colossus." It was printed in the exhibit catalogue. Harrison was herself the author of many popular works of fiction, including *Golden Rod* (1880), *Bar Harbor Days* (1887), *The Anglomaniacs* (1890), *Flower de Hundred: The Story of a Virginia Plantation* (1890), *A Daughter of the South* (1892), *Sweet Bells Out of Time* (1893), *A Bachelor Maid*

Liberty's hair as seen from behind

(1894), *A Son of the Old Dominion* (1897), *The Carcellini Emerald* (1899), and *The Count and the Congressman* (1908). Her autobiography, *Recollections Grave and Gay*, was published in 1911. Her husband, Burton N. Harrison, a prominent New York attorney, died in 1904, after which she moved to Washington, D.C.

Hayes, Rutherford Birchard (*b.* 4 October 1822, Delaware, Ohio; *d.* 17 January 1893, Fremont,

in the Statue of Liberty's torch, 1886–94. In 1889, Heap requested permission to try "the effect of electric light in the head of the Statue of Liberty, so arranged that the light will show through the windows under the rays." This new lighting effect was installed in 1892. With Millis, he prepared Statue of Liberty lighting reports (1887, 1890, and 1892). Still the lighting was unsatisfactory, and Heap recommended that the statue be painted white. Sculptor Auguste Bar-

Opening day: Aaron Hill (wearing hat) with wife Evelyn, her cousin, and children James and Constance Hill, at their new souvenir stand, 1931.

Ohio). President of the United States, 1877–81. President Hayes confirmed the selection of Bedloe's Island as the permanent site of the Statue of Liberty, which was made on his authority by General William T. Sherman in 1877.

Heap, David Porter (*b.* 24 March 1843, San Stefano, Turkey; *d.* 1910, Pasadena, California). Army engineer, U.S. Light-House Board. Major Heap worked with Lieutenant John Millis in attempting to increase the illumination power

tholdi was notified of the situation in May 1893. That September, he visited the United States and, heartily disappointed with the lighting system, sent a letter to Major Heap demanding that Liberty be gilded in gold or at least receive a luminescent varnish. But due to lack of funds, no action was ever taken. Heap served in the Army Corps of Engineers, 1865–1905, specializing in river and harbor engineering, fortifications, and lighthouse engineering. He retired with the rank of brigadier general. He was the author of *Ancient and Modern Light-Houses* (1889). *See also*

Light-House Board; Lighting; Millis, John; Torch.

Helios (Greek: sun). *See* Colossus of Rhodes.

Hewitt, Abram Stevens (*b.* 31 July 1822, Haverstraw, New York; *d.* 18 January 1903, New York, New York). Industrialist and politician. Hewitt, the son-in-law of iron and steel magnate Peter Cooper, made his fortune in the same business. He was elected to Congress as a Democrat in 1874. Congressman Hewitt introduced the congressional joint resolution to accept the Statue of Liberty in the House of Representatives in February 1877. In 1886, as a member of the House Appropriations Committee, he participated in winning federal financing of the inaugural ceremonies to be held on Bedloe's Island. Hewitt was chairman of the Democratic National Committee during the Tilden presidential campaign of 1876. Backed by Tammany Hall, he was elected mayor of New York City in 1886. He was a political ally and friend of Frédéric Coudert.

Hill, Aaron (*b.* 1895; *d.* November 1943, New York, New York) and **Hill, Evelyn** (*b.* 1901, Poland; *d.* 1990, New York, New York). Souvenir and restaurant concessionaires, Statue of Liberty, beginning in 1931. A veteran of World War I, Sergeant Aaron Hill was a soldier stationed on Bedloe's Island in the 1920s. He married Evelyn Kupferberg, a Polish immigrant. Their son, James I. Hill, was born on the island in 1925. After Aaron Hill's discharge, he managed the PX for the soldiers and visitors and, in 1931, purchased the souvenir stand from a captain stationed on the island. He continued the concession after the National Park Service replaced the army in 1933. Hill died at home in 1943, and his widow carried on the business, which became known legally as Evelyn Hill, Inc. In 1954, the business was transferred to a modern concessions building on the island. Their son, James, ran the concession for many

years until his retirement in 1995, when his son, Bradford Hill, succeeded him.

Hodel, Donald Paul (*b.* 23 May 1935, Portland, Oregon). Lawyer and U.S. secretary of the interior, 1985–89. Secretary Hodel dismissed Lee A. Iacocca as chairman of the Statue of Liberty–Ellis Island Centennial Commission in February 1986, following Iacocca's statement that it was not appropriate that members of the commission should also serve as members of the Statue of Liberty–Ellis Island Foundation. Aside from Iacocca, only J. J. Simmons and Armen Avedisian sat on both boards. Agreeing with Iacocca, Hodel terminated him as the commission's chairman. Hodel also held the position of secretary of energy, 1982–85.

Hudson-Fulton Celebration of 1909. Combined commemoration of two major events in U.S. history: the 300th anniversary of Henry Hudson's explorations of New York harbor and the Hudson River for the Dutch East India Company in September 1609 and the 100th anniversary of the first successful application of steam navigation on the Hudson River by Robert Fulton in 1807. It took place from 25 September to 11 October 1909 and was marked by parades and a spectacular review of naval and other vessels in New York harbor. In addition, there were many other public spectacles throughout New York City. The fashion of the day was the novel and widespread use of electricity to illuminate the city's buildings and monuments, and the Statue of Liberty did not escape this dazzling electrification, making the monument an even more impressive structure at nightfall. In addition, a "Statue of Liberty Enlightening the World" float was included in the great parade held in Manhattan. The lavishly decorated float consisted of a replica of the Statue of Liberty, 6 or 8 feet high; seated at a lower level in the front of the float were two female figures symbolizing the friendship of France and America, the sister republics.

Hugo, Victor (*b.* 26 February 1802, Besançon, France; *d.* 22 May 1885, Paris, France). Poet and novelist. On 29 November 1884, Victor Hugo visited the Gaget and Gauthier foundry where the Statue of Liberty had just been completed. Turning to Auguste Bartholdi, Hugo said: "To the sculptor, form is everything and nothing—nothing without the spirit, everything with the idea." The celebrated author, who was to many a symbol of France's striving toward democracy, was presented with an inscribed copper fragment of the goddess as a memento of his visit. In a letter to Richard Butler describing the visit, Bartholdi wrote, "You may have read in the papers that my mother bravely assisted during Victor Hugo's reception at the statue; our illustrious poet had tears in his eyes, as did my mother; in short, everyone was deeply moved." Equally brilliant as poet, playwright, and novelist, Victor Hugo's works include *Odes and Ballads* (1822), *Cromwell* (1826), *The Hunchback of Notre Dame* (1831), *Napoleon the Little* (1852), *Legend of the Centuries* (1859), *Les Misérables* (1862), *Quatre-vingt-treize* (1874), and *Torquemada* (1882). He was made a life senator in 1876. He died shortly after his visit to the Statue of Liberty and was buried in the Panthéon. *See also* Copper (illustration).

Richard Morris Hunt

Huguet, Auguste-Victor (*b.* 21 December 1822, Boulogne-sur-Mer, France; *d.* 18 January 1919, Boulogne-sur-Mer, France). Member of the French Committee, Franco-American Union; served on its Statue of Liberty Lottery Commission, 1879. Huguet, a well-known publisher, entered the political arena as a centrist reformer, serving with distinction as mayor of Boulogne-sur-Mer, 1871–73, and as a senator of the Third Republic, 1876–1909.

Hunt, Richard Morris (*b.* 31 October 1828, Brattleboro, Vermont; *d.* 31 July 1895, Newport, Rhode Island). Architect. Hunt was the designer of the pedestal of the Statue of Liberty, for which the American Committee commissioned him on 6 December 1881. After several of his designs were rejected, he was at last successful in a design submitted on 31 July 1884; it was accepted by the committee on 7 August 1884. Hunt received a fee of $1,000 for his design, which he donated to the fund to erect the statue. The son of Jonathan Hunt and Jane Maria Leavitt Hunt, Hunt was the first American to be educated at the Ecole des Beaux-Arts's architectural section, 1846–55. His works include the New York Tribune Building (1873–76), the Lenox Library (1870–77), the Vanderbilt estate Biltmore, in North Carolina (1890), and the Administration Building of the World's Columbian Exposition at Chicago (1893). He was one of the founders of the American Institute of Architects and served as its first secretary, 1857–60. He was also a member of the Union League Club. *See also* Architecture; Pedestal; Pedestal patent and copyright.

Iacocca, Lee (Lido Anthony) (*b*. 15 October 1924, Allentown, Pennsylvania). Business executive. Iacocca served as chairman of the Statue of Liberty–Ellis Island Centennial Commission, 1982–86. He was also chairman of the private fund-raising arm of the commission, the Statue of Liberty–Ellis Island Foundation, 1982–87, after which he continued on as its chairman emeritus. Iacocca and the foundation raised more than $300 million by 1986. Of that sum, approximately $86 million was applied to the restoration of the Statue of Liberty and landscaping work on Liberty Island. Iacocca was president of the Ford Motor Company, 1970–78, and became chairman of the Chrysler Corporation in 1979.

Imer, Edouard Auguste (*b*. 23 December 1820, Avignon, France; *d*. 13 June 1881, Haarlem, Netherlands). Painter. Imer accompanied Auguste Bartholdi, Léon Gérome, Léon Belly, and Narcisse Berchère to the Near East in 1855–56; they were seeking inspiration from the antiquities and culture of the Orient—"a return to roots." Imer was the son of an Avignon merchant and did not dedicate himself entirely to art until he settled in Paris in 1850. The most celebrated of his paintings are those that depict the south of France. Among his works are *Chemin de Provence* (1850), *Paysage des bords du Rhône à Avignon* (1850), and *Piédimont dans les Abruzzes* (1874).

Immigrants. The powerful impression that the Statue of Liberty left on millions of immigrants who entered New York harbor by steamship was an unexpected reward that would have made both Auguste Bartholdi and Edouard de Laboulaye proud. Although Bartholdi was deeply conscious of what he wanted the statue to look like from aboard ship, seeking a strong aesthetic impact at first glance, it is unlikely that he could have foretold its symbolism to immigrants. Their reactions to *Liberty Enlightening the World* were a mixture of wonder, awe, admiration, adoration, and even puzzlement, as these quotations show:

> When we got to America, we saw the Statue of Liberty and Mother said to me in German: "That means we are free." Austro-Hungarian (emigrated 1910)

> I remember we see Statue of Liberty. Gus asked me, "What's the statue?" And then we're looking . . . and his father say, "That's Christopher Columbus." And I put my two

An immigrant family on Ellis Island gaze at the Statue of Liberty

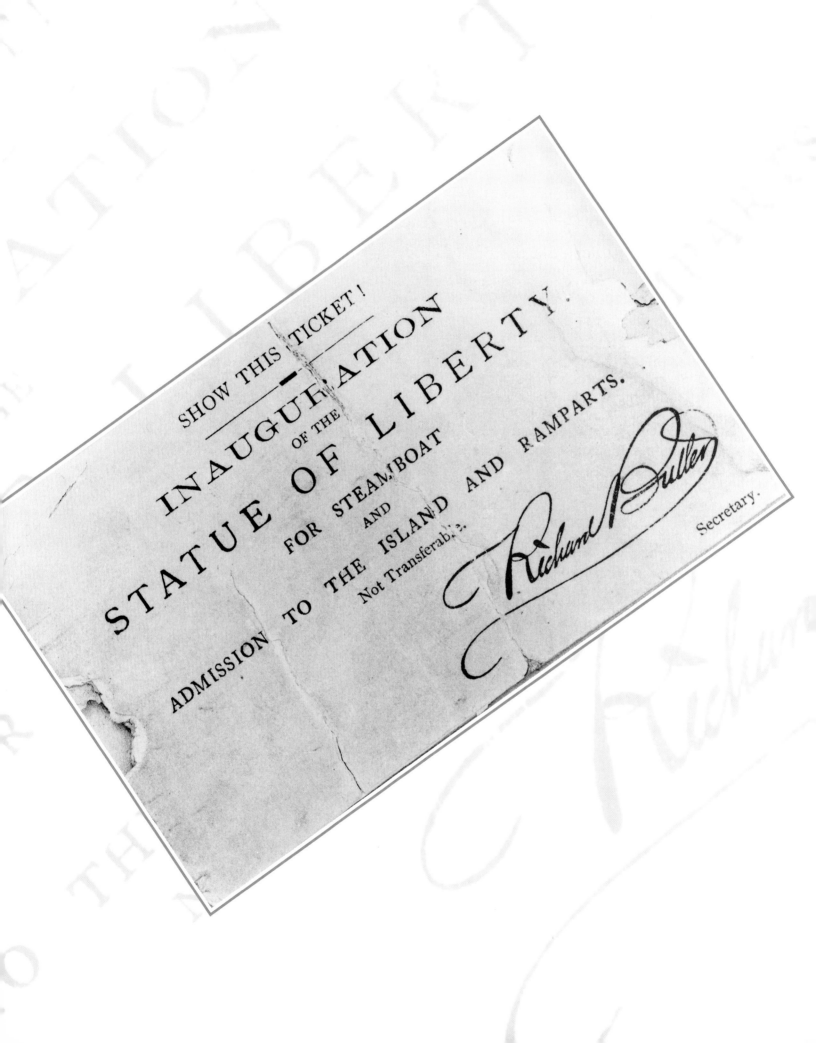

cents out. I say, "Listen, this don't look like Christopher Columbus. That's a lady there." Greek (emigrated 1911)

After thirteen days, we finally came here and I was so happy that I was now in America. I saw the Statue of Liberty. And I said to myself, "Lady, you're beautiful. You opened your arms, and you get all the foreigners here. Give me the chance to prove that I am worth it, to do something, to become someone in America." Greek (emigrated 1919)

When word got out that we were approaching land, everybody . . . ran on deck. We were packed like sardines, gazing with such excitement and wonderment. I saw the Statue of Liberty. It was so impressive, so majestic, so meaningful. Freedom! Opportunity! And most of all, it linked to us, America and France . . . we knew it was given to America by France. French (emigrated 1920)

When we were told we would be passing the Statue of Liberty, we all lined the deck. The thrill of seeing that statue there. And the tears in everybody's eyes. . . . It was more, not freedom from oppression, I think, but freedom from want. So that was the biggest thrill to see that statue there. German (emigrated 1920)

We were eleven days on ship. When we saw the Statue of Liberty, everybody started screaming and crying and hollering, they were just happy to see it, to be in America. Hungarian (emigrated 1921)

Some immigrants confused the Statue of Liberty with a Roman Catholic saint, proclaiming her "Santa Libertà," while others speculated whether she contained the tomb of Spain's explorer Christopher Columbus. Some were astonished and puzzled by her, while others had heard about the statue and were waiting for a glimpse. The Castle Garden and Ellis Island immigrant inspection stations came in the wake of Liberty's dignified welcome and left a bittersweet memory for millions who passed through to the states, towns, and rural districts of the United States (some to Canada), and to others who were rejected by immigration inspectors and returned by steamer to some foreign shore. Popular records and vaudeville sketches also reflected the good feeling the Statue of Liberty elicited from immigrants. An example can be heard in the 1922 Yiddish record *Die Imigranten* (S. Silberbush and Gus Goldstein), which contains comical talking scenes and also a moment when the Jewish immigrants, in passing by the gigantic sculpture, exclaim, "Hurrah to the Statue of Liberty." *See also* Castle Clinton National Monument; Ellis Island.

Inauguration. The statue of *Liberty Enlightening the World* was officially inaugurated in New York City on 28 October 1886, which had been declared a public holiday for the occasion. The sky was overcast with gray clouds, and there was a fine drizzle. The inauguration was divided into two events: a grand parade in the morning in Manhattan; a flotilla celebration in the harbor, followed by the dedication ceremony and unveiling on Bedloe's Island early in the afternoon; and, finally, a fireworks display in the evening. On the previous day, Mayor William R. Grace had given Auguste Bartholdi the Freedom of the City of New York "in gratitude to the . . . creator of the statue which will forever remain a splendid ornament of [the] metropolis." The Manhattan parade drew a crowd of about 1 million people.

It began at Fifth Avenue and Fifty-seventh Street. Grand marshal Charles P. Stone and the marchers and floats reached President Grover Cleveland's Madison Square reviewing stand by 11:30 in the morning. There, the president declared Bartholdi the "greatest man in America today," to which the sculptor graciously responded, "Through your courtesy, sir." The dignitaries in the reviewing stand, with the President and Monsieur and Madame

American Committee ticket to the inauguration and dedication of the Statue of Liberty, 1886

Bartholdi, included Viscount de Lesseps, William C. Whitney, and William Evarts. French and American flags fluttered everywhere, and the excited throng milled about in anticipation. A parade of twenty thousand marchers went by, proceeding from Fifth Avenue to Broadway, and down to the Battery. Musical airs such as the "Marseillaise," were heard. Marchers included army regiments; Zouaves; war veterans; the Rochambeau Grenadiers; the Italian Rifle Guards; French and Alsatian societies; Philadelphia, New York City, and Brooklyn constables; firemen; and elected officials in carriages. There were freemasons and the Knights of Pythias, and other patriotic and social clubs; there were collegiate groups and a hundred marching bands, and then the representatives from other parts of the nation. There were decorated floats and carriages and plenty of men on horseback. The parade ended with the moving spectacle of President George Washington's carriage passing by, drawn by eight dappled gray horses and escorted by the Continental Guards. By 1:00 P.M., the dignitaries and other sightseers were boarding vessels to see the parade of ships. President Cleveland reviewed this event from the poop deck of the *Despatch*. There were three hundred ships and boats of all descriptions—steamers, yachts, tugboats, and sailing ships—dominated by Rear Admiral Luce's seven men-of-war, which included the *Tennessee,* the *Saratoga,* the *Portsmouth,* and the *Jamestown*. The naval flagship was the *Gedney*. Admiral Luce, commander of the North Atlantic Squadron, was disappointed that the French fleet was unable to join them. The army commander, General Schofield, reviewed the event with his officers on Governor's Island.

At 3:15, there were deafening salvos of U.S. army artillery fire from Governor's Island, joined by the sound of steam whistles from the ships. The Statue of Liberty was then dedicated and unveiled in an elaborate Bedloe's Island ceremony presided over by President Grover Cleveland; Consul Albert Lefaivre of France;

Viscount Ferdinand de Lesseps of the Franco-American Union; and William M. Evarts, on behalf of the American Committee. *See also* Dedication; Martí, José Julián; Olmsted, Frederick Law.

Inman, John Hamilton (*b.* 6 October 1844, Landridge, Tennessee; *d.* 5 November 1896, New Canaan, Connecticut). Merchant and financier. Member of the American Committee, Franco-American Union. Inman, who served in the Confederate army from 1862 until 1865, organized his firm, Inman, Swann & Company, in 1870. In the same year, he founded the New York Cotton Exchange (1870), where commodities were traded. He also headed the Tennessee Coal, Iron & Railroad Company, and he sat on the New York Rapid Transit Commission.

Inscriptions. The only significantly historic inscription on the Statue of Liberty is that of the name of sculptor Auguste Bartholdi and the Gaget and Gauthier foundry where it was constructed. Written in French, it is on the copper base, beneath the statue's feet. It was inscribed at the foundry in Paris. *See also* "The New Colossus"; Tablet; Tablets and plaques.

Insect infiltration. In the spring of 1994, swarms of eastern subterranean termites were noticed in the boiler room and the museum area of the pedestal. Four colonies were discovered: two on the ground floors of the pedestal (the boiler room and the Statue of Liberty museum exhibit) and two outside the walls of Fort Wood (the Sally Port and Sally Port exit). Due to the widespread swarming in foraging tubes and display cases, the Statue of Liberty exhibit on the second floor had to be temporarily closed. Since the infiltration was so extensive, entomologists assumed that the pests had been introduced on the island during the 1984–86 restoration. A population of a single colony of termites can number between 100,000 and 1 million workers that forage up to a distance of 330 feet (about 100 meters) in their quest for food. Because termite damage to historic structures (particularly wooden structures) is costly and irreversible, preservation concerns dictated that the pests be killed. By October 1997, all four infestations had been eliminated through the use of hexaflumuron baits. Monitoring stations were then placed in the soil to detect any remaining or new populations on Liberty Island.

Interior. Upon entering the monument, visitors find themselves in the lobby, where they are confronted by the grand old torch displayed there. Visitors continue to the steps that take them up to the main staircase, which leads up to the pedestal. The main staircase rises to the colonnade level, with a rest platform. Then a few more steps lead to the outside balcony. Continuing up, visitors quickly reach the mezzanine level, where the helical or circular staircase takes them into the Statue of Liberty itself. From here, the climb is more dramatic owing to the narrowness of the helical staircase. Key parts of the internal structure of *Liberty Enlightening the World* are in full view. Visitors have attained their goal when reaching the crown platform where they may gaze out of the windows at the spectacular view of New York harbor.

The earliest staircase in the monument was installed in about 1886 and was a cast-iron ornamental affair. The first elevator in the pedestal was operated by cable pulleys and was installed by the Otis Elevator Company in 1906 or 1907. The current pedestal elevator was installed during the 1980s restoration and was designed for high capacity. To avoid congestion, it is double-decked. Its glass-enclosed space provides a clear view of the pedestal and the anchorage system of the statue. It is powered by hydraulic technology and is convenient to disabled visitors. Visitors riding in the elevator from the base get out at the colonnade level. *See also* Skeleton.

International Workers of the World. Trade union. Early in June 1934, the International Workers of the World (IWW) approached Su-

perintendent George Palmer to request permission to stage a special event at the Statue of Liberty: a celebration of what would have been Emma Lazarus's eighty-fifth birthday on 22 July 1934. According to Palmer, in those years, the IWW was suspected of being a front for the Communist party. Thus, the uneasy superintendent consulted with Jackson Price, legal counsel to the director of the National Park Service. He was advised not to decline the request. Permission was therefore granted, and at Price's suggestion, Palmer chaired the event.

Interpretation. Special techniques of teaching visitors about the significance of natural and historical sites. The National Park Service (NPS) has been influential in the development of interpretation. Freeman Tilden, author of the classic work *Interpreting Our Heritage* (1977), is especially noteworthy as a promoter of a NPS philosophy of interpretation. The approaches include the art of giving public lectures and ranger-guided tours. Although superintendents George Palmer and Oswald Camp and park rangers such as Russell Andrews provided the first regular NPS presence at the site as early as 1933, it was not until about 1936 that the first efforts seem to have been made to develop interpretive programs at the site through the efforts of the first park guides: William C. Webb, S. H. Pickering, Clarence Schultz, J. Fred Roush, Paul H. Younger, and Louis J. Hafner. Park historians Frank Barnes (1950–52), Albert Dillahunty (1952–54), Walter E. Hugins (1954–62), and Thomas M. Pitkin (1955–70) provided leadership during the second phase of interpretive planning. Programs over the years have included tours, torch talks, film festivals, puppet shows, ethnic music and dance programs, special exhibits, the development of brochures, and educational programs. *See also* National Park Service; Park rangers; Pickering, Simeon H.

Iron (puddled). Metal used in the construction of the Statue of Liberty's support system, known as the pylon. Puddled iron is distinguished from wrought iron by its possession of a larger quantity of impurities. Gustave Eiffel chose this form of iron over steel for the sake of its fibrous nature, which allows it to bend while breaking. The process of "puddling" iron removes the phosphorous, the material that gives steel its brittleness. The English ironmaster Henry Cort invented the puddling process of purifying iron in 1783. *See also* Construction (France).

Isère. Frigate of the French navy that transported the Statue of Liberty to the United States. A bark-rigged vessel of 1,000 tons burden and 1,350 displacement, it was one of six men-of-war used for the transportation of soldiers, munitions, and supplies to French colonies. It was painted white for tropical service. The ship was provided by the French Ministry of Marine by the direction of Prime Minister Jules Ferry. It took seventeen days to stow the 214 cases containing the Statue of Liberty. In a letter from Auguste Bartholdi to Richard Butler in December 1884, the sculptor wrote, "In May you will receive the statue aboard the state ship *l'Isère* which I shall inspect at Cherbourg one of these days soon. I shall put a man aboard it to

take care of the unloading . . . a man familiar with the whole procedure . . . who will classify the pieces on the ground." First Lieutenant Lespinasse de Saune was commander of the ship. The vessel set sail from Rouen, France, on 21 May 1885. The weather was stormy, and the ship encountered several terrific gales of wind. The coal having given out, the ship docked at Fayal, in the Azores Islands of Portugal, on 2 June, where it took on provisions and coal. The *Isère* departed Fayal on 4 June. During the remainder of the voyage, the weather was lovely and the sea was smooth. The ship arrived in New York on 17 June. On the same day, De Saune presented official documents to General Charles P. Stone, transferring the statue from the French Committee to the American Committee. Other French naval officers accompanying Lespinasse de Saune were Second Lieutenant Charles Amet and the ship's surgeon, Doctor M. Amiaud. The ship was diverted from colonial wars in order to bring the statue to the United States. Its usual function had been to transport French troops and munitions to Madagascar and French Indochina. It set sail for Brest, France, on the afternoon of 3 July 1885. Numerous presents, including boxes of cigars, cases of smoking and chewing tobacco, snuff, and cigarettes, were bestowed on each of the sixty-five crew members.

Isma'il Pasha (*b.* 31 December 1830, Cairo, Egypt; *d.* 2 March 1895, Istanbul, Turkey).

Ruler of Egypt, beginning in 1863, and khedive (Ottoman viceroy), 1867–79. A powerful reformer in the tradition of his illustrious ancestor Mehemet 'Ali, the Khedive Isma'il promoted the extension of Egyptian railways and telegraph, inaugurated the Suez Canal to international navigation, and improved the vital harbor of Alexandria. He further modernized Egypt by building libraries, secular schools and colleges, public theaters, a khedivial opera house, and fifteen lighthouses. He also set up a consultative parliament, reformed the law courts, and established publications along European lines. However, other reforms caused profound social upheaval in Egyptian society as the balance of power altered. The traditional religious elite lost many of its tax privileges, while royalty, nobles, bourgeoisie, and foreigners gained estates and other sources of wealth. At the time of Auguste Bartholdi's first meeting with the khedive during the Universal Exposition of 1867, he had just arrived in Paris, a romantic spectacle of the East. Bartholdi tried to win from him a commission to build a Suez lighthouse that was to take the form of a colossus called *Egypt Carrying the Light to Asia*. Isma'il Pasha finally rejected the proposal in 1869. The khedive also met Edouard de Laboulaye and attended his international congress of abolitionist societies, which was meeting in Paris during the khedive's visit in 1867. Owing to the Egyptian debt crisis, Sultan Abdul Hamid II dismissed Isma'il in 1879.

Unloading cases containing Statue of Liberty parts from the *Isère*, 1885

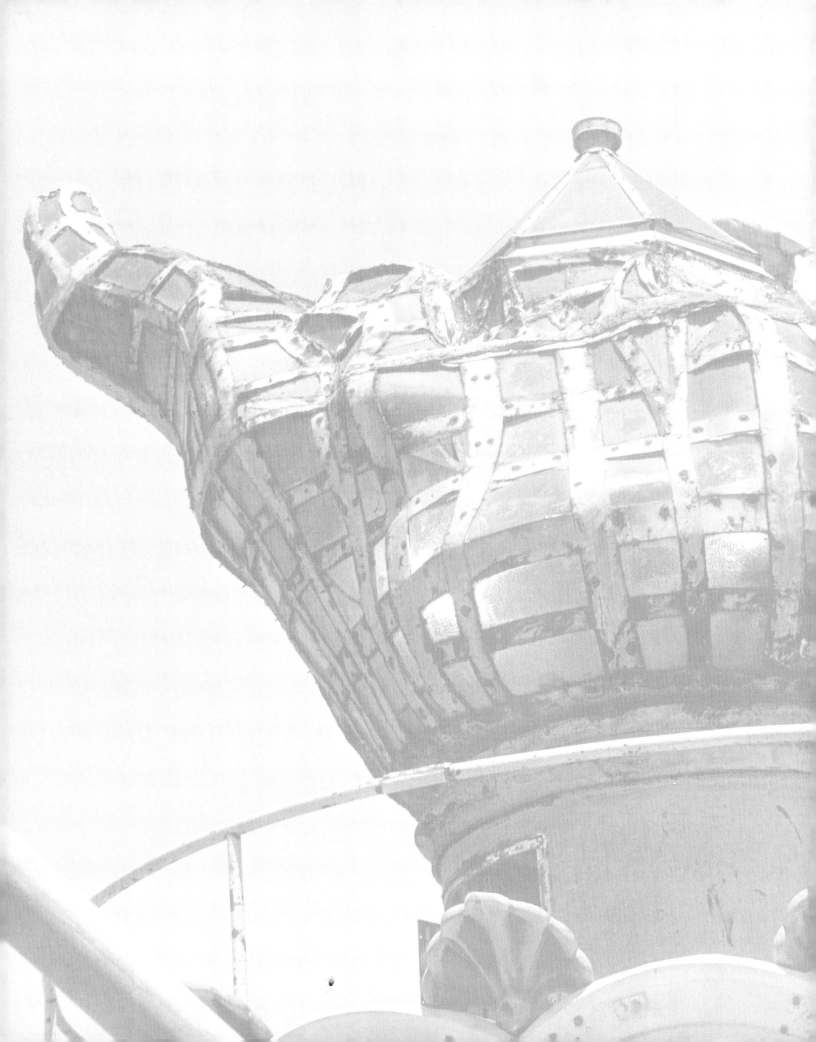

Jaurès, Benjamin (*b.* 3 February 1823, Paris, France; *d.* 13 March 1889, Paris, France). French vice admiral and politician. Jaurès was a political ally of Prime Minister Jules Ferry and a delegate representing the French Senate at the inauguration of the Statue of Liberty in 1886. During his naval career, Jaurès participated in several important maneuvers, including the October 1851 bombardment of Sebastopol during the Crimean War (he was in command of the warship *Napoléon*). He was active in Cochin-China and Tokin (Vietnam) on French imperialist business, 1860–61. In 1870, during the Franco-Prussian War, he was appointed commandant of the subdivision of Maine and Loire department and divisional general of the auxiliary army. In 1871, he was elected a deputy in the National Assembly; he was promoted to vice admiral a month later. He was elected a life senator in 1875. As a senator, he was a great ally of Ferry in promotion of that premier's policy of imperial expansion, for it was to Jaurès that Ferry owed thanks for persuading the National Assembly to permit him to establish the protectorate of French Indochina. Later in his career, Jaurès served as ambassador to Spain, 1878–82; ambassador to Russia, 1882–83; and minister of marine, 1889.

Jay, John II (*b.* 23 June 1817, New York, New York; *d.* 5 May 1894, New York, New York). Lawyer, diplomat, and reformer. Member of the Union League Club and the American Committee, Franco-American Union. Jay responded early to Edouard de Laboulaye's request for aid in setting up fund-raising activities for the Statue of Liberty, joining William M. Evarts and others in establishing the American Committee in 1877. He served on the Legislation subcommittee in 1877 and in 1883 joined the executive committee, chaired by Joseph Drexel.

Jay was a grandson of Chief Justice John Jay and son of William Jay. He was the director of the New York Young Men's Anti-Slavery Society, 1834; secretary of the Irish Relief Committee (during the potato famine), 1847; and U.S. minister to Austria-Hungary, 1869–75. He was also responsible for the eventual establishment of the U.S. civil service, due to his investigations of government corruption revealed in the Jay Commission Report (1877). Further, he was a founder of the Union League Club of New York and served as president twice (1866 and 1877), and he also held the presidencies of the American Historical Association (1890) and the Huguenot Society of America; he was the

founder of the American Geographic and Statistics Society (1852) and one of the founders of New York's Metropolitan Museum of Art (1870).

Johnson, Lyndon Baines (*b.* 27 August 1908, Stonewall, Texas; *d.* 22 January 1973, Johnson City, Texas). President of the United States, 1963–69. Implementing the Antiquities Act of 1906, President Johnson proclaimed Ellis Island a part of the Statue of Liberty National Monument on 11 May 1965. On 3 September of that year, the president, accompanied by a party that included his wife, Lady Bird Johnson, Vice President Hubert H. Humphrey, and Senators Robert Kennedy and Edward Kennedy, visited Liberty Island, where he signed a newly passed immigration bill into law. The law did away with preferential quotas that had favored immigration from the countries of northern and Western Europe.

Jones, George (*b.* 16 August 1811, Poultney, Vermont; *d.* 12 August 1891, New York, New York). Newspaper publisher. Jones, publisher of the *New York Times,* was a member of the Union League Club and the American Committee, Franco-American Union.

Jurisdiction. The first act of acceptance, jurisdiction, and responsibility for the Statue of Liberty was contained in the congressional resolution of 3 March 1877 and immediately signed into law by President Ulysses S. Grant. The American Committee first suggested this resolution to the president on 1 February 1877. The idea was for the U.S. government to accept formally France's gracious offer. President Grant forwarded the committee's resolution idea to Congress with an attached letter expressing his own personal support. The resolution accepted the gift and authorized the president to "designate and set apart a site" on either Bedloe's or Governor's Island, and to "cause suitable regulations to be made for its future maintenance as a beacon, and for the permanent care and preservation thereof as a monument of art and of the continued good will of the great nation which aided us in our struggle for freedom." Its sponsor, Senator Simon Cameron of Pennsylvania, hastily declared that the resolution would cost the U.S. government nothing.

On 28 October 1886, President Grover Cleveland formally accepted the Statue of Liberty at its dedication and inauguration ceremony on Bedloe's Island. Earlier, on 5 August, Congress had appropriated $56,500 for inauguration ceremonies and other expenses. This was the first time that federal money had been provided for the Statue of Liberty and established a precedent for its direct care and maintenance by Washington. The question of jurisdiction and administration of the statue also occurred during the summer of 1886. A U.S. Treasury Department letter asserted that department's jurisdiction through its agency the Light-House Board, owing to the statue's acceptance as a beacon in the 1877 resolution. But the Treasury letter observed that nothing could be done without executive authorization. Taking the hint, President Cleveland ended the dilemma on 16 November 1886 by ordering that the statue of *Liberty Enlightening the World* be put "under the care and superintendence of the Light-House Board, and that it be from henceforth maintained by said Board as a beacon." Over the years, Liberty proved to be ineffective as a beacon. Furthermore, there were complaints about the Light-House Board's maintenance of the site. Especially critical was Major A. C. Taylor, the army post commander of Fort Wood who, in a letter dated 30 June 1901, stated, "Inside and out, the statue of Liberty . . . is a distinct disgrace to our country." He found "no evidence that either money or work had been expended" since 1886 and declared that "this grand work of Art" would slowly deteriorate for want of care. *See also* Army; Legislation; Light-House Board; National Park Service.

K

Karm Island (Norwegian: *Karmøy*). Island located along the southwestern coast of Norway in the North Sea. Its Vigsnes mine is thought to be the source of the Statue of Liberty's copper. Kay Lande Selmer of Staten Island, New York, brought the historical connection to the attention of the public in 1985. Years before, she had learned of Liberty's metallic origins from her father, an emigrant from Karm Island. After her claim was made, the National Park Service agreed that a scientific test should be taken to prove or disprove it. John Robbins, a Park Service historical architect, provided a Statue of Liberty rivet for testing at Bell Laboratories in New Jersey. Through an emission spectrographic test, scientists carried out a comparative analysis of the copper radiation of the statue's rivet with a copper ore sample that had been taken from the Norwegian mine. The scientists agreed that Vigsnes was "a very likely source" for the Statue of Liberty's copper and asserted furthermore that it was "unlikely . . . different ore bodies would produce such similar results." It was later learned that a Franco-Belgian company had operated the mine at the time of the statue's development and construction and that its copper ores were taken by ship for delivery at Belgian and French seaports, such as Dunkerque, France, and then taken to copper mills for refining. French manufacturer Pierre-Eugène Secrétan, the donor of the copper used to build the Statue of Liberty, operated several copper refining mills outside Paris during the same period.

Kennedy, Archibald (*b.* 1685, Craigoch, Scotland; *d.* 14 June 1763, New York, New York). Prominent Scottish colonist who served for many years as New York's receiver-general and collector of customs. Noted for his honest public service, he also acquired considerable properties in New York City and New Jersey. On 22 January 1746, he bought Bedloe's Island from Adolph Philipse for the sum of £100 and one peppercorn on Michaelmas Day (29 September), one of the quarter days when rents came due. (The peppercorn was a token of completing the sale.) In 1710, Kennedy came to New York an adjutant officer of His Majesty's army. Twelve years later, he was appointed collector and receiver-general, a post he held until his death. He was a member of the City Council, 1721–32. His son, Captain Archibald Kennedy (d. 1794), a British loyalist, moved to Scotland at the end of the American Revolution upon inheriting the family's ancestral earldom of Cas-

sillis. His descendant, also named Archibald Kennedy (b. 1961), is the current marquis of Ailsa and earl of Cassillis.

Kennedy Island. Name for Liberty Island during the proprietorship of Archibald Kennedy, 1746–58. *See also* Bedloe's Island; Kennedy, Archibald; Liberty Island.

Keystone Bridge Company. Pittsburgh, Pennsylvania, iron and steel manufacturing and construction firm. In 1885–86, the company manufactured and supplied the Statue of Liberty's complete steel anchorage finished, placed, and painted at a cost of 4.8 cents per pound. One of its senior foremen, Clement MacMahon, supervised the installation of the anchorage system on Bedloe's Island. Keystone erected numerous iron railroad bridges, including those that spanned the Schuylkill River in Philadel-

phia; the Connecticut River in Middletown, Connecticut; and the Mississippi River in Keokuk, Iowa. The company, incorporated in 1872, was controlled by steel magnate Andrew Carnegie.

King, David H., Jr. (*b.* 1849, New York, New York; *d.* 20 April 1916, New York, New York). Building contractor. King was a key figure in the construction of the Statue of Liberty and was especially important in obtaining the necessary granite from the Beattie Quarry at Leete's Island, Connecticut. His many assistants included G. R. A. Ricketts, Colonel J. M. Morgan, William Kennedy, Michael Byrne, and Charles O. Long. King worked on many other contracting jobs in New York City during his career, including the construction of Madison Square Garden, the old Equitable Building, the Washington Arch, and the Mills Building (corner of

Broad and Wall streets). King held the presidencies of the New York Park Commission and the New York Dock Company; he retired from the latter position in 1909. He was a member of the Union League Club.

Koechlin, Maurice (*b.* 1856, Buhl, Alsace, France; *d.* 1946, Vetoz, Switzerland). Engineer. A senior employee in the firm headed by Gustave Eiffel, Koechlin played a role in the design and the calculations of the Statue of Liberty's skeleton framework. He was also prominent in engineering designs for the Eiffel Tower and the Cubzac Bridge, which spans the Garonne River. Koechlin emigrated to Switzerland and was naturalized as a Swiss citizen in 1876. He soon went to Paris, where he was engaged by Gustave Eiffel's engineering firm in October 1879. He worked for Eiffel for the rest of his career and eventually succeeded him as the firm's president. In 1936, the press acclaimed the diffident engineer for his contributions in building the Statue of Liberty. In 1939, he retired to Vetoz, Switzerland.

L

Laboulaye, André de (*b.* 1876, Paris, France; *d.?*). Diplomat who represented France at the fiftieth anniversary of the Statue of Liberty on Bedloe's Island in 1936. He entered the diplomatic service in 1898, eventually rising to the posts of counselor at Berlin, 1924–27, and the principal officer at the Foreign Ministry in the Quai d'Orsay, Paris, before serving as ambassador to the United States, 1933–37. André was the second son of René de Laboulaye and a grandson of Edouard de Laboulaye.

Laboulaye, (Antoine) Paul de (*b.* 1833, Paris, France; *d.* 1905, Paris, France). Diplomat. Educated at the University of Heidelberg (Germany). In England, he entered the French diplomatic service. He was attaché at Brussels (1870) and eventually rose to the posts of minister to Portugal (1878–85) and ambassador to Spain (1885–86). The height of his diplomatic career came while he served as ambassador to Russia, 1886–93, and he played a crucial role in the negotiation of the Franco-Russian Treaty of Alliance signed in 1894. Paul was the elder son of Edouard de Laboulaye and his first wife, Virginie Augustine Paradis (d. 1841).

Laboulaye, Charles de (*b.* 1813, Paris, France; *d.* 1886, Paris, France). Engineer, scientist, and industrialist and brother of Edouard de Laboulaye. After serving in the army, Charles operated a printing shop for a time with his brother. He was the author of many technical books, including *Dictionnaire des Arts et Manufacteurs* (1847), *De la Démocratie industrielle* (1847), *Des Bateaux transatlantiques* (1857), and *L'Art industriel* (1887).

Laboulaye, Edouard de (*b.* 1883, Paris, France; *d.* 1960?, Paris, France). Industrialist and orientalist. Laboulaye was a grandson of the Edouard de Laboulaye, Father of the Statue of Liberty. The younger Laboulaye was widely known for his association with numerous investments in French Indochina, including the development of railroads there. He was third son of René de Laboulaye and the author of *Chemin de fer de Chine* (1911) and an autobiography, *Images d'une Chine défunte* (1953).

Laboulaye, Edouard (René Lefebvre) de (*b.* 18 January 1811, Paris, France; *d.* 25 May 1883, Paris, France). Jurist, historian, politician. Founder and first president of the Franco-American Union; chairman of the French Committee. Laboulaye was the creator of the Statue of Liberty and developed it into a public monu-

Edouard de Laboulaye

ment with the assistance of sculptor Auguste Bartholdi.

Laboulaye was the son of Auguste René Lefebvre de Laboulaye and Aglaé Charlotte Juliette Martinon de Laboulaye. Originally from Auvergne, his paternal grandfather, Jean-Baptiste René Lefebvre de la Boulaye, rose to social dignity as His Majesty's Secretary in the Grand Chancellery of France, 1778–88. This high office conferred hereditary nobility on the family, evident in their use of the *particule de noblesse,* "de." Laboulaye was married twice. His first wife was Virginie Paradis (married 1832; d. 24 June 1841). Their sons were Paul (b. 1833), who became a diplomat, and René (b. 1835), who became a civil servant in the Finance Ministry and rose to the position of director of the Posts and Telegraph Administration. His second marriage (1844) was to Micheline Tronçon du Coudray, with whom he had a son, Lucien (b. 1845). Micheline de Laboulaye headed the women's division of the French Anti-Slavery Society (c. 1865–70) and was the author of a biography of Joan of Arc (*Vie de Jeanne d'Arc,* 1877).

Laboulaye became France's leading Americanist following the death of Alexis de Tocqueville in 1857. He had established his credentials as his country's expert on the U.S. Constitution, offering the first course ever taught in a French college on that subject in December 1849. In 1865, Auguste Bartholdi was invited to a dinner party at Laboulaye's estate at Glatigny, near Versailles. Bartholdi found himself somewhat out of his depth, as such distinguished liberal politicians and intellectuals as Count Charles de Rémusat, Count Agénor de Gasparin, and Henri Martin surrounded him. It was then that Laboulaye first discussed the idea of giving a monument to the United States to honor its independence from Great Britain. This idea flowed from a general discussion regarding the gratitude of nations. Laboulaye held the view that the relations between France and Italy were largely governed by political conflict, while this was quite absent in the relations of France and America, between which there was a genuine sympathetic bond.

Laboulaye proposed that the French and Americans should join together to build a commemorative monument that would pay tribute to the hundred years of friendship of the two nations. This view may have been provoked by a combination of events in the United States: the abolition of slavery, the victory of the Union in the Civil War, and the assassination of President Abraham Lincoln. But Laboulaye was not ready to act: Napoléon III was still emperor, and he did not want to run afoul of the regime, so the matter was dropped until the end of the Second Empire. In 1871, Bartholdi was once more a dinner guest at Glatigny, surrounded by Laboulaye and his liberal political allies. The company included Oscar de Lafayette, Louis Wolowski, Count Charles de Rémusat, and Count de Gasparin. But the combination of the Egyptian failure and the loss of the Franco-Prussian War and the Germanization of Alsace-Lorraine had changed him. Bartholdi was more experienced and now ready to accept the unusual commission of Laboulaye. The scholar reiterated his conceptions for a monument to American liberty and independence (possibly showing Bartholdi the seal of the Second Republic, to which the Statue of Liberty is so similar as to be almost a reproduction). While Bartholdi accepted Laboulaye's statue of Liberty and Independence, Laboulaye was forced to acquiesce to the sculptor's obsession of making a colossus of it. Convinced that this concession would keep the sculptor motivated and ensure that the commission would be carried out to the end, Laboulaye dispatched the artist to the United States with letters of introduction to his circle of friends at the Union League Club and elsewhere. Enthusiastically Laboulaye declared that Liberty would have a "body of iron and a soul of fire."

Laboulaye's early intellectual views were influenced by the methodical discipline of the German historical school. He wrote a book on the great German legal scholar Friedrich von Savigny, *Essai sur la vie et les doctrines de Savigny* (1842). However, liberal writers such as Benjamin Constant, Alexis de Tocqueville, Paul Royer-Collard, and Alexandre Vinet were more important in shaping his political views. He also developed a deep and abiding interest in the legal institutions of European antiquity, especially those of Rome. He produced a fine historical study on the legal status of women: *Recherches sur la condition civile et politique des femmes depuis les Romains jusqu'à nos jours* (1843). He continued his close study of Roman law in his next book, *Essai sur les lois criminelles des Romains concernant la responsabilité des magistrats* (1845). Further, he was a frequent contributor to his friend Wolowski's legal journal, *Revue de législation et de jurisprudence*. His interest in contemporary legal problems seems to have arisen as a result of the Revolution of 1848 and the overthrow of the liberal Orleanist monarch, King Louis-Philippe. He served on two government commissions: one to study education and the other regarding constitutional matters. He soon resigned from both commissions, for, among other things, he was disappointed with the Constitution of the Second Republic (1848–51), a document that provided for only a single-chamber parliament. Strongly preferring a two-chamber legislature, Laboulaye argued that such a constitutional arrangement would fall prey to extremism. The Napoleonic coup d'état of 1851 introduced political censorship and restored the monarchy. These various events directed Laboulaye's scholarly interest toward modern democratic institutions, in particular the study of the U.S. Constitution. He began writing his *Histoire des Etats-Unis,* a work filled with the philosophy and the thoughts that would create his Statue of Liberty. It is a literary equivalent of the monument. But Laboulaye and his group were confronted by the specter of the Second Empire that threatened those who sought to promote liberal ideas. He watched as his bolder liberal colleagues at the Collège de France were one by

one dismissed; this was a warning to Laboulaye, and he took it seriously. He restricted his college lectures to the constitutions of ancient Roman (1852–57) and Gaulish, Teutonic, Merovingian, and Salic legal and political institutions (1857–62).

During this period Laboulaye came under the influence of three American writers: William Ellery Channing, Horace Mann, and Benjamin Franklin. Many of his ideas about the United States were derived from study of their works. He wrote abundantly about them, producing translations, essays, articles, and books. Channing's views on slavery had a profound effect on Laboulaye, and they prepared him for the role he was to play as an abolitionist and supporter of President Abraham Lincoln and the Union cause during the Civil War. Laboulaye concurred with Horace Mann's views that better education for the masses was the way to solve social ills. Laboulaye said, "Establish schools, and you chase away ignorance, crime and misery, and you diminish hatred, for you will make the country wealthy and great by the well being, morality and happiness of each." Benjamin Franklin's moral and economic writings deeply impressed Laboulaye. He liked Franklin for teaching people to reconcile themselves to duty and good conduct. All of these writers, but especially Channing, inspired Laboulaye to venture into politics. His first try was in 1863, when he declared that he would stand for the imperial parliament, known as the Legislative Assembly (Corps législatif) for a constituency in Paris. But he withdrew when the liberal ex-premier Adolphe Thiers entered the race. In 1864, Laboulaye, standing in a parliamentary by-election, campaigned for the principles of democracy and liberty and proclaimed, "Each citizen is master and responsible for his actions and for his life; it is the rule of law in place of the rule of government. I ask for freedom for all, freedom of the person, of the Church, of the school, of the commune, of the department and, above all else, freedom of the press, which is the organ of the public con-

Statue of the young Marquis de Lafayette arriving in America (sculptor: A. Bartholdi, 1872)

science, the incomparable means of popular education and controlling all powers, (and) is the supreme guarantor of all rights." Further, he advocated self-government for the city of Paris. He was endorsed enthusiastically by the *Journal des Débats,* which noted that he represented the old liberal traditions of Alexis de Tocqueville, Benjamin Constant, and Paul Royer-Collard. Notwithstanding this support, he was nevertheless defeated badly, running a distant third. Undaunted, the great scholar again stood for the Legislative Assembly for the 1866 elections; he contested a seat from a constituency in the Lower Rhine department in Alsace. But in spite of generous financial and moral assistance from his friend, the liberal legislator Emile Ollivier, he again was defeated.

Laboulaye made a last and equally unsuccessful bid for a Legislative Assembly seat in the Seine-et-Oise department in the 1869 elections. At about the same time, the government began to relax its firm hold over the nation. From 1867 to 1869, the Emperor Napoleon introduced a series of liberal reforms. In 1869, he appointed Ollivier prime minister, and in a May 1870 plebiscite, the French people approved a new liberal constitution for the empire by a vote of 7,358,786, with only 1,571,939 opposed. During the preelection campaign, Laboulaye abandoned his more radical republican colleagues and urged a vote in favor of the new constitution, for he saw in it a genuine move toward parliamentary democracy. However, he was denounced by his abandoned colleagues and in the fracas was compelled to suspend his classes at the Collège de France. After the plebiscite, Prime Minister Ollivier, in forming a new cabinet, seriously considered Laboulaye for a ministerial post, but the emperor was unfavorable.

When Paris was besieged during the Franco-Prussian War, Laboulaye left the city (and his home at Glatigny-Versailles) and went to Normandy, where he organized ambulances. Upon his return, he found that his house had been occupied by Prussian troops and, curiously, found that they had put his wife's crucifix in a place of prominence and decorated it with boughs. The fall of the Second Empire breathed new life into Laboulaye's political ambitions, and he was elected to the newly established National Assembly for a Parisian constituency in the by-election of 2 July 1871. He took his seat with his fellow conservative republican deputies of the *centre gauche*. Laboulaye assumed the chairmanship of the Parliamentary Commission on Education and in 1873 was named to the influential Committee of Thirty, whose task was to draft a series of constitutional documents that were destined to become the key provisions of the Constitution of the Third Republic (1875–1940). During parliamentary sessions in January 1875, Laboulaye and his ally Henri Wallon won National Assembly acceptance of a republican government for France. In February, parliament passed legislation creating a second chamber—a 300-member Senate, 225 of whom were to be indirectly elected by electoral colleges in the departments. New laws also established the office of president of the Republic, a Chamber of Deputies, and the office of prime minister. In December 1875, Laboulaye was one of seventy-five men elected to be life senators (this was a special honor). Laboulaye hailed the adoption of the new constitutional laws of France as a reflection of "the common right of free peoples."

In 1872, Laboulaye returned to his earlier interest in the condition of women. He demonstrated publicly his support of legal rights for women by presiding over a banquet given by the Women's Rights Association (Association pour le droit des femmes). The association advocated full legal and voting rights for women.

The achievements of these political aims gave Laboulaye freedom to return to his dream of building the Statue of Liberty. In 1875, granting final approval to Bartholdi's study model for the monument, Laboulaye and his liberal associates formed the Franco-American Union for the fund-raising campaign and established its governing board, also known as the French Committee. The members included his colleagues in the Senate and National Assembly. In July 1880, Laboulaye and the Franco-American Union celebrated the completion of the campaign, having raised over 400,000 francs. But success had come too late; Laboulaye did not live to come to America to unveil his *Liberty Enlightening the World. See also* Bartholdi, Auguste; Bigelow, John; Franco-American Union; French Anti-Slavery Society; French Committee; Union League Club; Wolowski, Louis.

Lafayette, (Count) Edmond de (*b.* 1818, La Grange, Blesneau, France; *d.* 1890, Paris, France). Politician. Member of the French Committee, Franco-American Union, 1883–86. Lafayette was a grandson of the marquis de Lafayette (1757–1834) and brother of Oscar de Lafayette. Unlike his more revered brother Oscar, Edmond gained somewhat the reputation of a political opportunist. A moderate republican, he served in the Constituent Assembly, 1849; National Assembly, 1871–75; and as life senator, 1875–90.

Lafayette, (Count) Oscar de (*b.* 1816, Paris, France; *d.* 1882, Paris, France). Politician. A grandson of the marquis de Lafayette (1757–1834), he was a member of honor of the French Committee, Franco-American Union, 1876–82. He began his career as an artillery officer, attaining the rank of captain. A moderate republican in politics, he served in the Chamber of Deputies, 1846–48; the Constituent Assembly, 1849; and the newly reconstituted National Assembly, 1871–75; he was also a life senator, 1875–82. His brother was Edmond de Lafayette, and their sister was married to Count Charles de Rémusat (1797–1875), a friend of Edouard de Laboulaye.

Lafayette Statue (New York). Gift of the French government in gratitude for American relief during the Franco-Prussian War. The government awarded Auguste Bartholdi the commission for this monument shortly after his return from a visit to the United States (1871). He unveiled a plaster model at the Paris Salon of 1873. In 1874–75, the complete bronze statue was cast at the Barbedienne foundry. It was brought to the United States and unveiled with fanfare on 6 September 1876 in Union Square, New York City. The celebration parade lasted four hours. It included U.S. National Guard regiments; French, Belgian, Canadian, Italian, and Swiss veterans; and societies, clubs, and masonic lodges. The sculptor's friend, Henri de Stucklé, designed its pedestal (which was paid for by the French community's Lafayette Committee). The statue shows a young marquis de Lafayette arriving in America to aid the American revolutionaries. A *Courrier des Etats-Unis* correspondent wrote, "This is really the nineteen-year-old Lafayette animated by youthful ardor and fired by the noble passion for liberty."

Lafayette Statue (Paris). An American reciprocal gift to France for the Statue of Liberty. Fund raising for the statue began in 1898 when school children all over the country were asked for penny and nickel donations. Within a year, $50,000 had been raised, and the committee selected Paul Bartlett as the sculptor. Although a model for the statue was displayed on 4 July 1900, it was not until June 1908 that the bronze equestrian statue of the marquis de Lafayette was finished. It was unveiled in the garden of the Louvre in Paris, where it was permanently exhibited.

Landscape and vegetation. Liberty Island is not conducive to vegetation due to high winds, salty sea water, and poor soil. The island was largely cleared of its early vegetation by the 1890s. Prior to this period, notice was usually taken only of the commonest trees and plants such as might be seen on the nearby New Jersey shore or Staten Island. The construction of military barracks and other buildings beyond the walls of Fort Wood and on the island's north side began in the 1880s and reached a climax

during World War I. The removal of early trees and shrubbery was essential to the utilitarian demands of the army, although the island's oldest surviving trees—horse chestnut, oaks, and maples—date from the military years. In 1931, the Statue of Liberty's first civilian superintendent, William A. Simpson, installed a series of rather curious flowerbeds on the lawn that surrounded the pedestal. The beds were edged by a geometrical arrangement of bricks in the shape of stars and moons. This striking brickwork arrangement remained until 1934, when they were removed by order of Simpson's successor, Superintendent George Palmer, who observed wryly that the beds were more suited to a gas station than a national monument.

With the departure of the army from Bedloe's Island in 1937, the National Park Service began to transform the island into a park. The old army buildings would be replaced with new landscaping and vegetation designed to enhance the pleasure of tourists who visited the Statue of Liberty. In 1939, the master plan, designed to accomplish these goals, was adopted and largely fulfilled by 1965. In 1952, a new channel was dredged, and the northwestern end of Bedloe's Island was enlarged by 2 to 3 acres with earth from the operation. The sea wall was rebuilt in 1938–39 and again in 1952.

The island's vegetation consists largely of trees, hedges, turf, and ground clover. For visitors, the current landscape begins with the Boat Dock; from there the Arrival Promenade orients visitors with informational signage and access to the Park Service Administrative Building and visitors' center, as well as the Concession Building. This area leads to Flag Pole square, which affords a splendid view of Manhattan through the linden trees; from there, the Central Mall, lined by hedges and linden trees, leads to the entrance of Fort Wood and the Statue of Liberty. Other landscaped areas are the Pedestal Lawn surrounding Fort Wood and the monument; the Northeast and Southwest Side Lawns (with cherry trees); and the perime-

Political cartoon critical of Pierre Laval during World War II

ter path with a fence barrier at the water's edge. There are also staff residential quarters and maintenance buildings. *See also* Army; Bedloe's Island; Ferry service; Insect infiltration; Liberty Island; Master Plan of 1939; National Park Service; Newton, Norman; Visitation.

Lanier, Charles (*b.* 19 January 1837, Madison, Indiana; *d.* 7 March 1926, New York, New York). Banker. Member of the American Committee, Franco-American Union; served on the Finance subcommittee, 1884–86. A partner of Winslow, Lanier & Company, from 1860, he was also associated with the Central Union Trust and the Southern Railway Company.

Laval, Pierre (*b.* 28 June 1883, Châteldon, Puy-de-Dôme, France; *d.* 15 October 1945, Fresnes, France). Politician and statesman. In October 1931, Prime Minister Laval, accompanied by his daughter Joséphine, made an official visit to the United States to hold high-level talks with President Herbert Hoover. His steamship arrived in New York, and before taking a train to Washington, he and his daughter participated in the lighting ceremony of the Statue of Liberty's new and highly improved floodlighting system installed by the Westinghouse Electric Company. Joséphine Laval pressed the button that sent a signal to an aviator who, high above the statue, illuminated *Liberty Enlightening the World* more powerfully than ever before.

Pierre Laval, a socialist, was prime minister thrice: 1931–32, 1935–36, and 1942–44. On the last occasion, he openly collaborated with the Nazi Germans, for which he was condemned to death as a traitor and executed in 1945. *See* Lighting.

Lazarus, Emma (*b.* 22 July 1849, New York, New York; *d.* 19 November 1887, New York, New York). Poet. Lazarus composed the famous sonnet, "The New Colossus," in aid of the Pedestal Fund on 2 November 1883. She was the fourth of six daughters and one son of Moses Lazarus (1813–85), a sugar refiner, and

HIS ARM WILL TIRE – HERS NEVER WILL

his wife, Esther Nathan Lazarus. The family were descendants of Portuguese Sephardic Jewish immigrants. Her books of poetry were *Admetus and Other Poems* (1871), *Songs of a Semite* (1882), and *The Dance to Death* (1882). Prose works include the novel *Alide: An Episode of Goethe's Life* (1874) and *The Spagnoletto* (1876), a five-act historical tragedy. Lazarus not only wrote her own poetry but also translated French, German, Italian, and Hebrew poetry into English and also translated the great Ladino poetry of medieval Spain. Inspired by George Eliot's novel *Daniel Deronda,* and dismayed by the anti-Jewish pogroms in Russia and Romania, she took up the Jewish charitable work for refugees and on many occasions visited Ward's Island, where a large number were detained by Castle Garden officials. She became an aid worker for Jewish immigrants at Ward's Island and was deeply moved by the plight of the Russian Jews she met there. She believed that Jewish emigration to a homeland in Palestine would solve the problem, and visited Europe in aid of Jewish nationalism in 1883 and 1885–87. Senator William M. Evarts and Constance Cary Harrison asked her to compose a poem to aid the Bartholdi Pedestal Fund. Inspired by the Ward Island refugees, she wrote her powerful sonnet, "The New Colossus." Lazarus became terminally ill with cancer in August 1884, shortly after her return to New York City. The thirty-eight-year-old writer died at her home and was buried in Cypress Hills cemetery. She was lamented by such notable literary figures as John Greenleaf Whittier, Robert Browning, John Burroughs, Constance Cary Harrison, George W. Cable, John Hay, and Harriet Beecher Stowe. *See also* Harrison, Constance Cary; "The New Colossus"; Pedestal Art Loan Exhibition.

Leete's Island. Located on a peninsula in Connecticut, this was the location of the Beattie Quarry from which the granite for the Statue of Liberty's pedestal was obtained. The granite was transported by boat across the Long Island Sound and Atlantic Ocean to Bedloe's Island in New York harbor. *See also* Granite; King, David H.

Legislation. The primary legislative acts and official authorizations governing Liberty's legal history in the United States is founded on the following legal documents:

1. Joint congressional resolution of 1877 to accept Liberty as a work of art and beacon, sponsored by Congressman Abram Hewitt of New York and Senator Simon Cameron of Pennsylvania. It passed the House on 22 February and the Senate on 27 February. President Ulysses S. Grant approved it on 3 March 1877.

2. In accordance of the provisions of the joint resolution, President Rutherford B. Hayes, on the recommendation of General William T. Sherman, selected Bedloe's Island as the permanent site for the Statue of Liberty, 1877.

(left) Emma Lazarus

(opposite page) The story of the arrival of the *Isère* in *Frank Leslie's Illustrated Newspaper,* 27 June 1885

3. First federal funding ($56,500): sundry civil appropriations bill (4 August 1886).

4. Executive order of President Grover Cleveland placing the statue under the Treasury Department, Light-House Board, effective 22 November 1886.

5. Executive order of President Theodore Roosevelt transferring the statue from the Treasury to the War Department (Army), 30 December 1901, effective March 1902.

6. President Calvin Coolidge, by right of the Antiquities Act of 1906, proclaims and decrees the statue and Fort Wood a national monument, under the administration of the War Department, 15 October 1924.

7. Executive order of President Franklin Roosevelt transferring the statue and Fort Wood from the War to the Interior Department, 1933.

8. Two executive orders of President Roosevelt transferring the statue and Fort Wood by name from the War to the Interior Department, issued 10 June and 28 July 1933.

9. Executive order of President Franklin Roosevelt transferring the remainder of Bedloe's Island from the War to the Interior Department, 7 September 1937.

10. President Dwight Eisenhower signs a joint resolution of Congress renaming Bedloe's Island "Liberty Island," August 1956.

11. President Lyndon B. Johnson, by right of the Antiquities Act of 1906, proclaims and decrees Ellis Island to be henceforth a part of the Statue of Liberty National Monument, 11 May 1965. *See also* Antiquities Act; Congressional Joint Resolution of 1877; Enabling authorization.

Leslie, Frank (*b.* 21 March 1821, Ipswich, England; *d.* 10 January 1880, New York, New York). Publisher and illustrator. Leslie's periodicals carried richly illustrated articles on the Statue of Liberty's fund raising and construction in the 1880s. Frank Leslie (his original name was Henry Carter), who immigrated to the United

NEW YORK.—ARRIVAL OF THE FRENCH TRANSPORT STEAMER "ISÈRE," WITH THE BARTHOLDI STATUE ON BOARD, AT THE BASE OF THE PEDESTAL, BEDLOE'S ISLAND, FRIDAY, JUNE 19TH.—THE SALUTE OF WELCOME BY THE FLEET.

FROM A SKETCH BY A STAFF ARTIST.—SEE PAGE 302.

States from England in 1848, was the founder and publisher of *Frank Leslie's Illustrated Newspaper* (established 1855), *Frank Leslie's Weekly Magazine,* and *Lady's Journal.* After his death, his widow, Miriam Follin Leslie (1836–1914), successfully continued the business. She later married William Wilde, brother of Oscar Wilde.

Lesseps, (Viscount) Ferdinand Marie de (*b.* 19 November 1805, Versailles, France; *d.* 7 December 1894, La Chenaie, France). French diplomat and canal developer. Lesseps was a cousin of the Empress Eugénie, the consort of Napoléon III. He launched his diplomatic career in 1825 and held appointments in Portugal, Tunisia, and Egypt. In 1856, he won a concession from the Egyptian viceroy to construct the Suez Canal. It took nine years to complete and was opened in November 1869. De Lesseps joined the Franco-American Union in 1883 and was selected to succeed Edouard de Laboulaye as its president. As president of the Union, he inherited the achievements of Laboulaye: fund raising for Liberty had already been completed, and the construction of the statue itself was nearly finished. In 1884, the viscount ceremonially presented the Statue of Liberty to the U.S. minister to France and in 1886 did the same honors in New York in the presence of the president of the United States. On seeing the statue in the harbor, he declared, "I can only call it a triumph. It represents the progress of the two nations. It tells of liberty on these shores. Let the American people abide by its precepts!" He was accompanied by one of his twelve children, seventeen-year-old Ferdinande "Tototte" de Lesseps. Viscount de Lesseps also developed plans to construct the Panama Canal, but the scheme failed. After his death, American promoters successfully revived the project, and the canal was completed in 1914.

Libertas (English: "Liberty"; French: "Liberté"). The Statue of Liberty is a modern allegorical representation of this goddess of ancient Rome. Libertas, the personification of liberty and personal freedom ordained by the Roman state, emerged from the Roman law of freedom (*libertas*) and was fully deified in the fourth century B.C. in an official state cult under the name of Jupiter Libertas. Her original association with Jupiter, king of the gods, was due to the legal origin. Her worship was more common among individuals than within social groups: she was a personal goddess. Freed slaves were especially devoted to her. A famous votive offering to Libertas was a painting depicting a First Punic War battle in which slaves are shown securing their manumission; it was placed in a temple (*aedes*), built for her in 238 B.C. In the following century, the Roman statesman and reformer Tiberius Sempronius Gracchus (168–133 B.C.) built an even more glorious temple to Libertas on the Aventine hill. This temple, probably of Greek design, would have been furnished with her idol, a sacrificial altar, lamps, basins for ceremonial washings, and benches. In the first century B.C., the orator Asinius Pollio placed a statuary idol of the goddess in the Roman Forum. There was also an Atrium Libertatis (atrium of Liberty) in a part of the Forum of Trajan that was known as the Ulpian Basilica.

The temples of Libertas had state priests who presided over the ceremonial offerings of sacrifices and prayers and the celebration of public festivities to her glorification. During these celebrations, cult images and objects dedicated to the goddess were displayed to worshippers. Her sacred attributes included the *vindicta,* the *pileus,* the sceptre and, at her feet, a broken vase and a cat. The *vindicta* was the rod or staff with which a slave was tapped to grant manumission. The *pileus* (Phrygian bonnet or cap of freedom) was worn by emancipated slaves to proclaim their status as freedmen. The sceptre signified the goddess's dominion over mankind; the cat, which had not yet been domesticated in Rome, represented the natural instinct for freedom; and the broken vase symbolized the end of confinement.

As with all other Roman gods, the most com-

(Clockwise, from left)

Libertas, goddess of freedom, in profile. In her right hand she bears the *pileus libertatis* (cap of freedom); in her left hand, the sceptre (Roman denarius coin issued by Brutus, c. first century B.C.)

Reverse of the Libertas denarius coin with signature of Brutus

Head of Libertas, Roman denarius coin, c. first century A.D.

mon religious ceremony for Libertas was a sacrifice. A magistrate, a club, or any devotee could offer an ox, pig, sheep, or bird to the goddess. While a priest chanted prayers, an attendant led an animal to the flower-decorated altar; any resistance was considered a bad omen. The creature's head would then be sprinkled with meal, salt, and incense. A *victimarius* (sacrificial butcher) would stun it with a swift blow of a mallet to the head and then cut its throat with an axe or a knife. As the blood ran out, its entrails were examined by a *haruspex* priest for bad omens; it was then roasted over the altar fire. Some portions were reserved for the goddess, while the rest was served in a feast held in the sacred precincts of the temple. Simple offerings to the goddess included flowers, clay images, vegetables, and cakes. The feast day of Libertas fell on 13 April, a day known as the Ides of April, sacred to Jupiter.

Under the regime of Julius Caesar, the cult of the goddess became associated with political liberty: in 48 B.C., Caesar issued *denarii* coins bear-

ing the likeness of the goddess to strengthen his claim of being a liberator of the Romans. But his assassins, Brutus and Cassius (who had accused him of despotism), exalted Libertas on their own *denarii,* showing two daggers and a *pileus.* During the Roman Empire, beginning with the reign of Augustus Caesar, her importance as an icon of political liberty expanded even further; some even associated her with constitutional government. Libertas was only one of many personifications of abstract ideas and virtues brought into Rome's pantheon. Other fully deified abstracts of the Republican period were Fortuna (luck), Concordia (harmony), Salus (welfare and health), Victoria (military victory), Spes (hope), Fides (faith and fidelity), Ops (abundance of crops and help), and Virtus (military courage). Those of the empire included Clementia, Indulgentia, Justitia, Pax, Providentia, Securitas, and Pudicitia (chastity).

Libertas enjoyed a revival as a philosophical and political symbol of liberty and democracy in the eighteenth century. The form of the an-

tique deity, once conspicuous on Roman coinage, now found herself on modern French and American coins and medals. Although artists rendered her image according to the spirit of the time and their own varying ability and tastes, she was consistently recognizable, for most artists continued to depict her in Roman style, with the sacred features, the elegant robes of antiquity, and the *pileus.* She appeared on American coins as early as 1793 and would maintain her position prominently throughout the nineteenth century. The revival of the goddess on coinage, medals, paintings, and other forms of art established the precedent necessary for her ultimate return in the form of the statue of *Liberty Enlightening the World.* European artists early recognized that the goddess Libertas was a suitable allegorical symbol for the United States.

In 1791, Giuseppe Ceracchi, the neoclassical sculptor, visited the United States and, anticipating Laboulaye and Bartholdi by eighty years, offered to sculpt and build a colossal monument

to the deity. His commission was to be $30,000. The statue was to be 100 feet high, and Libertas was to be depicted "descending in a carriage drawn by four horses, darting through a volume of clouds which conceals the summit of a rainbow . . . in her right hand she brandishes a flaming dart, which is dispelling the mists of Error, illuminates the universe." Again the idea of illumination is present. The proposal was rejected.

It is scarcely surprising that objections were raised on Judeo-Christian grounds to building a statue of the goddess in New York harbor. Perhaps the clearest denunciation came from an article that appeared in the *American Catholic Quarterly* (vol. 5) in 1880, the year in which the French completed their successful subscription campaign to build the monument. The article, "Worship of Liberty Decried," made the following observation: "There seems no hope of a speedy deliverance from this state worship of Libertas. She is to remain on our coins, and the gigantic bronze figure will soon tower on the little island in the beautiful bay of New York. Massive and grand, beautiful in outline and in pose, holding her torch to proclaim that mankind receives true light, not from Christ and Christianity, but from heathenism and her gods."

But these sentiments did not take hold and, the public waxed enthusiastic over their great goddess; she was even blessed by Protestant ministers at her inauguration in 1886. In 1937, an altar of liberty was put up for a special event at the Statue of Liberty National Monument with the permission of the National Park Service. The altar bore a resemblance to those that existed in ancient Rome.

Libertas has journeyed a long way indeed. The Christians who had put out the goddess's sanctuary flames in the fifth century would perhaps be astonished (if not appalled) to see their spiritual descendants come perilously close to relighting those flames in the nineteenth century. But Liberty is viewed as the symbol of democratic institutions and individual freedom, not

as an idol of Roman religion, notwithstanding her origin. Hence she has won the hearts of all who believe in these principles.

La Liberté. French film production made in tribute to the Statue of Liberty's fiftieth anniversary in 1936 by Jean Kemm, in cooperation with Leopold Netter, who had presented it originally as a stage play, *Bartholdi un sin Rabmanella* ("Bartholdi and His Little Winegrower"), which was presented in the Alsatian Theatre in 1934.

Liberty. Roman goddess. *See* Libertas.

Liberty Altar. The altar of Liberty was set up at Bedloe's Island in September 1937 to commemorate the 150th anniversary of the U.S. Constitution and honor the goddess of liberty. It stood in front of the staircase giving entrance to the portals of the pedestal, the Statue of Liberty looming above. The front of the altar was decorated with thirteen stars at the top and, in the center below, a large image of the Liberty Bell; an inscription on the left side read "1787," while on its opposite was "1937." The following items were placed on the altar: a replica of the Statue of Liberty (about 4 feet high) standing on an entablature of a Doric pillar (her torch was surmounted by a curious electric globe); on either side of the goddess were two large candlesticks each fitted with three tall white candles, and two small American flags. Draped behind the altar was an enormous American flag, attached to the top of the staircase parapet perhaps 12 feet above. Wreaths and flowers were placed as offerings to Liberty at the base of the altar. The event was sponsored in part by the Mayor's Committee on the 150th anniversary of the adoption of the Constitution and in part by the National Park Service, which was represented by Superintendent Oswald E. Camp. Crowds of guests and reporters came to the island, where they listened to speeches and witnessed a naturalization ceremony for immigrants. An actor did an effective impersonation

The Altar of Liberty with park guide William C. Webb, Bedloe's Island, 1937

(left) First page of the music and lyrics of the "Liberty Cantata" of Gounod and Guiard

(opposite page, top) Auguste Bartholdi's watercolor painting of Liberty enlightening the world

(opposite page, below) Temporary plaque for the newly named Liberty Island, 1956

of George Washington. A New York harbor fireboat provided more entertainment with a display off the East Dock. The program concluded with a fantastic emission of smoke from the Statue of Liberty's torch, as if to symbolize the smoke of burned offerings, or perhaps to convey the deity's approval of the festivities.

Liberty Bell. Dating from the American Revolution, the Liberty Bell is the traditional symbol of United States freedom from Great Britain. It was cast in England in 1753 and brought to Philadelphia that year, where it cracked in a test

ring. It was twice recast there before being hung in the steeple of the assembly house in June 1753. It was rung in 1776 in the same building, which was renamed Independence Hall. It weighs about 2,080 pounds (936 kilograms), its lip is 12 feet (3.6 meters) in circumference, and it measures 3 feet (approximately 1 meter) from lip to crown. An engraved motto reads: "Proclaim Liberty throughout All the Land unto All the Inhabitants Thereof" (Leviticus 25:10).

Liberty Cantata. Dramatic choral hymn presented at the Paris Opera on 25 April 1876 as a

part of the Franco-American Union's fund-
raising effort to build the Statue of Liberty. Its
full name was *La Liberté éclairant le monde.*
Charles Gounod composed the music, and
Emile Guiard wrote the lyrics. The evening
event at the Palais de l'Opéra was introduced by
a brief address given by the sixty-five-year-old
Edouard de Laboulaye, who was dressed in a
tunic buttoned to the top, "revealing only the
line of the white neck; clean shaven; the hair
grey, worn long and brushed back." An extrav-
agant musical program, with selections by
Aubert, Fauré, Rossini, and Gounod's *Ave
Maria,* followed Laboulaye's remarks. A male
chorus of some seven hundred then sang the
Liberty Cantata. The musical part of the program concluded with what was mistakenly described as the American national anthem, "Hail
Columbia." The event was not well received by
the critics, and it raised only 8,291 francs; a full
house would have brought in 22,000 francs. For
more than a hundred years the Liberty Cantata
was quite forgotten, but as the Statue of Liberty
approached its hundredth anniversary, the musical motet was revived for a second performance. It was first rescored and translated into
English rhyme by conductor Hugh Ross, before
being sung by his Schola Cantorum and a group
from the All-City High School Chorus in its
American debut at Alice Tully Hall in New
York City on 11 April 1986.

Liberty Enlightening the World. Official En-
glish translation of the original French name of
Liberty, *La Liberté éclairant le monde.* Alternate
English translations are *Liberty Illuminating the
World* and *Liberty Lighting the World.*

Liberty Island (formerly Bedloe's Island). A
12.7-acre island in New York harbor, lying near
the New Jersey shore; the site of the Statue of
Liberty. Although Auguste Bartholdi con-
stantly referred to Bedloe's Island as Liberty Island and frankly expressed a desire that the
island's name be officially changed, nothing was
done until more than fifty years after his death.

Just before the seventieth anniversary of Liberty's unveiling, the American Museum of Immigration fund raisers initiated the change of name. They also contrived to include a passage in the legislation that directly referred to their own organization by name; this served as a sort of federal sanction to their campaign to found the American Museum of Immigration. This legislation, endorsed by President Dwight D. Eisenhower, was approved as a joint resolution of Congress and signed into law by the president on 3 August 1956. *See also* Bedloe's Island; Landscape and vegetation.

Liberty Loan. A U.S. government fund-raising campaign to help win World War I. The government sold "Liberty War Bonds" in different denominations. The example was taken from

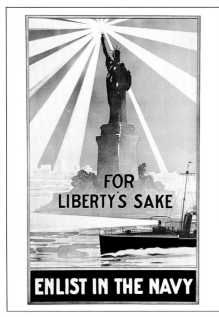

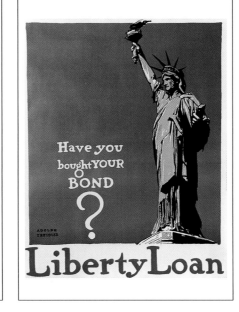

(left) Liberty Loan (artist: G.R. Macauley)

(right) U.S. Food Administration advertisement, World War I

(below, left) Naval recruitment advertisement, World War I (Boston Public Safety Committee)

(below, right) Liberty Loan of 1917 (artist: Adolph Treidier)

Great Britain's successful war bond campaign. The Statue of Liberty was adopted for the campaign for two reasons: the nature of the profoundly pro-French nature of the war and the connection of the statue with immigrants. The very name "Liberty Loan" immediately reminded people of the statue. Taking a further lesson from the British (and the French), the Liberty Loan was introduced by an aggressive poster advertising campaign, the most famous one being artist G. R. Macauley's drawing of Liberty pointing directly at the viewer, with the caption: "YOU Buy a Liberty Bond." The success of this and others led to the government's setting up a special Division of Pictorial Publicity, composed of volunteer artists and chaired by the celebrated illustrator Charles Dana Gibson (1867–1944). His staff included illustrators

(left) Second Liberty Loan of 1917 (artist: Eugene DeLand)

(right) Second Liberty Loan of 1917: immigrants bound for Ellis Island view the Statue of Liberty

(below, left) Third Liberty Loan: "Weapons for Liberty." Armed Goddess of Liberty and Boy Scout, World War I

John C. Leyendecker, Joseph Pennell, and the Frenchman Sem. Many famous people became fund raisers for the Liberty Loans, led by such silent film stars as Mary Pickford, Douglas Fairbanks, Charles Chaplin, and Marguerite Fisher and the Italian opera singer Enrico Caruso, whose country was an ally in the war.

Liberty Weekend (3–6 July 1986). Weekend extravaganza of the centennial anniversary of the Statue of Liberty, hosted by President Ronald Reagan. The guest of honor for the occasion was President François Mitterand of France. President Reagan declared, "We are the keepers of the flame of liberty; we hold it high for the world to see." In unveiling the newly restored Statue of Liberty on 4 July 1986, President Reagan pressed a button that sent a laser beam across the water to the statue. Gradually, dramatically, and splendidly, a light show unveiled the colossus and her new torch, and then a dazzling fireworks display was let off, its fantastic lights encircling the hundred-year-old statue. Liberty Weekend celebration included Operation Sail, a flotilla of hundreds of civilian and naval vessels in New York harbor. *See also* Anniversaries; Reagan, Ronald.

Light-House Board (U.S. Department of the Treasury). First federal agency to have responsibility for the care and maintenance of the Statue of Liberty (1886–1902). Because Congress had designated the Statue of Liberty for use as a beacon in 1877, President Grover Cleveland assigned jurisdiction of the new monument to the Light-House Board. The new beacon was located in the Light-House Board's Third District, with headquarters on Staten Island. Despite constant work, the efforts of such Light-House Board officials as Lieutenant John Millis and Major David Porter Heap to improve the lighting power of the Statue of Liberty met with failure. In response, President Theodore Roosevelt transferred jurisdiction of the Statue of Liberty to the War Department on 30 December 1901 (effective March 1902). The Light-House Board

had been created by an act of Congress in 1852 to administer lighthouses and lightships throughout the country. In 1910, the board was renamed the Bureau of Lighthouses. In 1939 it ceased to be an independent agency when it was transferred to the U.S. Coast Guard.

Lighting. The Statue of Liberty was designated a beacon in the congressional resolution signed into law by President Ulysses Grant on 3 March 1877. The resolution authorized the president to "designate and set apart a site" for the statue on either Governor's or Bedloe's Island and to "cause suitable regulations to be made for its future maintenance as a beacon, and for the permanent preservation thereof as a monument of art and of the continued good will of the great nation which aided us in our struggle for freedom." After having been presented to the people of the United States in the ceremony of 28 October 1886, there was a delay in lighting the goddess. It was not until 7.35 P.M. on 1 November 1886 that the public had a chance to see the effects of the freshly installed steam-powered electric lighting apparatus. Due to disappointing results (the light was dim), the illumination was turned off on 7 November for further work; it was relighted on 22 November. President Cleveland duly placed the monument under the care and superintendence of the Light-House Board, U.S. Department of the Treasury, effective 22 November 1886. The board was to maintain Liberty as a beacon, as stipulated in the 1877 resolution. The American Committee received the donation of an electric plant and lighting equipment for use in electrifying the torch and flame. The man permanently in charge of the electrification was Lieutenant John Millis of the U.S. Army Corps of Engineers, and the first head light keeper was A. E. Littlefield, for whom an ex-military infirmary constructed of brick was fitted up as a residence.

In January 1887, Liberty was lighted with fourteen arc lamps—nine in the torch and five others positioned strategically below at the angles of Fort Wood. A steam dynamo pow-

Liberty Weekend fireworks, 4 July 1986

ered them. Dissatisfied with this arrangement, the Light-House Board, on 4 February 1887, requested a congressional appropriation of $32,500 to build a permanent lighting plant and erect buildings, a wharf, and other necessities for physical maintenance. Congress responded within a few weeks by tagging an extra $19,500 for the lighting plant for Liberty onto the sundry civil appropriations bill. With this money, Lieutenant Millis, though unable to make the torch an aid to navigation, was yet able to beautify the new statue significantly. In 1892, another unsuccessful effort was made to solve the illumination problem. In 1897, an oil-generated engine was installed to power the lighting system.

In 1916, the lighting system in the torch was completely replaced and successfully intensified by a floodlighting system installed by the General Electric Company. Gutzon Borglum supervised the removal of copper and the installation of amber-colored cathedral glass as a replacement. He placed more of this glass at the flame's upper portion to enhance the lighting. The torch now emitted 250,000 lumens of constant light. Also, 95,000 lumens of automatically flickering lights were added to create the effect of authentic fire. An exterior floodlighting system for the statue and pedestal was also installed.

On the night of 26 October 1931, Joséphine Laval stood on the 102nd floor of the Empire State Building in Manhattan and turned on yet another new floodlighting installation at the Statue of Liberty. The daughter of France's visiting premier, Pierre Laval, passed her hand over a Knowles grid glow relay tube, which sent a signal via radio to Army Air Corps Captain Albert Stevens, who was circling above the statue in an airplane, from which a photographic aerial "bomb" was released. The light from this "bomb" activated an electric eye in Liberty's hand, which threw switches that turned on the powerful floodlamps. The whole system was donated and installed by the Westinghouse Electric Company under the supervision of engineer Alfred Paulus. There were ninety-six lighting units, forty of them equipped with 1,000-watt

Light-House Board caretaker inside the Statue of Liberty or pedestal, c. 1890s

lamps to illuminate the pedestal; the remaining fifty-six units were equipped with 1,000-watt lamps, which produced a narrow beam of light focused on Liberty herself; 15,600 watts of electric power were installed for illumination in the torch. In December 1931, W. F. Dietz of the Westinghouse Company sent a report of the work to Colonel U. S. Grant III of the Army Corps of Engineers in Washington, D.C.

Although the lighting was intensified in 1945 (Westinghouse Electric Company) and again for America's bicentennial celebration in 1976, it was not until the 1982–86 Liberty restoration that the system underwent serious change. Technological advances made it possible to install a lighting system that could duplicate natural daylight. Since then, the statue has been illuminated by warm lights that show the details of sculpture and the pedestal. The metal halide lamps send a high-intensity, narrow beam of light that focuses on specific parts of the statue, such as the face or the tablet. There are forty lamps of 250 watts each, providing 320,000 lumens of light over the statue's body. Sixteen 250-watt tungsten halogen lamps are installed under the railing of the torch, and forty-two 120-watt, 6-voltage spotlights throw narrow beams of light on the torch from below. In addition, four 1,000-watt medium floodlights send a powerful stream of light from the statue's head. H. M. Brandston prepared the lights, which were produced and perfected by the General Electric Company. *See also* Heap, David P.; Light-House Board; Millis, John; Palmer, George A.;Torch.

Lion of Belfort. War memorial. Representative of Auguste Bartholdi's patriotic art in the colossal tradition, the *Lion of Belfort* is a memorial to the vigorous French defense of the town and citadel of Belfort, Lorraine, during the Franco-Prussian War (1870–71). The stubborn resistance of Colonel Pierre Denfert-Rochereau (1823–78) and his troops ensured that Belfort would remain part of France by the terms of the Treaty of Frankfurt (10 May 1871). The

Superintendent George Palmer briefly reignites the torch during World War II, May 1945

monument is constructed on a rock formation that dominates the town. Following the completion of a fund-raising campaign initiated by the Belfort municipal council (92,000 francs was collected by 1875), Bartholdi set up a work camp on the outskirts of Belfort. Most of the labor was done by a large number of stonecutters. The pink sandstone *Lion,* which measures 72 feet long (22 meters) and 36 feet high (11 meters), was dedicated in 1880. Its inscription reads, *"Aux Défenseurs de Belfort, 1870–71"* ("To the Defenders of Belfort, 1870–71"). Bartholdi produced a smaller version of the *Lion* located in Denfert-Rochereau Square, Paris.

Literature. The earliest book on the new statue was Auguste Bartholdi's *Statue of Liberty Enlightening the World,* edited by Allen Thorndike Rice and published by the North American Review in 1885. This slim promotional volume (timed for the year of the statue's arrival in New York) was intended to help the American Committee raise funds to complete the pedestal. Copies sold for seventy-five cents each. Booklets appearing after the statue's inauguration were John J. Garnett's *Statue of Liberty: Its History, Conception, Construction and Inauguration–Official Programme* (1886) and Ross Conway Stone's *A Way to See and Study the Statue of Liberty Enlightening the World* (1887).

In the first few decades after Liberty's transfer to America, she chiefly inspired short literary pieces and journalistic commentary that appeared in a variety of periodicals. The first widely published book seems to have been Frances Rogers's juvenile book, *Big Miss Liberty* (1938), doubtless inspired by the statue's fiftieth anniversary celebrated two years before. The darkening political struggle developing in Europe and the military invasions of China and Ethiopia must also have contributed to a renewal of media attention to the symbolism of the Statue of Liberty. A more visitor-friendly atmosphere emerged when the president transferred the statue and then all of Bedloe's Island to the jurisdiction of the National Park Service

in 1933 and 1937, respectively. The care of trained park rangers keenly interested in helping visitors and tourists understand the monument's history and significance was a clear change from the former presence of soldiers and military police.

With World War II came Rodman Gilder's *The Statue of Liberty Enlightening the World* (1943) and in the postwar years, Hertha Pauli and E. B. Ashton authored the first major book on the monument, *I Lift My Lamp: The Way of a Symbol* (1948). This work is notable for its exploration of the statue's sociopolitical origins in both France and America.

A modern critical and biographical work on Edouard de Laboulaye is Walter Gray's *Interpreting American Democracy in France: The Career of Edouard de Laboulaye* (1994). Auguste Bartholdi biographies are Jacques Betz's *Bartholdi* (1954) and Pierre Vidal's illustrated *Frédéric-Auguste Bartholdi: Par la Main et par l'Esprit* (1994). Other works emphasizing Bartholdi are a juvenile book, Willadene Price's *Bartholdi and the Statue of Liberty* (1959); André Gschaedler's *True Light on the Statue of Liberty and Its Creator* (1966); and Jean-Marie Schmitt's *Une Certaine Idée de la Liberté* (1985). Works on Gustave Eiffel include Bertrand Lemoine's *Gustave Eiffel* (1980) and Bertrand Marrey's *La Vie et l'oeuvres extraordinaires de Monsieur Gustave Eiffel* (1984). R. M. Hunt is treated in several studies, including Paul Baker's *Richard Morris Hunt* (1980).

General works on the statue include *The Statue of Liberty* by immigration historian Oscar Handlin and the Editors of Newsweek Book Division (1971) and art historian Marvin Trachtenberg's enlightening work, *The Statue of Liberty* (1976). The centennial of Liberty spawned new interest in the statue with such books as *Statue de la Liberté* (1984) by Christian Blanchet and Bertrand Dard; the New York Public Library's *Liberty: The French-American Statue in Art and History* (1986), a combined effort of some fifteen scholars; Claude Gauthier's *La Statue de la Liberté: Une signe pour vous*

The *Lion of Belfort*

AVX DEFENSEVRS DE BELFORT 1870-71

The Statue of Liberty Enlightening The World.

Described by the Sculptor BARTHOLDI

Published for the Benefit of the Pedestal Fund
BY THE
NORTH AMERICAN REVIEW
30 LAFAYETTE PLACE,
NEW YORK.

(1986); and Bertrand Lemoine's *La Statue de la Liberté* (1986). The 1982–86 refurbishment of the monument is dealt with in *The Restoration of the Statue of Liberty* (1986) by Richard Hayden and Thierry Despont, with Nadine Post, and *The Statue of Liberty Restoration* (1990), edited by Robert Baboian, Blaine Cliver, and Lawrence Bellante. Fund raising and the political aspects of the restoration are treated in Ross Holland's *Idealists, Scoundrels and the Lady* (1994); while editors Wilton S. Dillon and Neil G. Kotler were joined by other scholars to produce *The Statue of Liberty: Making a Universal Symbol* (1993), a book of reflective essays that treat culture, history, politics, and engineering. Art historian Albert Boime has produced critical essays about the statue in two books: *Hollow Icons: The Politics of Sculpture in Nineteenth Century France* (1987) and *Unveiling of the National Icons* (1998).

Since 1960, the statue has been an especially popular topic with juvenile writers, and books have appeared by Charles Mercer; James Bell and Richard Abrams; Susan Burchard; and Eve Bunting, whose *A Picnic in October* (1999) was the last book to be published on the statue in the twentieth century. In addition, Benjamin Levine and Isabelle F. Story in 1952 and Paul O. Weinbaum in 1986 produced informative tourist guidebooks to the monument.

Observations about the statue appear in the novels of renowned authors such as Franz Kafka (*Amerika,* 1927) and Graham Greene (*The Quiet American,* 1955), and she was the subject of both a short story by William Irish ("The Corpse in the Statue of Liberty*,*" 1934) and a *fiction noir* novel by French writer Michel Rio (*La statue de la Liberté,* 1997). *See also* Gilder, Rodman; Lazarus, Emma; "The New Colossus"; Pauli, Hertha; Rogers, Frances.

Lockett, Samuel Henry (*b.* 1826; *d.* 1891). Colonel, Confederate army, professor of mechanical engineering at Louisiana State University, and Egyptian army officer. Served as assistant engineer under General Stone in the construction of the foundation of the pedestal of the Statue of Liberty.

Long, Charles O. (*b.* 1845, Pottsville, Pennsylvania; *d.* May 1904, New York, New York). Superintendent and guardian of the Statue of Liberty, c. 1884–1904. Long was an associate of contractor David H. King. His assistant was James McLaughlin, c. 1884–87 and 1895–1900. His father, Colonel Jacob M. Long, built the Harlem gasworks in the early 1850s.

Longfellow, Henry Wadsworth (*b.* 27 February 1807, Portland, Maine; *d.* 24 March 1882, Cambridge, Massachusetts). Poet and educator. Auguste Bartholdi and the poet Longfellow met in Massachusetts during the sculptor's first trip to the United States (1871). Longfellow, quite taken with the French proposal, made the following entry in his diary: "August 2nd. M. Auguste Bartholdi, French sculptor, calls with a letter from Agassiz. A pleasant, lively, intelligent man, a republican and an Alsatian. He has a plan for erecting a bronze Colossus on Bedloe's Island in New York harbor—a statue of Liberty—to serve at night as a lighthouse. It's a grand plan; I hope it will strike the New Yorkers." Longfellow's career as a professor of languages at Harvard University was distinguished. Moreover, his poetry, rich in stories and rhyming verse, made him famous. His works included *Ballads* [with "The Wreck of the Hesperus"] (1841), *Poems on Slavery* (1842), *Evangeline* (1847), *The Golden Legend* (1851), *Hiawatha* (1855), *The Courtship of Miles Standish* (1858), and *Tales of a Wayside Inn* [with "Paul Revere's Ride"] (1863).

Lotos Club. One of the oldest literary clubs in the United States, founded in 1870 by a circle of young writers, journalists, and critics for the purpose of "rest and harmony." Whitelaw Reid, the editor of the *New York Tribune,* became its president in 1872. Mark Twain, who had been ad-

The 1885 souvenir fund-raising booklet, *The Statue of Liberty Enlightening the World,* written by Auguste Bartholdi and translated into English by publisher Allen Thorndike Rice

mitted to membership in 1873, dubbed the Lotos "The Ace of Clubs." The club gave a banquet in Auguste Bartholdi's honor on 16 September 1876, following the unveiling of his statue of the marquis de Lafayette. It was one of the first acts of public acclaim he received in the United States, and he cherished the memory. Such luminaries as Frederick A. Schwab (banquet chairman), English novelist Joseph Hatton (1841–1907), publisher Samuel French, architect Henri de Stucklé, Charles Viele, John Elderkin, Daniel Bixby, William J. Florence, British-American art critic Montague L. Marks, and others attended the dinner. At that time, the clubhouse was located at 2 Irving Place, off Fourteenth Street, next to the Academy of Music.

Another banquet was given in Bartholdi's honor on 14 November 1885 at its new permanent location at Fifth Avenue, near Forty-sixth Street. He was lauded by such personalities as Whitelaw Reid, Chauncey Depew, Joseph Pulitzer, Richard Butler, Algernon S. Sullivan, John Elderkin, General Horace Porter, General John Halderman, H. W. Cannon, F. R. Coudert, Colonel Thomas W. Knox, S. S. Packard, Chandos Fulton, General E. F. Winslow, Felix Moscheles, George H. Story, and many others. Tributes were paid to the Franco-American Union, and to the memory of its founder, Edouard de Laboulaye. George Alfred Townsend recited a witty poem, "Lines to Bartholdi." Its last stanzas were:

> The Son of France his kindling glance
>   Threw o'er this radiant Edom,
>   And like a Bayard of romance
>   Knelt to the strength of freedom;
>   He saw arise athwart our skies
>   A Goddess ever living,
>   Illumination in her eyes
>   And flame to darkness giving.
> Lift high thy torch and forward march,
>   O dame of Revolution!—
>   All heaven thy triumphal arch,
>   All progress thy solution;

> And from the earth and all its dross
> May man behold the story—
> Friendship is pious as the cross,
> And only Art is glory.

Such lines might have annoyed Edouard de Laboulaye, who opposed the attachment of any revolutionary symbolism to the Statue of Liberty, but they were truly in the spirit of free-thinking clubmen such as Townsend. The word *lotos* was taken from Lord Tennyson's poem, *The Lotos Eaters,* from which two lines were selected as the club's motto:

> In the afternoon they came unto a land
>   In which it seemed always afternoon

Lottery. Fund-raising scheme in France organized by the Franco-American Union. This type of gambling had been banned in France since 1836, exceptions being permitted by the minister of the interior only in the case of charity or support of the arts. Noting this, Senator Henri Martin applied for a permit to set up a lottery on behalf of the Franco-American Union on 8 January 1879. The minister, Charles Lepère, signed the official decree of consent on 9 May 1879. It established the Commission for the Franco-American Lottery and named as members Senator Jean-François Bozérian (chairman), the watchmaker and jeweler Adolphe Japy, the American painter Henry Baker, Alsatian artist Gustave Jundt, and the journalist Pierre Véron. Within three months, the Lottery Commission had issued 300,000 tickets at 1 franc each. Designed by Auguste Bartholdi, these tickets were sold at tobacconist shops throughout France and were also available in the United States. Winners had a chance at seventeen grand prizes of 35,000 francs each. There were also five hundred prizes worth from 50 to 400 francs apiece. Additional prizes included government donations of decorative porcelain Sèvres pieces and fine engravings, after such masters as Sir Hans Holbein, Leonardo da Vinci, Jean Ingres, and Léon Gérome. In addition, the Ministry of Education provided twelve expensive illustrated books.

Love Island. A seventeenth-century colonial name for Liberty Island, c. 1668–73. Named for Colonel Francis Lovelace, the English colonial governor. This name was used during much of Lovelace's administration, but was abandoned shortly after, following the Dutch navy's reconquest of New York. The island's name was then changed to Bedloe's Island, after its Dutch proprietor.

Lovelace, Francis (*b.* 1621, Hurley, England; *d.* 1675, Oxford, England). English colonial governor of New York and New Jersey, 1667–73; deputy governor of Long Island, 1665. Lovelace was a strong royalist who was rewarded by Prince James, duke of York, after the Restoration in 1660, with colonial offices. His policy as governor was to placate the Dutch elite (including Isaac Bedloe) and improve relations with the Native Americans. Highlights of his administration included suppression of a rebellion in New Jersey, the purchase of Staten Island (13 April 1670), and the settlement of German Palatine refugees. He also tried to improve transport and communication within the colony. In August 1673, he lost the colony to the Dutch fleet during the Third Anglo-Dutch War. Without a colony to govern, Colonel Lovelace returned to England to face the wrath of his prince, James. With the support of King Charles II, the duke formally dismissed him as governor and imprisoned him in the Tower of London. *See also* Bedloe, Isaac; Love Island.

M

Macé, Jean (*b.* 1815, Paris, France; *d.* 1894, Monthier Aisnes, France). Politician and author. Macé was a member of the French Committee, Franco-American Union, which raised the funds to build the Statue of Liberty. He is famous for his uncompromising advocacy of both republicanism and secular education for France. He expressed both views through his journal, *La République* (1848–51), and the French League of Teaching, which he founded in 1866. After the creation of the Third Republic, he was elected a life senator (1883). Macé was the author of many books, including *L'Histoire d'une bouchée de pain* (1861).

MacMahon, Clement (*b.* 17 March 1834, Philadelphia, Pennsylvania; *d.* 1 March 1909, Bellwood, Pennsylvania). Construction foreman, Keystone Bridge Company, c. 1865–90. MacMahon worked on Bedloe's Island in the placing of the steel anchorage system of the Statue of Liberty in 1885.

Madison Square. New York City neighborhood and park located between Twenty-third and Twenty-sixth streets. To encourage public interest and donations, the torch and arm of the Statue of Liberty were on public display in Madison Square Park from 1877 until 1882. The square and park were named in honor of President James Madison in 1814.

Manhattan skyline. At 305 feet (93 meters), the Statue of Liberty was the tallest structure in New York City upon completion in 1886. However, it was later superseded by such structures as the ornate Singer Building (1911; 612 feet/186.5 meters); the Gothic style Woolworth Building (1913; 792 feet/241 meters); the art deco Chrysler Building (1930; 1,047 feet/319 meters); the world's most famous skyscraper, the Empire State Building (1931; 1,250 feet/381 meters); and the World Trade Center (1976; 1,350 feet/412 meters). All of these structures can be seen from both the crown of the Statue of Liberty and the observation balcony at the top of the pedestal.

Marquand, Henry Gurdon. (*b.* 11 April 1819, New York, New York; *d.* 1902, New York, New York). Banker and philanthropist. A member of the American Committee, Franco-American Union, he served on the finance subcommittee, 1884–86. He was also a connoisseur of paintings and served as president of the Metropolitan Museum of Art.

Arm and torch of Liberty on display in New York City's Madison Square Park, 1877

Martí, José Julián (*b.* 28 January 1853, Havana, Cuba; *d.* 19 May 1895, Dos Ríos, Cuba). Lawyer, writer, and Cuban nationalist. Martí, covering the story of the Statue of Liberty's inauguration on 28 October 1886 for *La Nación,* an Argentine newspaper, wrote, "Liberty, it is thine hour.... And all these luckless Irishmen, Poles, Italians, Bohemians, Germans redeemed from oppression or misery, hail the monument to Liberty, because they feel that through it they themselves are uplifted and restored.... In her presence, eyes once again know what tears are. She seemed alive, wrapped in clouds of smoke, covered by a vague brightness, truly like an altar with steamers kneeling at her feet." Further commenting on the ordinary people, he wrote, "Look at them run to the waterfront for a glimpse of the Statue, happy as castaways.... They are the dregs, those who shun crowded streets and well-dressed people: pale rag pickers, lightermen, hunchbacks, Italian women in dotted shawls, from east to west, from the narrow, teeming streets in poorest parts of town." He described the Manhattan inaugural parade in these words: "A bayonet stream, kilometers of red shirts, of grey, blue, green militia. The big, white splotch of the naval . . . caps, and on a lorry a miniature Monitor steered by a little boy in a sailor suit. Blue uniformed artillery; heavy-footed police; cavalry with yellow on the lapels . . . and cheers rising in the park and flying from mouth to mouth until they die, stifled by the cannon thunder.... Disabled veterans and judges riding in carriages. And the Negroes." Martí was an ardent fighter for Cuban independence from

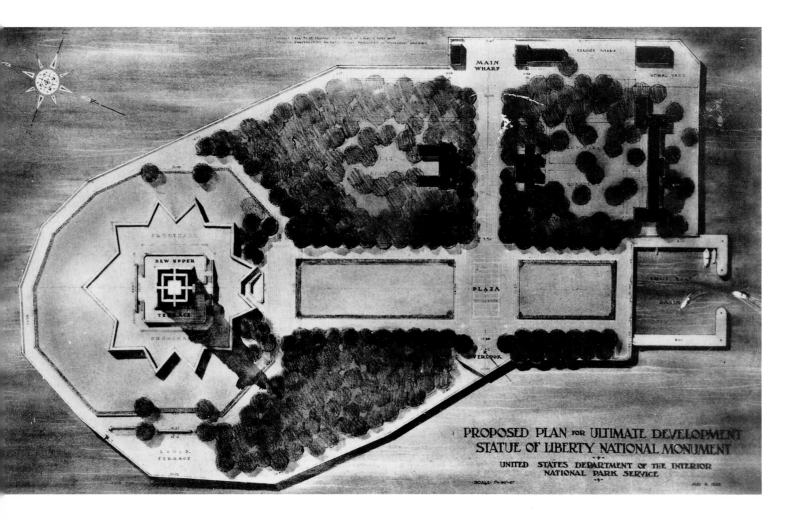

PROPOSED PLAN FOR ULTIMATE DEVELOPMENT
STATUE OF LIBERTY NATIONAL MONUMENT
UNITED STATES DEPARTMENT OF THE INTERIOR
NATIONAL PARK SERVICE

Spain and a vigorous opponent of slavery. He emigrated to the United States in 1880, passing through the Castle Garden immigration station in New York. He was the leader of the Partido Revoluciano Cubano and editor of the Cuban exile newspaper, *Patria*. In 1895, Martí returned to Cuba at the head of a rebel military force. Royal Spanish troops repelled the force, and Martí was killed in the battle.

Martin, (Bon-Louis) Henri (*b.* 1810, Saint Quentin, France; *d.* 1883, France). Historian and politician. Educated as a notary, Martin joined Paul Lacroix, the book collector and author known as the "Bibliophile Jacob," in a vast project to write the history of France in "48 volumes." Extracts were taken from old histories and chronicles. The first volume was published in 1833; Martin completed seventeen volumes more from 1837 to 1854. His other books included *De la France, de son Génie et de ses Destinées* (1847) and *L'Unité italienne et la France* (1861). Martin joined Laboulaye, Count Gasparin, and others in the fight against slavery by helping to found the French Anti-Slavery Society in 1865; he served as an advisory councilor to the body. In the same year, Martin was one of the guests at Laboulaye's famous dinner at which the latter proposed giving a monumental gift to the United States as a token of friendship. He was elected to the Chamber of Deputies in 1871 and became a senator in 1876. He was inducted into the French Academy in 1878.

Masonic symbols. *See* Freemasonry.

Master Plan. National Park Service (NPS) beautification plan for landscaping and improvements at Bedloe's Island approved in 1939. It was implemented over a number of years and completed by 1965. The work included repairs to the Statue of Liberty, such as the replacement of its corroded iron armature bars and rivets and removal and cleaning of the crown's spikelike rays. Repairs were also made to the pedestal stairway. Around the island, the old army barracks were demolished, the acreage was graded, the topsoil was spread and seeded, and the sea wall and the old East Pier were replaced. A series of new buildings were constructed, including an NPS administration building, a concession building, and staff houses. Improvements in 1952 included channel dredging, island enlargement, and construction of a new sea wall. *See also* Landscape and vegetation; National Park Service; Newton, Norman.

Measurements. *See* Dimensions.

Military Police. The Military Police occupied the Bedloe's Island army post, 1923–37, replacing the Army Signal Corps. They maintained a brig (military prison) within the walls of Fort Wood in which to detain unruly soldiers. When the first National Park Service superintendent, George Palmer, arrived in 1934, the Military Police commandant was Colonel Huskey, who gave him quarters and explained conditions on the island. *See also* Army.

Millaud, Edouard (*b.* 1834, Tarascon, France; *d.* 1912, Paris, France). Magistrate and politician. Member of the French Committee, Franco-American Union. A relentless advocate of republican government, Millaud served as a National Assembly deputy, 1871–80.

Millis, John (*b.* 31 December 1858, Wheatland, Michigan; *d.* 20 March 1952, Cleveland, Ohio). Army engineer, U.S. Light-House Board. The highest-ranked graduate of West Point Military Academy class of 1881, Lieutenant Millis was an expert in electrical lighting systems. From November 1886 until 1890, he worked with Major David Porter Heap to devise and super-

(opposite page) Proposed Master Plan for the Statue of Liberty National Monument

(below) Military Policemen at Bedloe's Island, c. 1930

vise the installation of electrical illumination at the Statue of Liberty. They sought to make the lighting in the statue and its torch an effective aid for ships' navigators. As Light-House Board engineer secretary, from around 1896 until the end of the century, he was again drawn to the unsolvable lighting problems at the statue. After a long career, which included engineering duties in France during World War I, Millis retired with the rank of colonel in 1922. *See also* Heap, David Porter; Light-House Board; Lighting; Torch.

Miss Liberty. Musical comedy. After a successful Philadelphia tryout, *Miss Liberty* made a dazzling Broadway debut at the Imperial Theatre on 15 July 1949 and ran 308 performances. Irving Berlin composed its songs, and playwright Robert E. Sherwood wrote the story. Moss Hart directed it, and choreographer was Jerome Robbins.

The story revolves around the rivalry of two New York City publishers, Joseph Pulitzer of the *World* and James Gordon Bennett of the *Herald,* as they use every means they can muster to learn who the supposed mystery girl was whom Auguste Bartholdi had used as his model for the Statue of Liberty (a case of mistaken identity, since the model was the sculptor's mother). The stars of this vastly entertaining

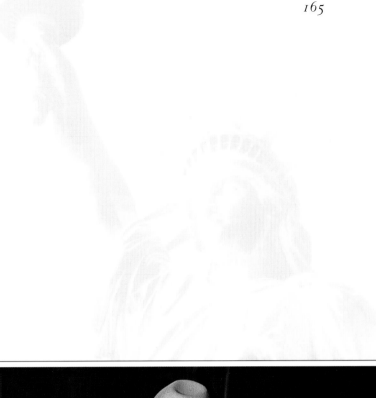

production were Eddie Albert (as Horace Miller), Allyn McLerie (as Monique Dupont, the mystery girl), Mary McCarty (as Maisie Dell), Ethel Griffies (as the Countess), and Herbert Berghof (as Auguste Bartholdi). Although the storyline was criticized as "flimsy," several songs electrified the show, especially "The Most Expensive Statue in the World," "Let's Take an Old Fashioned Walk," "Paris Wakes Up and Smiles," "Only for Americans," and "Give Me Your Tired, Your Poor." Although it never returned to Broadway, the show has gone through many small-time revivals.

Miss Liberty of 1886. At the time of the inauguration of the Statue of Liberty in 1886, New York City officials elected Clara Voorhis as Miss Liberty. She appeared in a black satin dress and was described by one journalist as being "all smiles and roses." Voorhis (1866–1962) was the daughter of John R. Voorhis, a Democratic politician in the latter part of the nineteenth century and the beginning of the twentieth. She later became the wife of William H. Newell, an importer of haberdashery.

Moffitt, David L. Horticulturist and civil servant. Moffitt served as superintendent of the Statue of Liberty National Monument, 1976–87, residing at Liberty Island with his wife and children. During his tenure, the monument underwent the most widely publicized restoration in the history of the United States. In 1977, Moffitt began several unsuccessful attempts to persuade Washington to set up a commission to plan for the centennial anniversary of the Statue of Liberty. The idea was finally taken up when Ronald Reagan assumed the presidency in January 1981. During the restoration years, Moffitt's activities included negotiating with labor unions, acting as a liaison between the Park Service and the Statue of Liberty–Ellis Island Foundation, working on the gold leaf project for the torch, testifying before Congress, and giving many media interviews. Moffitt later served as superintendent of Colonial National Historical Park in Virginia.

Monuments. *Liberty Enlightening the World* comes from a long tradition of colossal monumental art. Auguste Bartholdi admired the huge monumental sculptures of his teacher Antoine Etex. Bartholdi later fell under the influence of ancient Egyptian colossal sculpture during his trip to that country in 1855–56. From 1867 to 1869, he failed in an attempt to persuade Isma'il Pasha, the ruler of Egypt, to commission him to build a colossal lighthouse for the Suez Canal in the form of a woman and to be known as *Egypt Carrying the Light to Asia.* In 1871, he joined a group of senior liberal politicians, which included men such as Edouard de Laboulaye, Henri Martin, Count Charles de Rémusat, and Victor Borie. He won a commission

1880s engraving of the world's highest monuments

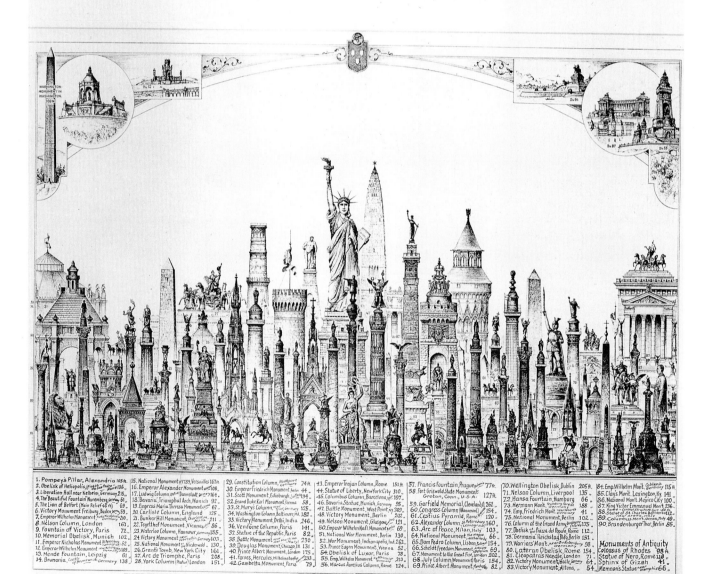

The Highest Monuments

A print contemporary with the erection of the Statue of Liberty unveiled in 1886.

from them to build a colossal statue of the Roman goddess Libertas, which symbolized the personification of freedom and, perhaps more vitally, the group's moderate French democratic republicanism (it has served as an official symbol of all five French republics). Since republicanism represented only a single political faction in France, it was decided that the monument was to be made as a gift to the people of the United States. Bartholdi wanted the statue to compare favorably with and, where possible, even exceed the height of the world's great monuments, past or present. He was greatly taken by such monuments as *San Carlo Borromeo,* the Vendôme column, the *Virgin of Puy,* the colossal statue of Emperor Nero, and the legendary Colossus of Rhodes. His views on colossal statuary are expressed in his book, *The Statue of Liberty Enlightening the World* (1885); in *Les Colosses anciens et modernes* by his friend, E. Lesbazeilles; and in Charles Talansier's article, "La Statue de la Liberté," in *Le Génie Civil* (1883).

Moran, Edward (*b.* 19 August 1829, Bolton, England; *d.* 9 June 1901, New York, New York). Painter. Moran specialized in maritime scenes depicting U.S. history. He unveiled his 1876 oil painting, *Commerce of Nations Rendering Homage to Liberty,* to the American Committee at their first session, held at the Century Association, on 2 January 1877. Joseph W. Drexel eventually bought the painting. Moran's related oil paintings were *The Statue of Liberty at Night* (1876), *Reception of the French Steamship Isère in New York Bay* (1885), and *Unveiling of the Statue of Liberty, 1886* (1886).

Morgan, Edwin Denison (*b.* 8 February 1811, Washington, Massachusetts; *d.* 14 February 1883, New York, New York). Politician and philanthropist. Morgan joined William M. Evarts, Parke Godwin, James Pinchot, and Clark Bell on the legislative subcommittee of the newly established American Committee of the Franco-American Union. Auguste Bar-

Levi Parsons Morton driving the first rivet into Liberty's pylon, Paris, 1881

tholdi was present at this historic meeting held at the Century Association on 2 January 1877. Morgan enjoyed a successful and long career in Whig and Republican politics, having served as state senator (1850–58), governor of New York (1859–63), and U.S. senator (1863–81).

Morton, Levi Parsons (*b.* 16 May 1824, Shoreham, Vermont; *d.* 16 May 1920, Rhinebeck, New York). Politician and diplomat. Morton was the U.S. minister plenipotentiary who drove in the first rivet at the ceremony of 24 October 1881 to mark the beginning of the phase when the statue's copper sheets and armature were at last to be riveted on the skeletal framework. On 4 July 1884, Morton officially

accepted the completed Statue of Liberty in Paris and signed the deed of gift on behalf of the president and the people of the United States.

Morton was a successful Wall Street banker when he entered public life as a congressman in 1879. He served as minister plenipotentiary to France, 1881–85; vice president of the United States, 1889–93; and governor of New York, 1895–97.

Museum services. The Statue of Liberty National Monument's museum division was established in 1972 to administer the American Museum of Immigration. Currently, the division serves the public through its various departments and administers the Ellis Island Immigration Museum, Statue of Liberty Exhibition, and the Bartholdi Gallery on Liberty Island. Its staff is divided into the park's Collections, Exhibits, Reference Library, Oral History, Archives, and Audio Visual departments.

Music and song. Many composers have directly and indirectly used the Statue of Liberty in their music. The best known are perhaps the official Liberty Cantata, composed by Charles Gounod and Emile Guiard for the Franco-American Union in 1876; Harry Kennedy's 1886 "Liberty Anthem" (a hymnal chorus for mixed voices); "Liberty" (1916) by Ted S. Barron; "Ten Million Men and a Girl" (1942) by John Redmond, Jim Cavanaugh, and Jack Edwards; "She Will Be Standing in the Harbor" (1943) by Carmen Lombardo and John Jacob Loeb; and Irving Berlin's "The Most Expensive Statue in the World" and "Give Me Your Tired, Your Poor" (a musical version of "The New Colossus") for the Broadway show *Miss Liberty* (1949).

Sheet music cover for "Liberty: The Song of our Land," by Ted S. Barron, 1916

N

Napoléon III (Charles Louis Napoléon Bonaparte) (*b.* 20 April 1808, Paris, France; *d.* 9 January 1873, Chislehurst, England). Emperor, 1852–71, and president, 1848–52. Napoléon III was a son of Prince Louis Bonaparte (king of the Netherlands), and a nephew of Emperor Napoléon I. His regime, the Second Empire, with its absolutist nature was the focus of liberal opposition during its eighteen years of existence. The drive to build the Statue of Liberty was the expression of the democratic constitutionalism advocated by united factions of liberals, republicans, and constitutional monarchists (Orleanists). Edouard de Laboulaye and his fellow moderate liberals sought ways to influence all French governments, real or potential, to safeguard all civil rights and uphold democratic constitutionalism. For many French people, including Laboulaye, this included even Napoléon's government. For example, Laboulaye shocked ardent republicans and antimonarchist fanatics alike by his endorsement of the emperor's proposal to establish a liberal constitutional monarchy in 1870. For, to Laboulaye, the goal was always to encourage authentic steps to democracy, be it either in the form of a republic or a monarchy. *See also* Second Empire; Second Republic.

National Park Service. Federal agency of the U.S. Department of the Interior having jurisdiction of the Statue of Liberty since 1933. The National Park Service (NPS) introduced educational and interpretive programs at the monument in the 1930s and has developed these programs over the years. The first two superintendents, George Palmer and Oswald Camp, provided leadership in developing the first Park Service programs at the Statue of Liberty. Early employees included Russell Andrews of Oregon (the first park ranger) and historical aides Simeon Pickering and William C. Webb. In 1939, the agency approved a master plan to change Bedloe's Island into a national park that would provide a pleasant environment for visitors. This project was largely achieved by 1965. The Park Service presided over two important restorations of the Statue of Liberty, the first during the years 1937–39 and the second during the years 1982–86. The American Museum of Immigration (AMI) was inaugurated at the site in 1972, and the Statue of Liberty Exhibit joined it in 1986. Ellis Island, an abandoned immigration station, came under NPS jurisdiction in 1965 when it was made part of the Statue of Liberty National Monument. The main building was restored and reopened as the Ellis Is-

His Imperial Majesty Napoléon III, Emperor of France

land Immigration Museum in 1990. The island was opened to visitation, and the NPS developed new interpretive programs appropriate to the site. In addition, curatorial and library services (including an oral history project) were expanded. For many years, the park staff has been divided into the administrative, interpretation, maintenance, management, museum services, and protection (U.S. Park Police) divisions; the staff usually numbers about 150 employees. Park concessionaires include the Statue of Liberty–Ellis Island Circle Line ferry and food and gift shop operators Evelyn Hill, Inc. (Liberty Island), and Aramark, Inc. (Ellis Island).

The National Park Service was created by an act of Congress in 1916 and administers some 378 national parks, monuments, battlefields, historic sites, memorials, recreation areas, seashores, and so forth. *See also* Demonstrations; Interpretation; Jurisdiction; Museum Services; Park rangers; Protection; Superintendents.

"The New Colossus." Emma Lazarus's now-celebrated piece of verse was composed at the request of her friend Constance Cary Harrison and American Committee chairman William M. Evarts for the Pedestal Art Loan Exhibition, held in December 1883. The original manuscript, written in ink and dated 2 November 1883, was included in the Pedestal Art Loan Exhibition's auction to help raise funds to build the Statue of Liberty's pedestal. The work takes the form of a classic Italian sonnet of fourteen lines:

The New Colossus

Not like the brazen giant of Greek fame,
    With conquering limbs astride from land
    to land;
Here at our sea-washed sunset gates shall
    stand
A mighty woman with a torch, whose flame
    Is the imprisoned lightning, and her
    name

Mother of Exiles. From her beacon-hand
    Glows world-wide welcome; her mild
    eyes command
The air-bridged harbor that twin cities
    frame.

"Keep ancient lands, your storied pomp!"
    cries she
With silent lips. "Give me your tired, your
    poor,
Your huddled masses yearning to breathe
    free,
The wretched refuse of your teeming shore,
Send these, the homeless, tempest-tost to me,
I lift my lamp beside the golden door."

Although it cannot be said to have been in any way popular at the time of its appearance, its power was noticed, for it was occasionally printed in publications including the *World* and the *New York Times,* which ran the sonnet in October 1886 when the popularity of Liberty poems was particularly high. In 1887 (the year of Emma Lazarus's death), Ross Conway Stone quoted the sonnet in his book, *A Way to See and Study the Statue of Liberty Enlightening the World.* Impressed, he made this observation: "As the navies of the world, guided by this light, pass by the mighty flambeau to our docks, the dullest star or lowliest immigrant is plainly told in the universal language of symbolism that he is in the land of liberty." In 1888, "The New Colossus" was included in *The Poems of Emma Lazarus,* published by Houghton Mifflin. The sonnet was largely forgotten afterward.

In about 1901, Georgina Schuyler, browsing in a bookshop, found an old book with the sonnet included in its text—possibly Stone's. She had known Emma Lazarus and was greatly touched by her late friend's poem. Schuyler, enlisting the aid of Richard Watson Gilder (another friend of Emma Lazarus), organized a civic effort to resurrect this lost work and bring it to public notice. She and her friends had it inscribed on a large bronze tablet and presented it

Original bronze plaque of Emma Lazarus's sonnet "The New Colossus" (plaque donor: Georgina Schuyler, 1903)

THE NEW COLOSSUS.

NOT LIKE THE BRAZEN GIANT OF GREEK FAME.
WITH CONQUERING LIMBS ASTRIDE FROM LAND TO LAND;
HERE AT OUR SEA-WASHED, SUNSET GATES SHALL STAND
A MIGHTY WOMAN WITH A TORCH. WHOSE FLAME
IS THE IMPRISONED LIGHTNING. AND HER NAME
MOTHER OF EXILES. FROM HER BEACON-HAND
GLOWS WORLD-WIDE WELCOME; HER MILD EYES COMMAND
THE AIR-BRIDGED HARBOR THAT TWIN CITIES FRAME.
"KEEP ANCIENT LANDS. YOUR STORIED POMP!"
        CRIES SHE
WITH SILENT LIPS. "GIVE ME YOUR TIRED. YOUR
        POOR.
YOUR HUDDLED MASSES YEARNING TO BREATHE FREE.
THE WRETCHED REFUSE OF YOUR TEEMING SHORE.
SEND THESE, THE HOMELESS. TEMPEST-TOST TO ME.
I LIFT MY LAMP BESIDE THE GOLDEN DOOR!"

———

THIS TABLET, WITH HER SONNET TO THE BARTHOLDI STATUE
OF LIBERTY ENGRAVED UPON IT. IS PLACED UPON THESE WALLS
IN LOVING MEMORY OF
EMMA LAZARUS
BORN IN NEW YORK CITY. JULY 22ⁿᵈ 1849
DIED NOVEMBER 19ᵀᴴ 1887.

in a formal ceremony to the army post commander at Bedloe's Island on 6 May 1903. It was mounted inside the pedestal for public display.

The sonnet was widely popularized in the late 1930s by such people as Louis Adamic and became even more popular during World War II. It was dramatically read in *Hold Back the Dawn,* a 1941 motion picture about the plight of a refugee portrayed by French actor Charles Boyer. The tablet with "The New Colossus" is currently mounted in the Statue of Liberty Exhibition gallery, Liberty Island.

New York Produce Exchange. Commodities market founded in 1861. In 1885, it established its headquarters at 2 Broadway in Manhattan. It was at this location that an excursion of French delegates (mostly members of the Paris Board of Trade) were brought on 27 October 1886, where they were given a special reception by the president of the exchange, James McGee. In a brief address, he declared the sculpture of the goddess of liberty a mystic symbol, representing the key to all progress: commerce lighting her torch and flame, the pioneer of civilization.

Newton, Norman Thomas (*b.* 21 April 1898, Corry, Pennsylvania; *d.* 1992). Landscape architect. Newton's Master Plan of 1939 was the first comprehensive scheme to make the Statue of Liberty's surroundings attractive to visitors. Liberty Island's landscape design and general physical appearance today is the result of it. Throughout a long career, Newton was involved in designing parks, historic sites, buildings, and land developments. He worked in the National Park Service from 1933 to 1939 and was a professor of architecture at Harvard University, 1939–66. Newton was also an aviator, having served in the U.S. Army Air Forces in both world wars, for which he attained the rank of colonel. *See also* Master Plan of 1939.

Nicknames. Common nicknames for the Statue of Liberty include: America's Freedom, America's Great Lady, America's Great Symbol, America's Icon, America's Light, America's Refuge, America's Treasure, Aunt Liberty, Bartholdi Statue, Bartholdi's American, Bartholdi's Daughter, Embodiment of Freedom, "Everybody's Gal," Fortress of Freedom, France's Gift, French Gift, Gift of Friendship, Giant Goddess, Giant Lady, Goddess of Democracy, Goddess of Liberty, Grande Dame, Great Goddess, Great Lady, Great Statue, Green Goddess, Her Ladyship, Holy Freedom, Keeper of Dreams, The Lady, The Lady Higher Up, Lady Liberty, Lady of Liberty, Lady of the Harbor, Lady on a Pedestal, Lady with a Torch, Light of Freedom, Miss Liberty, Mother of Exiles, Mother of Freedom, New Colossus, Saint Liberty, Spirit of American Independence.

Nimbus. Halo surrounding the head of a figure in art, serving as an emblem of a god or a saint. It took different forms throughout the ages, although most commonly it appeared in the form of a disc or a plate above the head. Because of its similarity to the sun's rays, this form is thought to have originated in the worship of Helios, the divine personification of the sun in ancient Greek religion. Von Erlach's 1721 engraving of the Colossus of Rhodes (Helios) depicts rays of sunlight emanating from the god's head. In Liberty, the nimbus takes the form of rays that brilliantly radiate from her head and diadem, doing double service as nimbus rays and beacon light. Although found widely in neoclassical imagery, it is probably the state iconography of the French Second Republic that determined the form Liberty was to take. Eugène-André Oudiné's medallion of the "French Republic" and Jean-Jacques Barre's Seal of the "Democratic French Republic One and Indivisible," both struck in 1848, are virtually twins of the Statue of Liberty. The same nimbus, the Roman dress, and the face and figure appear on the lady in the harbor. Edouard de Laboulaye and his associates, deeply involved in the constitutional issues of their late and

Liberty's nimbus from above

Close-up of Liberty's nose

lamented Second Republic, would have known the seal and the medallion, showing the form the monument was to take in America. *See also* Libertas.

Nose. The nose measures 3 feet, 8 inches (1.1 meters). During the Liberty restoration of the 1980s, unsightly cracks on the nose, most notably on the nostril, were repaired. The smaller cracks were mended by the "wolf-mouth" assembly technique, a traditional method of joining two large pieces of metal by means of cutting them into the pattern of a sawtooth and making them level to a feather edge, and so interlocking them. They are then hammered together. The damaged nostril presented a greater challenge. A mold was taken of the original, and then a new repoussé piece was made. Small tears and cracks were mended by the wolf assembly method, in some instances, simple hammering together was sufficient.

Noyes, Edward Follensbee (*b.* 3 October 1832, Haverhill, Massachusetts; *d.* 7 September 1890, Cincinnati, Ohio). Soldier, diplomat, politician. As President Rutherford Hayes's chief diplomat in Paris, Noyes attended various functions for the Statue of Liberty, including the banquet that celebrated the completion of the French fund-raising campaign in July 1880. During the Civil War, Noyes was a Union army colonel and then brevet brigadier general. He continued his public service as governor of Ohio, 1872–74; U.S. minister to France, 1877–81; and judge of the superior court, 1889–90.

O

Observation balcony. Located at the top of the pedestal, just below the Statue of Liberty's feet. From the balcony, millions of visitors from the United States and countries throughout the world have enjoyed spectacular views, descrying objects within a radius of fifteen miles. Typically seen from both the balcony (and the crown of the statue) are the following: to the south, the New York City borough of Staten Island and the shore of Raritan Bay, New Jersey; to the southeast, the Verrazano Narrows and its bridge (connecting Brooklyn to Staten Island); to the east, the New York City borough of Brooklyn and Governor's Island. Northward are the Brooklyn Bridge in the East River, joining Brooklyn to Manhattan; the borough of Manhattan, with its world-famous skyline; the Hudson River; and the George Washington Bridge. To the southwest is the Bayonne Bridge, joining Staten Island to New Jersey. Due west is the New Jersey shore, Liberty State Park, and Jersey City. *See also* Crown; Manhattan skyline; Pedestal; Visitation.

Olmsted, Frederick Law (*b.* 26 April 1822, Hartford, Connecticut; *d.* 23 August 1903, Waverly, Massachusetts). Landscape gardener. Member of the Union League Club. Olmsted supervised the clean-up of debris on Bedloe's Is-

land in October 1886 following the completion of the construction of the Statue of Liberty by General Stone and his engineers, contractors, and laborers. Olmsted's task was to ensure that Fort Wood and its public entrance would provide a reasonably neat appearance for the 28 October 1886 inaugural ceremonies of the goddess of liberty. There were seventy-five laborers and twelve grounds workers, nearly all of them Italians. The men removed rubbish and refuse, painted the cannons black, demolished the old shanties inside the fortress, and repaired the visitors' landing pier. While Olmsted supervised this, several other jobs were being done in which he may also have had a hand. The work included the construction of a platform for the ceremonies and the removal of the scaffolding from Liberty's feet. Further, a large canvas veil masking her countenance was removed on a day when Auguste Bartholdi appeared on the island; a new one, designed to resemble the French tricolor flag, was put up in its place. Olmsted is famous for his designs for New York's Central Park and the Chicago World's Fair of 1893.

Olózaga, (Don) Salustiano de (*b.* 8 June 1805, Oyón, Alava, Spain; *d.* 26 September 1873, Enghien, Paris, France). Politician, diplomat, and

George A. Palmer with American and Japanese visitors on Liberty's observation balcony in the 1930s orator. Elected a deputy to Spain's parliament, the Cortes, in 1832, he rose to opposition leader by 1835. In 1840, he was named ambassador to France but returned to Spain in 1843 and was appointed prime minister. But when accused of dissolving the Cortes without the queen's assent, he was promptly ousted and fled to Portugal. He eventually settled in Paris and assumed the leadership of Spanish liberal exiles there. He led the Spanish Anti-Slavery Society and represented it at the international congress of abolitionist societies organized by Edouard de Laboulaye in Paris in 1867. When Queen Isabel II was overthrown in favor of a republic in 1868, Olózaga helped to write the text of the new constitution and also served as Spanish ambassador to France, 1868–73. Olózaga, an able diplomat and an eminent lawyer, was also noted for his splendid oratorical skills. He was the author of the classic book, *Estudios sobre elocuencia política* (1871), as well as other works. He was buried in the cemetery of San Nicolas in Madrid.

Opinion. In the nineteenth century there were a wide range of views on the Statue of Liberty. Opinion in France tended to divide itself into political factions. Its enthusiastic republican and liberal sponsors were often confronted by conservative royalists who were aware that it was a statue symbolic of the democratic system of government. Many constitutional monarchists, however, found Liberty's dignified bearing and symbols (such as the torch of enlightenment) an expression of views that posed no threat to their political goals. Their leader, the count of Paris, cautiously praised the monument without feeling that he had compromised the hope of establishing constitutional monarchy in France.

In the United States, Liberty was warmly accepted as a lasting tribute to American democracy and Franco-American friendship. Additionally, there was a strong tendency of the Republican party leadership and its Union League clubmen to see the statue as a celebration of the Union's victory in the Civil War and the emancipation of slaves. Chinese immigrant Saum Song Bo, citing the injustice evident in the Chinese Exclusion Act of 1882, questioned America's commitment to liberty:

The word liberty makes me think of the fact that this country is the land of liberty for men of all nations except the Chinese. I con-

sider it an insult to us Chinese to call on us to contribute toward building . . . a pedestal for the statue of Liberty. The statue represents Liberty holding a torch which lights the passage of all nations who come into this country. But are the Chinese allowed to come? As for the Chinese who are here, are they allowed to enjoy liberty as men of all other nations enjoy it? Are they allowed to go about everywhere free from the insults, abuse, assaults, wrongs, and injuries from which men of other nationalities are free? . . . Whether this statute against the Chinese or the statue to Liberty will be the more lasting monument to tell future ages of the liberty and greatness of this country will be known only to future generations.

At the inauguration festivities for the statue in 1886, Cuban journalist and independence advocate José Martí writing for the Argentine press thought Liberty represented the struggle of oppressed peoples such as the Irish, Poles, Italians, Czechs, Alsatians, Jews, Germans, African Americans, and mulattoes. Feminists were drawn to the statue as well. The New York Woman Suffrage Association sent a boatload of suffragettes into New York harbor to protest the exclusivism of the dedication ceremony; they praised the goddess of liberty, but roundly denounced the Bedloe's Island ceremony as a farce, for of the two thousand guests attending it, only a handful were women. Across the Atlantic, critical murmurs were heard in London too. The *Times* called the unveiling of the goddess of liberty "a curious festival." The editor mockingly inquired why "Liberty should be exported from France, which has so little therof, to America, which has so much."

Origins. *See* Bartholdi, Auguste; Civil War; Coinage; Copyrights and patents; Emancipation Movement; Enlightenment; Freemasonry; Laboulaye, E. R.; Libertas; Monuments; Nimbus; Shackle; Slavery; Tablet.

Oyster Islands. Early colonial name for the three islands that lay off the coast of New Jersey. Only Bedloe's Island and Ellis Island remain; the third and smallest of the islands—only a sandbar—is now submerged beneath the waters.

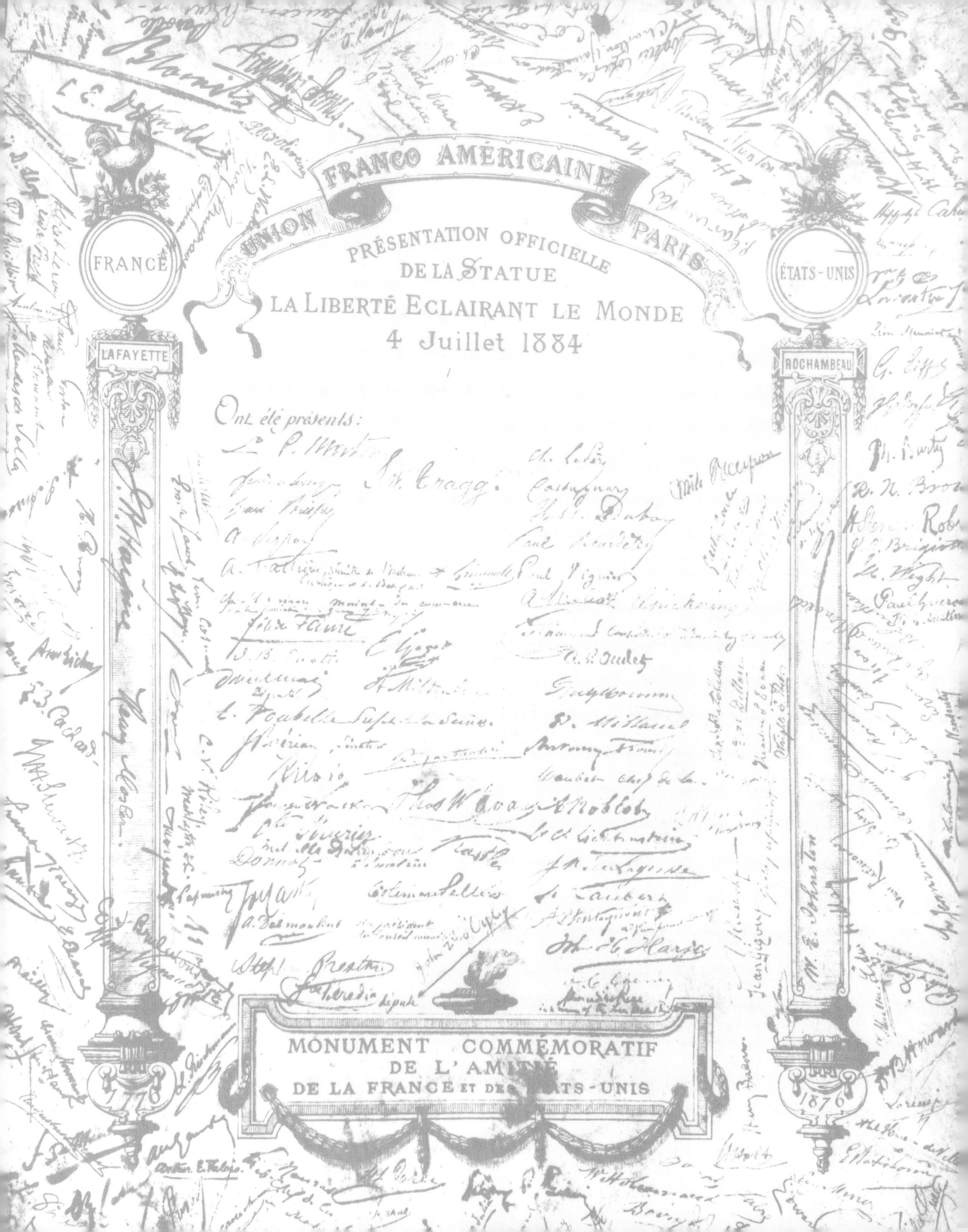

UNION FRANCO AMÉRICAINE PARIS

FRANCE

ÉTATS-UNIS

LAFAYETTE

ROCHAMBEAU

PRÉSENTATION OFFICIELLE
DE LA STATUE
LA LIBERTÉ ÉCLAIRANT LE MONDE
4 Juillet 1884

Ont été présents:

MONUMENT COMMÉMORATIF
DE L'AMITIÉ
DE LA FRANCE ET DES ÉTATS-UNIS

1778

1876

Palmer, George A. (*b.* 1909; *d.* 1990, New Jersey). Civil servant. George Palmer served as the first National Park Service superintendent of the Statue of Liberty National Monument, 1934–35 and 1937–45. He developed early Park Service interpretive programs at the site and oversaw the implementation of parts of the park's Master Plan of 1939. Palmer also relighted the Statue of Liberty's torch, which had been extinguished during World War II, following the Allied victory in 1945.

Paris, Count of (HRH the Prince Louis-Philippe-Albert d'Orléans) (*b.* 24 August 1838, Paris, France; *d.* 8 September 1894, England). Orleanist claimant to the throne of France and grandson of King Louis-Philippe. In 1876, Edouard de Laboulaye invited the count of Paris to visit the Statue of Liberty construction site, but acceptance had to be delayed. At last, in 1878, the count made his royal visit to the Gaget and Gauthier foundry and Liberty workshop in the Rue de Chazelles. Doubtless well acquainted with the role that his own ancestor, King Louis XVI, had played as a key source of military and economic aid to the American colonists during their Revolution, the count was pleased "to express in person his fellow-feeling . . . with the defenders of the American constitution" (ap-propriately cautious words from a prince). In addition, the count praised Auguste Bartholdi's talent and admired the moderating image that was achieved in creating the goddess of liberty.

Park rangers. National Park Service officials responsible for the preservation of Park Service sites, providing visitor educational programs, and ensuring visitor safety and protection. The first ranger at the Statue of Liberty was Russell Andrews of Oregon who worked at the monument from 1934 to 1935. Thousands of men and women have followed in Andrews's steps as park rangers at the Statue of Liberty National Monument. Most rangers at the monument work in the interpretation division. *See also* Interpretation; National Park Service; Protection.

Patents. *See* Copyrights and patents.

Patina. Green film verdigris that forms naturally on copper and bronze by long exposure. A patina provides copper with an enduring stability against atmospheric elements and effectively reduces corrosion over the years. When the Statue of Liberty was constructed on Bedloe's Island, it was the color of a copper penny, but it gradually underwent a color change known as patination. Three stages of copper patination have been identified: stage 1, the surface is copper colored; stage 2, it is brownish-black; stage 3, it is greenish-blue. According to chemical analyses, there was a delay of patina growth on Liberty due to sulfur in the atmosphere of New York harbor. From the time of its dedication in 1886, it would have taken approximately twenty years for a thick film of patina to encapsulate the Statue of Liberty; today, owing to a much greater concentration of sulfur in the atmosphere, it would take only eight years. Analyses made in the 1980s revealed the following components (primarily minerals) in the Statue of Liberty's patina: the major components were cuprite, brochantite, antlerite, antacamite, and posnjakite; the minor components were malachite, copper II formate, copper II acetate, copper II nitrate, copper II oxalate, fatty acids, and trace minerals. *See also* Corrosion.

Pauli, Hertha Ernestine (*b.* 1909, Vienna, Austria; *d.* 1973, New York). Author and actress. With her husband E. B. Ashton, immigrant Hertha Pauli was the coauthor of *I Lift My Lamp: The Way of a Symbol* (1948), the first substantial history book on the Statue of Liberty. This work is noteworthy for its historic and political detail as well as its period interpretation of the site, which deeply reflects the post–World War II political climate and the search for democratic principles. Pauli began her career as an actress on the German stage and radio (1927–33), but returned to her native Austria, where she was employed as a literary agent for five years. After coming to the United States as a refugee in 1940, she took up writing, producing several books, including *Silent Night: Story of a Song* (1943), *The Story of the Christmas Tree* (1944), *The Golden Door* (1949), *Bernadette and the Lady* (1956), *Christmas and All the Saints* (1956), and *Gateway to America* (1965). *See also* Literature.

Pedestal. Grand "footstool of Liberty" designed by the eminent architect Richard Morris Hunt. The pedestal forms the second vital element in the artistic composition of *Liberty Enlightening the World.* The form of the pedestal is based on a pencil drawing that Hunt submitted to the American Committee on 31 July 1884; it was accepted on 7 August 1884. Like Liberty, it is of gigantic proportions—more than appropriate for the requirements of the colossus. It rises to a height of 89 feet (27.4 meters) and is essentially a concrete structure covered by granite stone. It has 20-foot-thick (6-meter-thick) concrete walls and contains the Statue of Liberty's massive anchorage. Noble and classical in the Beaux-Arts tradition, its arrangement of rough and smooth stonework creates a splendid sense of harmony and repose. Further, it possesses a dignity equal to the statue owing to its Doric pattern. The pedestal's architectural features include a pillared loggia, a cornicework of moldings in an echinus-abacus sequence, a parapet (balcony), and an especially handsome socle. This last element includes forty ornamental escutcheons that were intended to bear the coats of arms of the forty states that then made up the Union. The entire structure stands atop a pyramid-shaped foundation.

Anticipating the acceptance of Hunt's drawing, the American Committee engaged General Charles P. Stone, a military engineer, to supervise the construction of the pedestal and its foundation. An assistant engineer responsible for drawings, computations, and work inspection was engaged to assist Stone. The first man to hold this position was Colonel Samuel Lockett, who was succeeded by George F. Simpson. Ground was broken for excavation work in April 1883. The construction of the concrete foundation began on 9 October 1883 and was completed on 17 May 1884. The total weight of the pedestal's foundation is 23,500 tons net. It measures 91 square feet at the bottom and rises upward to a height of 52 feet, 10 inches (approximately 15 meters), measuring 67 square feet (about 20 meters) across the top. In the center is an open shaft that measures 10 feet square (about 3.2 meters). At the time of its completion, the foundation was the world's largest solid

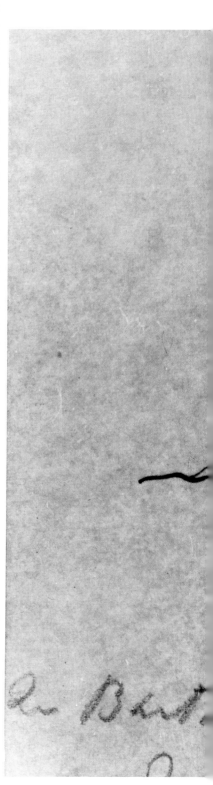

Monuments mexicains

Nº 1

mass of surface concrete. The work contractor was civil engineer F. Hopkinson Smith, who was assisted by bridge builders Alexander McGaw, John Drake, and Alfred Boller, who was the consulting engineer for the project. The final cost of $93,830.94 was twice as high as the initial estimates due to expensive excavation work.

General Stone's foundation design takes the shape of a sharply truncated stepped pyramid, executed in a manner resembling early sketches that Auguste Bartholdi had drawn of the monument. On 5 August 1884, the edifice and its forthcoming pedestal were consecrated with a Masonic ceremony. This was the laying of the cornerstone, a 6-ton block of granite. The cornerstone block was suspended in the air and then, following Grand Master William A. Brodie's spreading of the mortar with the silver trowel, it was lowered into position. The Masonic officers then tested the stone with their "jewels." It was found acceptable "by the square of virtue," by the level of "equality," "plumb" for "rectitude of conduct." Following three blows by the gavel, the cornerstone was declared truly laid. And after enunciating the symbolic words, "So mote it be," it received the consecration of corn (symbol of plenty), wine (symbol of gladness), and olive oil (symbol of peace). This grand ceremony initiated the construction of the pedestal.

Richard Morris Hunt's original design for the pedestal called for the use of granite throughout, but the American Committee rejected this as prohibitively expensive, and General Stone's recommendation to economize by the use of concrete faced with granite was adopted. David H. King was contracted to engage laborers and obtain supplies (such as the pedestal's forty-six courses of granite from Leete's Island, Connecticut). It was hoped that the pedestal would be completed in midautumn, but work was slower than anticipated, and when funds ran dry, work was suspended for the winter of 1884–85. With no money, the elite American Committee was compelled to accept the assistance of Joseph Pulitzer, who launched a

(opposite page) One of Richard Morris Hunt's rejected designs for the pedestal

(left) This design for the pedestal by Richard Morris Hunt was rejected because of its excessive height

(below) Early photograph of Richard Morris Hunt's winning design for the pedestal as it appeared under construction on Bedloe's Island in 1886

grandly popular fund-raising campaign in his newspaper, the *World*. Work soon resumed on the pedestal, and it was completed in April 1886. *See also* American Committee; Dimensions; Fort Wood; Foundation; Granite; Hunt, Richard M.; King, D. H.; Leete's Island; Observation balcony; Pedestal campaign; Stone, Charles P.

Pedestal Art Loan Exhibition. A fund-raising event for the pedestal held at the National Academy of Design in December 1883. William Merritt Chase, James Carroll Beckwith, Edwin Davis, and Ichabod T. Williams organized the exhibition and the art dealer Daniel Cottier selected the pictures. Constance Cary Harrison arranged the auction of art works and manuscripts. It was she who invited numerous writers to contribute an original manuscript for her auction portfolio. Emma Lazarus was one of these writers. It is because of Harrison's request that Lazarus came to write her sonnet, "The New Colossus." Others involved in the exhibit included Cornelius Vanderbilt, Jr., F. Hopkinson Smith, and Emma Lazarus's future brother-in-law, Montague L. Marks. The exhibition raised $15,000. Art critic Maureen O'Brien has credited this event with having strengthened the foundations of American art.

Pedestal campaign. This campaign was launched in 1877 to raise money through public subscription to construct the pedestal of the colossal Statue of Liberty. An American or Pedestal Committee was established in March 1877 with William M. Evarts as its chairman and twenty-two other members. An initial appeal was published in the *New-York Times* on 6 February 1877. At about the same time, the arm and torch of Liberty were brought up from Philadelphia and placed in Madison Square. In 1882, the American Committee secured the services of expert fund raiser Mahlon Chance and sent him west on a tour for the pedestal. Chance made speeches everywhere he traveled and excited a good deal of interest. Money came in from several states; one Chicagoan sent in $500.

Wealthy New Yorkers were among the leading donors to the campaign. John Jacob Astor gave $5,000; Joseph Drexel, $5,000; the Union Ferry Company, $2,000; Henry Villard, $1,000; Cornelius Vanderbilt, $500; Phineas T. Barnum, $250; and other large sums came from William M. Evarts, James Pinchot, and Louis Delmonico. The Chamber of Commerce contributed the balance in the Union Defense Fund. The committee sponsored the selling of all manner of souvenirs and gave public entertainments, such as balls, concerts, and vaudeville performances. Root and Tinker published a popular lithograph, and photographs and stereopticons of the construction were widely sold. The Brooklyn Academy presented a pedestal benefit on 12 May 1884, which raised $12,000. In Manhattan, the Academy of Music at Madison Square put on four amateur theatricals that raised thousands of dollars. The sophisticated Art Loan Exhibition at the National Academy of Design (December 1883–January 1884) made a profit of $15,000. The Brooklyn Art Association raised several thousand dollars by sponsoring an exhibit of oil paintings, many of which were loaned by the banker George Seney. Fund raising was going well, though slowly. On 8 October 1883, Joseph Pulitzer, publisher of the *World*, flayed New York's wealthy in this editorial: "We have more than a hundred millionaires in this city, any one of whom might have drawn a cheque for the whole sum without feeling that he had given away a dollar; any one of whom would have willingly spent the amount in flunkyism or ostentation. Towards a foreign ballet dancer or opera singer their hearts and pockets would have opened. But do they care for a Statue of Liberty, which only reminds them of the equality of all citizens of the Republic?"

Despite its astonishing early successes, the American Committee was finding it more difficult to raise funds as time progressed. At this point, the committee, preeminently a Republican body, decided to use its powerful political influence to solve the problem. But these efforts

Pedestal campaign fund-raising event at New York's famous Casino Theatre, 7 April 1885

aroused strong resistance in the Democratic party, which squelched every request for public assistance. In the spring of 1884, Democratic governor Grover Cleveland of New York vetoed a $50,000 appropriation for the pedestal, declaring it an unconstitutional use of state funds, and in March 1885, Congressional Democrats in Washington killed the sum of $100,000 for the pedestal that Republicans had attached to the deficiency appropriation bill. On 12 March 1885, the American Committee's treasurer, H. F. Spaulding, issued a gloomy financial report. Of $182,491.40 raised, only $3,000 remained, and $100,000 more was needed to complete the pedestal. The political efforts having failed, the committee was now nearly reduced to begging. At this point, Auguste Bartholdi intervened. He wrote his fund-raising souvenir booklet, *The Statue of Liberty Enlightening the World,* and then sent the sculptor Max Baudelot over from Paris to make a model of Liberty for cast reproductions. The firm Brundage and Newton manufactured them under Bartholdi's patent. The American Committee sold the statuettes in three sizes: the 6-inch model for $1.00, the 12-inch one for $5.00, and the 36-inch version (for use as a lamp) for $10.00. But the most successful effort to complete the fund raising was made by newspaper publisher Joseph Pulitzer. The *World* launched a dramatic campaign to raise the last $100,000, calling for donations to be sent directly to the newspaper, which would be forwarded to the American Committee. Pulitzer then provided his readers a splendid motive for giving: he promised to publish every donor's name in his newspaper, no matter how small the sum. In the first week, more than two thousand dollars came in; by 11 August 1885, the *World* had achieved its goal. The campaign had brought in $102,006.39 from 121,000 donors—farmers, clerks, factory hands, printers, vaudevillians, policemen, immigrants, housewives, and children. The American Committee was delighted, and Pulitzer received invitations to dine from the previously closed doors of upper-class society. It was then esti-

mated that an extra $40,000 would be needed to anchor and assemble the statue on top of the pedestal. This called for more fund-raising efforts, which included the continued selling of souvenirs and offering benefit performances, all of which proved successful. One such gala benefit stage show was presented at the Casino Theatre, at Thirty-ninth Street and Broadway, at 1.30 P.M. on 7 April 1886. The program included such limelight stars as Lillian Russell, Richard Mansfield, Robert B. Mantell, and Ovide Musin, and Rudolph Aronson's Casino Orchestra performed French music. The audience, an elegant crowd with the likes of Mr. and Mrs. William K. Vanderbilt and Daniel Frohman in its midst, was dazzled. A *World* reporter described the event with gusto: "What the managers call a jam, the press calls a success, and the players call an ovation." With the Statue of Liberty approaching completion, plans were now being made for improving the surroundings on Bedloe's Island, installing an electric lighting system, and planning the elaborate inaugural ceremonies. Having successfully raised some $323,000 in donations during the pedestal campaign and with William M. Evarts now a senator, the American Committee felt confident about approaching Congress once again. Evarts and the committee insisted that the 1877 resolution accepting the statue implied a legal obligation to assume responsibility for the final costs. In May 1886, President Grover Cleveland accepted the argument and recommended a congressional appropriation. Thus Evarts overcame the last Democratic opposition with an appropriation of $56,500 (down from $106,000), which was finally passed on 4 August 1886.

Pedestal Committee. *See* American Committee; Pedestal committees.

Pedestal committees. The first committees founded to raise funds for Liberty's pedestal appeared in September 1876 in Philadelphia and New York and were convened by members of the Union League Club in both cities. John Jay was the chairman of the New York committee, but it was evidently a temporary body and engaged in nothing but discussion. A permanent body—the American Committee—would not be formed until January 1877. *See also* American Committee; Boston; Philadelphia Committee.

Pedestal patent and copyright. On 14 July 1885, Richard Morris Hunt received patent protection for a term of seven years from the U.S. Patent Office for his design of Liberty's pedestal. In it, he described the pedestal as taking the form of a truncated pyramid, ornamented by a portico, a molding, a castellated border, pillars, medallions, pilaster ornaments, cornice, frieze, pediment, and cap molding. His witnesses were Edgar Tate and Edward M. Clark. Hunt previously received copyright protection from the Library of Congress on 14 April 1885. *See also* Copyrights and patents.

Peyron, Alexandre (*b.* 1823, France; *d.* 1892, France). Naval officer and politician. Admiral Peyron was the minister of marine and colonies during the second government of Prime Minister Jules Ferry, 1883–85, a position that put him in charge of the French navy. The prime minister, an enthusiastic supporter of the Statue of Liberty project, instructed the admiral to arrange for a naval transport ship to convey the newly completed statue to the United States. Admiral Peyron chose a troop transport vessel for the task. The ship selected, the man-of-war *Isère,* had just returned from its usual duty of transporting French soldiers to two areas of French colonial activity, Madagascar, and Cochin-China (the southern region of Vietnam). The ship was made ready at the Rouen docks, and 214 crates, packed with the pieces of the Goddess Liberty, were carefully loaded. The ship departed for the United States on 21 May 1885 and arrived in New York harbor on 17 June 1885. Alexandre Peyron was a career naval officer and had commanded the French fleet at Toulon.

Philadelphia Centennial Exhibition of 1876. First great American world's fair. The exhibition was authorized by Congress in 1871 to celebrate the hundredth anniversary of American independence and was managed by the United States Centennial Commission. It lasted from April to November 1876 and was visited by over 10 million people. Colonel John Forney persuaded the Franco-American Union to exhibit the arm and torch of the still-unfinished Statue of Liberty at the fair. This was particularly beneficial to the Union, as it would show Americans the sincerity and boldness of the sculpture. The colossal arm and torch caused a sensation; people were delighted to pay the entrance fee to climb through the arm and stand at the railing of the glorious flambeau. Auguste Bartholdi was allowed to attend the exposition as an official delegate of France, due to the influence of Senator Edouard de Laboulaye, president of the Franco-American Union. *See also* Bartholdi Visit of 1876–77; Forney, John W.

Philadelphia Committee. An American branch of the Franco-American Union. The committee was set up in the autumn of 1876 as a possible alternate fund raiser in case New York should falter. The body was composed of prominent Union League clubmen and headed by Colonel John W. Forney. The committee's members were interested in obtaining the completed Statue of Liberty for their own city as a memento of the Philadelphia Centennial of 1876. The body's existence was short due to the successes of the American Committee in New York.

Phrygian bonnet. *See Pileus libertatis*

Pickering, Simeon Horace (*b.* 1894, Salt Lake City, Utah; *d.* 1987). Civil servant. Pickering was a National Park Service employee at the Statue of Liberty, c. 1938–65; guard, 1938–40; guide, 1940–47; historical aide, c. 1947–65. With Oswald Camp, William C. Weber, and others, Pickering contributed to the historical interpretation of the Statue of Liberty in its early years as part of the National Park system. Earning $1,500 per year as a park guide, his duties consisted of meeting visitors, taking them to the statue, answering questions, giving lectures, performing police duties, and, in the absence of the clerk-cashier, collecting elevator fees. Pickering was also an amateur artist and photographer. *See also* Interpretation; Visitation.

Pileus libertatis ("cap of freedom" or "liberty bonnet"). This headdress was an attribute sacred to the Roman goddess Libertas, who was commonly depicted holding it in her hand. Under Roman law, a slave could be granted his freedom in an informal mode of manumission called *pileo* ("by means of the pileus"). This stipulated that the slave gained freedom by testamentary provision of the master and required him to follow his dead master's funeral procession wearing on his head the *pileus libertatis,* or Phrygian cap (made usually of red felt), ceased to be a slave, and became a *libertus,* a freedman—hence, the powerful symbolic effect of the *pileus libertatis* throughout history. The cap was employed in Rome's many political struggles, such as when Saturninus, having seized the capitol, hoisted one atop his spear, to make it known to all that slaves who joined his rebellion should be set free. Marius used the symbol against Sulla, while the conspirators responsible for the scandalous murder of the dictator Julius Caesar marched forth with a *pileus* elevated on a spear in token of the return of political liberty to Rome. The French Revolution saw the *pileus* revived as the Liberty bonnet, the emblem of the revolutionaries and the Reign of Terror. *See also* Libertas.

Pinchot, James W. (*b.* 1831, Milford, Pennsylvania; *d.* 1908). Merchant, lawyer, and philanthropist. Pinchot served on the executive board of the American Committee charged to build the pedestal for the Statue of Liberty; he was also its first treasurer. An interest in promoting art led him to become one of the first sub-

scribers of the Metropolitan Museum of Art. In later years, his son Gifford drew his attention to forestry and conservation concerns, inspiring him to become active in the founding of the School of Forestry at Yale University. He also served as vice president of the American Forestry Association and was a lifelong member of his club, the prestigious Century Association in New York.

Plaques. *See* Tablets.

Potter, Henry Codman (*b.* 25 May 1835, Schenectady, New York; *d.* 1908, New York, New York). Protestant Episcopal clergyman. The Right Reverend Bishop Potter delivered the benediction on Bedloe's Island at the inauguration of the Statue of Liberty on 28 October 1886. Afterward, the assembly of some 2,000 guests were dismissed and reembarked on steamers that returned to their piers in Manhattan. Potter was ordained an Episcopal minister in 1858. He was elevated to coadjutor bishop of New York in 1883. In 1887, he succeeded his uncle, Horatio Potter, as bishop of New York. Potter was the author of many works, including *The Gates of the East* (1877), *Sermons of the City* (1881), *The Scholar and the State* (1897), and *The Industrial Situation* (1902).

Potts, Frederick A. (*b.* 1836; *d.* 1888). Merchant and philanthropist. Member of the American Committee, Franco-American Union. Potts served on the executive committee, 1883–86.

Presentation. The Statue of Liberty was completed in Paris in June 1884 and presented to the United States in a formal ceremony held in a shed at the Gaget and Gauthier foundry yard, 26 Rue de Chazelles, on 4 July 1884. The company of distinguished Frenchmen and Americans included Chamber of Deputies president Jules Brisson, various cabinet ministers and senators, Colonel Liechtenstein (official representative of French president Jules Grévy), Senator Edmond de Lafayette, and the baroness de Pages (a grandniece of the marquis de Montcalm). Also present were Count d'Abzac; M. Caubert; Philippe Burty, the eminent critic; Senator Dietz-Monnin; Count Sérurier; two painters, the Alsatian Jean-Jacques Henner and Armand Dumaresq; Mayor Koechlin-Schwartz of the Eighth Arrondissement; and Doctor Ricord of Baltimore. Also among the Americans were Consul General George Walker, Theodore W. Evans, former senator Baldwin of Michigan, former governor Cheney of New Hampshire, Senator James B. Eustis of Louisiana, painter Henry D. Bacon, and stockbroker Henry F. Gillig. Afterward, a banquet for twenty-four guests was given at the house of Senator and Madame Arbel. The guests included Monsieur and Madame Bartholdi, Levi Parsons Morton, viscount de Lesseps, Dietz-Monnin, H. F. Gillig, J. de Castro, Maître Caubert, and Ricord. The presentation deed read as follows:

The 4th of July, anniversary day of American Independence. In the presence of Monsieur Jules Ferry, Minister of Foreign Affairs and President of the Council of Ministers [i.e. Prime Minister]. Count Ferdinand de Lesseps, in the name of the Committee of the Franco-American Union, and of the national manifestation of which that committee has been the organ, has presented the colossal statue of *Liberty Enlightening the World,* the work of the sculptor Bartholdi, to His Excellency Mr. Morton, the United States Minister to Paris, praying him to be the interpreter of the national sentiment of which this work is the expression. Mr. Morton, in the name of his compatriots, thanks the French-American Union for this testimony of sympathy from the French people; he declares that in virtue of the powers conferred upon him by the President of the United States, and the Committee of the work in America, represented by its honorable President, Mr. William M. Evarts, he accepts the statue, and that it shall be erected in conformity with the vote of Congress of

S. Horace Pickering's painting *The Statue of Liberty at Night* (oil on canvas, 1940)

the 22nd of February 1877, in the harbour of New York as a souvenir of the unalterable friendship of two nations. In faith of which there have signed: In the Name of France, M. Jules Ferry, Minister of Foreign Affairs, M. Jules Brisson, President of the Chamber. In the Name of the United States, Mr. Morton, Minister of the United States. In the Name of the French-American Committee, Ferdinand de Lesseps, E. de Lafayette.

Press. Numerous publications followed the Statue of Liberty story during the nineteenth century. In Philadelphia, Colonel Forney's *Press* covered it, and in New York City a host of newspapers of various political and social persuasions reported it. One notable publisher was American Committee member George Jones of the *New York Times,* whose paper included criticism as well as support. Other supportive periodicals were Charles Dana Gibson's Union League Club newspaper, the *Sun;* the pro-Evarts *Evening Post* (previously owned by William Cullen Bryant and Parke Godwin until 1881); Godwin's own *Commercial Advertiser;* and two newspapers controlled by James Gordon Bennett, Jr., the *Herald* and the *Evening Telegram* (Bennett had lived in Paris and had friends in the French Committee of the Franco-American Union). The *Courrier des Etats-Unis,* the leading French-language newspaper, followed the story with unabated enthusiasm; its best-known editor at the time was Léon Meunier, a member of the French Committee of New York. Joseph Pulitzer's *World,* realizing the statue's social and political significance, launched relentless attacks against New York City's wealthy for failing to pay for Liberty's pedestal out of their own pockets. The era's leading illustrated publications were also absorbed by the story. The *Daily Graphic, Frank Leslie's Weekly, Puck,* and *Life* offered readers informative articles and drawings. Other interested publications included Robert Allen, Jr.'s *Mercantile Journal* and Albert Pulitzer's *Morning Journal. See also Daily Graphic;* Godwin,

Parke; Jones, George; Leslie, Frank; Pulitzer, Joseph.

Pressené, Edmond de (*b.* 3 June 1824, Paris, France; *d.* 8 April 1891, Paris, France). Clergyman, orator, and politician. Pressené was a member of both the French Anti-Slavery Society and the French Committee, Franco-American Union, and a close political ally of Edouard de Laboulaye. Pressené became a Protestant minister in 1847, and his eloquent and passionate preaching soon attracted a large following. His sermons, which touched on many controversial issues, were especially striking on the question of religious liberty and toleration. He founded and edited the *Revue chrétienne,* a journal characterized by his vigorous writing and his liberal viewpoint. After the fall of the Second Empire, he served as a deputy in the National Assembly, 1871–76, and was elected a life senator, 1883–91. Among his works are *L'Eglise et la Révolution* (1864) and *L'Origines* (1882).

Protection. Policing at the Statue of Liberty was the responsibility of the soldiers stationed at the Bedloe's Island Army Post from 1886 through 1937, when authority passed entirely to the care of park rangers. For many years, the chief security problems were suicide attempts and graffiti damage. In the 1960s, public demonstrations began, and eventually so did takeovers of the monument and even bomb threats. A bomb explosion in the monument in 1980 caused both an increase in security and more careful plans for visitor safety. Many techniques were developed to enhance park security, including the use of specially trained Statue of Liberty bomb dogs. Since the 1970s, the National Park Service has often been compelled to call in the U.S. Park Police to advise and assist in various law enforcement matters. These contacts finally resulted in Superintendent Ann Belkov's arranging for the U.S. Park Police to take over park security permanently in 1995. *See also* Army; Demonstrations; Fort

Statue of Liberty presentation document (Franco-American Union, 1884)

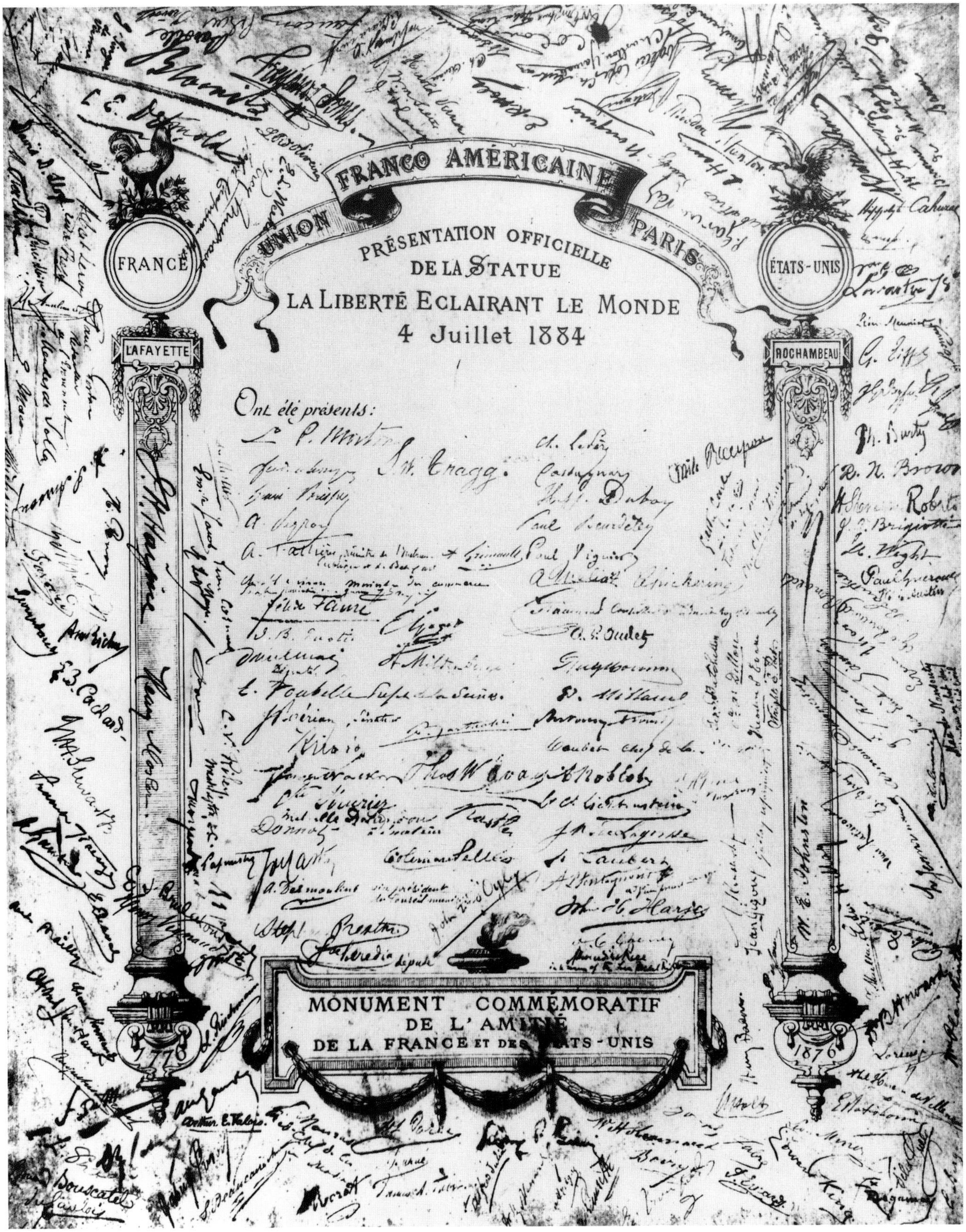
UNION FRANCO AMÉRICAINE PARIS
FRANCE
ÉTATS-UNIS
PRÉSENTATION OFFICIELLE
DE LA STATUE
LA LIBERTÉ ECLAIRANT LE MONDE
4 Juillet 1884
LAFAYETTE
ROCHAMBEAU
Ont été présents:
MONUMENT COMMÉMORATIF
DE L'AMITIÉ
DE LA FRANCE ET DES ÉTATS-UNIS
1776
1876

6,220.

The World.

230,220

Circulation of THE SUNDAY WORLD
that of any other Newspaper Published
Hemisphere.

The Average Circulation of THE SUNDAY W
Is larger than that of any other Newspaper
on the Western Hemisphere.

XVI., NO. 8,757. NEW YORK, TUESDAY, AUGUST 11, 1885---WITH SUPPLEMENT. PRICE TWO CEN

MURDERED IN HIS HOME.

A WEALTHY BROOKLYNITE SHOT DOWN BY A HIDDEN FOE.

Albert R. Herrick, Whose Place of Business Is at No. 60 William Street, this City, Dies Before He Can Tell Who Fired the Fatal Shot—The Police Without a Clue.

ONE HUNDRED THOUSAND DOLLARS!

TRIUMPHANT COMPLETION OF THE WORLD'S FUND FOR THE LIBERTY PEDESTAL.

Story of the Greatest Popular Subscription Ever Raised in America—How the Republic Was Saved from Lasting Disgrace—An Event for Patriotic Citizens to Rejoice Over—A Roll of Honor Bearing the Names of 120,000 Generous Patriots—The Flags of France and the American Union Floating in Sisterly Sympathy—Over $2,300 Received Yesterday—The Grand Total Foots Up $102,006.39—A Generous Lady Pays $130 for the Washington Cent.

THIS PEDESTAL TO LIBERTY WAS PROVIDED BY THE VOLUNTARY CONTRIBUTIONS OF 120,000 PATRIOTIC CITIZENS OF THE AMERICAN UNION THROUGH THE NEW YORK WORLD FINIS CORONAT OPUS

Wood; Military Police; National Park Service; Superintendents.

Pulitzer, Joseph (*b.* 10 April 1847, Makó, Hungary; *d.* 29 October 1911, Charleston, South Carolina). Newspaper publisher. Pulitzer was the son of Philip Politzer, a Hungarian Jew, and Louise Berger, a Catholic of German ancestry. At Hamburg, Germany, he was persuaded to emigrate to the United States in 1864. Upon arriving in Boston, he went to New York and joined the Union army. Discharged in July 1865, he moved to Saint Louis, Missouri, where he worked as a journalist for Carl Schurz's German-language newspaper, the *Westliche Post.* In 1878, Pulitzer bought two newspapers, the *Saint Louis Post* and the *Dispatch,* and merged them into the *Post-Dispatch.* In 1883, he purchased the *New York World* for $346,000 from Jay Gould and converted it into a highly profitable publication known as the *World.* Under his hand the paper resorted to sensationalism and was recognized by its large headlines, profuse illustrations, crime stories, publicity stunts, cartoons, and such popular crusades as the pedestal campaign for the Statue of Liberty. Although a Democrat, Pulitzer eventually launched a vigorous fund-raising drive to help the Republican-controlled American Committee give the statue her "footstool." In his editorial of 16 March 1885 he wrote: "We must raise the money! The WORLD is the people's paper, and it now appeals to the people to come forward. . . . The statue . . . was paid for by the workingmen, the tradesmen, the shop girls, the artisans—by all irrespective of class or condition. Let us respond in like manner. Let us not wait for the millionaires to give this money." By 11 August, the *World* had collected $102,000, bringing the pedestal campaign to a victorious end. Auguste Bartholdi, impressed by this feat, persuaded Pulitzer to commission him to build a new statue, *Washington and Lafayette.* Pulitzer agreed, paying 40,000 francs for its completion. *Washington and Lafayette* was Pulitzer's gift to France for the Statue of Liberty. Unveiled in 1895, it stands in the Place des Etats-Unis in Paris. *See also* Pedestal campaign; Press; *World.*

Joseph Pulitzer

R

Reagan, Ronald (*b.* 6 February 1911, Tampico, Illinois). President of the United States, 1981–89. President Reagan rededicated *Liberty Enlightening the World* at the spectacular Liberty Weekend celebration that followed its restoration in 1986. Two years earlier, the president spoke of her at the Republican National Convention in these words: "Her heart is full, her door is still golden, her future still bright. She has arms big enough to comfort and strong enough to support. For the strength in her arms is the strength of her people." First Lady Nancy Reagan activated a mechanism that relighted the torch on 4 July 1986.

Ronald Reagan became a motion picture actor in 1937, advancing from B-films to star status within two years of his arrival in Hollywood. His best-known films include *Brother Rat* (1938), *Dark Victory* (1939), *Knute Rockne—All American* (1940), *Kings Row* (1940), *This Is the Army* (1943), *The Voice of the Turtle* (1947), *Bedtime for Bonzo* (1952), *Tennessee's Partner* (1955), and *The Killers* (1964). Reagan made his mark on television as the star of *General Electric Theater* (1954–62) and *Death Valley Days* (1962–66). He also served as president of the Screen Actors Guild, 1947–52, 1959–60. He began his public service career as governor of California, 1967–75.

Religion. Although not officially a religious monument, for the modern world, the Statue of Liberty derives its intellectual power and its symbolic form and noble bearing from traditions of art and representation from the ancient Roman goddess Libertas and her world. *See also* Libertas; Liberty Altar.

Rémusat, (Count) Charles de (*b.* 1797; *d.* 1875). French politician, scholar, and journalist. A close friend and political ally of Edouard de Laboulaye, Rémusat dined often at his friend's estate at Glatigny and was included in the now historic dinners (1865, 1871) at which the sculptor Auguste Bartholdi was commissioned by Laboulaye (and his allies) to take up the venture of constructing and giving a statue of liberty to the United States as an expression of their political philosophy. A prominent liberal, Rémusat served in the Chamber of Deputies, 1830–48, and was minister of the interior in the 1840s. He went into exile following the coup d'état that ended the reign of King Louis Philippe in 1848. However, he returned to politics following the collapse of the Second Empire and served in the National Assembly, 1871–75; he was foreign minister in the cabinet of Louis-Adolphe Thiers, 1871–73. Among his many writings were *Essais de philosophie* (1842), *Angleterre au XVIIIe siècle*

Ronald Reagan on Governor's Island in 1988. On President Reagan's left is Soviet President Mikhail Gorbachev, and on his right, Reagan's vice president, George Bush

(1856), *Channing* (1857), and *Histoire de la philosophie en Angleterre de Bacon à Locke* (1875). He was married to a granddaughter of the marquis de Lafayette; their son was Paul de Rémusat.

Rémusat, Paul Louis Etienne de (*b.* 1831, Paris, France; *d.* 1897, Paris, France). Politician and writer. Member of the French Committee, Franco-American Union, 1875–86. In 1875, Edouard de Laboulaye selected Paul de Rémusat as a member of the French Committee to take a seat that would have gone to his father (and Laboulaye's friend), Count Charles de Rémusat, who had just died. The younger Rémusat was elected to the National Assembly in 1871 and was later a senator, c. 1870s–80s.

Replications. Numerous small-scale replications of the Statue of Liberty have been cast as outdoor sculpture since the 1880s. The first replica produced was the bronze Statue of Liberty located on the Ile des Cygnes in Paris. It was commissioned in 1884 by the American residents of Paris as a gift for the city. A plaster example was temporarily on display in the Place des Etats-Unis, c. 1885–86. The bronze statue, 36 feet (10.97 meters) high, was cast at the Thiébaut Frères foundry and was dedicated on the Pont de Grenelle by French President Sadi Carnot on 4 July 1889. An immense crowd witnessed the ceremony, which included speeches by Foreign Minister Eugène Spuller and U.S. ambassador Whitelaw Reid. The president un-

veiled the replica following Reid's address. In 1968, the Pont de Grenelle was completely rebuilt, and the statue was installed at its current location on the Ile des Cygnes.

Thiébaut Frères cast approximately five 9-foot-tall replications in bronze. One was for the city of Bordeaux (1887; destroyed in World War II); one was commissioned by Gaget & Gauthier for Hanoi, Vietnam, at the time a French protectorate (1887; disappeared 1945); one was for the southwestern French town of Lunel (c. 1889; destroyed in World War II); and one was for the town of Saint-Affrique, near Albi, (1889; destroyed in World War II). The German army melted down all of those listed as destroyed for use as ammunition. Only one statue avoided this fate: that which stands in the Jardin du Luxembourg in Paris, which Thiébaut Frères had cast for Auguste Bartholdi in 1900. A 9-foot-high bronze replica was cast for Izon, France (1926; also destroyed in the war) by the sculptor Toussaint of Bordeaux and given to Izon by Monsieur Rey-Jeanton.

Two founders cast iron replicas of the statue in France. The Société Antoine Durenne produced three replications: one for the town of Roybon (1906), a 9-foot-high replica for Semoutiers (1956), and a 36-foot-high bronze copy installed on top of the Liberty National Life Insurance Company in Birmingham, Alabama (1958). The second founder, the Société Anonyme des Hautes Fourneaux et Fonderies du Val d'Osne, produced a 9-foot-high replication for Poitiers (1903) and another for Buenos Aires, Argentina (c. 1906). It is not known precisely which of the two foundries produced the very similar 9-foot-high replicas that stand in the towns of Saint-Cyr-sur-Mer (c. 1903); Saint-Etienne, near Lyon (1915); and Cambrin, in northern France (1926).

A 44-foot-high polyester replica was constructed in Italy (1965–66) for use in the French motion picture *Le Cerveau,* which starred Jean-Paul Belmondo. The film's plot concerned gangsters who steal the Statue of Liberty. After completion of the film, the replica was almost destroyed; but thanks to Belmondo's intervention, it was saved by collector André Marie and installed permanently in the town of Barentin in 1973. The Boy Scouts of America were responsible for the sale of 206 replicas of Liberty that were installed in public parks throughout the United States from 1949 through 1983. The 8-foot-tall copper replicas were manufactured by the Friedley, Voshardt Company of Kansas City, Missouri, and sold for $300 each. Manufacturer Jack C. Whitaker dreamed up the idea, declaring it a "Crusade to strengthen the Arm of Liberty." The quality of the replicas was criticized by the National Sculpture Society.

Other notable American replicas of the Statue of Liberty are the 55-foot-high wrought iron one standing atop New York City's Liberty Warehouse; a 7-foot-tall replica in Paragould, Arkansas (1920); and two 30-foot-high copper replicas sculptured by Leo Lentelli and mounted atop the Liberty National Bank, Buffalo, New York. During World War II, the Motion Picture War Activities Committee commissioned a 55-foot-high replica, which was erected for temporary display in Times Square, New York City, in 1945. It was made of cement, plaster, and wood. Notable foreign replications include an 11-foot-high limestone statue in Guangzhou, China (rebuilt 1981; the original, which stood 5 feet high, was built in 1918 and destroyed during China's Cultural Revolution); a 30-foot-high replica atop the Lowe and Carr Building, Leicester, England, carved out of grey stone for the Liberty Shoe Company in 1922; and a 6-foot-high replica in front of the Liberty Hotel, Bangkok, Thailand (1967).

Repoussé. Artistic technique of hammering or beating copper into a sculpture or decorative form. Auguste Bartholdi employed it in modeling the Statue of Liberty at the suggestion of architect Eugène Viollet-le-Duc. The technique required hammering the copper sheets by hand, ensuring that the sculpture would exhibit relatively minute artistic detail. Furthermore, this technique made the statue solid yet light,

Repoussé artisans working on a portion of Liberty (Paris, c. 1883)

promising endurance and longevity. Finally, hammering separate sheets of copper into distinct pieces of the statue guaranteed an easy way of packing and transporting the parts once they were ready for delivery to the United States. The repoussé technique, in use since ancient times, is believed to have been the method the Greeks employed in constructing the Colossus of Rhodes, one of the seven wonders of the ancient world. Viollet-le-Duc used this method to assist in restoring medieval buildings in mid-nineteenth century France.

Restoration of 1937–39. Two New Deal agencies, the Public Works Administration (PWA) and the Works Progress Administration (WPA), undertook restoration and maintenance work at the Statue of Liberty. The monument was closed to the public from May through December 1938. WPA laborers replaced the corroded armature sections in the statue and removed the crown's rays in order to replace their rusted supports. The faulty and rusted cast-iron steps in the pedestal were replaced with a reinforced concrete staircase that reached to the foot of the statue. The WPA also demolished most of the old army buildings, regraded and seeded the island's eastern end, repaired the old East Dock, and built granite steps for the new public entrance at the statue's rear. The WPA maintenance crew left Bedloe's Island in 1941.

(opposite page) Restoration workers preparing for removal of Liberty's nimbus rays, c. 1938

(left) Liberty without her halo, c. 1938

Restoration of 1982–86. Launched by President Ronald Reagan in May 1982 with the founding of the Statue of Liberty–Ellis Island Centennial Commission, chaired by Chrysler Corporation head Lee A. Iacocca. The commission was to act as an "umbrella group coordinating private activities on behalf of both installations." It was also authorized to advise the secretary of the interior on preservation, projected facility use, and centennial celebration programs. The commission then set up a foundation to raise funds through a massive fund-raising campaign.

Before restoration work began, a diagnostic study of the statue found that the head is offset approximately 24 inches and the frame of the shoulder some 18 inches from the central pylon. It is believed that this mistake was made during assembly in Paris. In addition, one of the flares in the torch's flame was discovered to have been altered; this is believed to have occurred after the torch was shipped back to Paris in 1882. A freestanding 300-foot aluminum scaffolding was constructed from the base of the pedestal and rose above the torch. Its upper 150 feet did not touch Liberty; it was approximately 18 inches from the statue at every point, thus not interfering with the statue's movements under the force of strong winds. A 400-foot ramp was constructed from the water's edge, continuing over the walls of Fort Wood, leading to the pedestal's base. From there, an elevator carried materials and workers as high as the torch. Every effort was made to preserve the statue's green patina because it protects the metal colossus from corrosion.

The statue, which was closed 1984–86, was found to be stained in many places. Because of this, it required pressure washing over the whole body in order to clean away all stains and bird droppings. The statue's armature and rivets were completely replaced. The damaged nostril was mended by taking a mold of the original part and making a repoussé replacement. Cracks in the right eye, lips, chin; missing hair curls; badly patched folds of the dress; and

detached shackles at Liberty's feet were repaired. Minor tears were hammered together and then sealed from the inside. In removing and cleaning the crown's rays, the outside edges were found to be made of bronze and the top and bottom of brass instead of copper. *See also* Scaffold.

Rice, Alexander H. (*b.* 30 August 1818, Newton, Massachusetts; *d.* 22 July 1895, Melrose, Massachusetts). Politician and paper manufacturer. Member, Boston Committee, Franco-American Union. Rice was prominent in Republican politics and served as mayor of Boston, 1856–57; U.S. congressman, 1859–67; and governor of Massachusetts, 1876–78.

Richardson, Henry Hobson (*b.* 29 September 1838, Saint James's Parish, Louisiana; *d.* 27 April 1886, Brookline, Massachusetts). Architect. Richardson was famous for his voluptuous romanesque revival buildings in the 1870s. Richardson was one of the first Americans to study under Eugène Viollet-le-Duc at the Ecole des Beaux-Arts, Paris. Auguste Bartholdi met Richardson on his visit to Massachusetts in 1871. He is thought to have been the only American architect capable of having rivaled Richard Morris Hunt in designing a pedestal for the Statue of Liberty.

Rivets. The various parts of Liberty are joined together by 12,000 rivets or bolts—especially long pins driven through the copper sheets, the armature bars, and the central pylon or frame. A special ceremony was held to commemorate the driving of the first rivet. It was held in Paris on 24 October 1881, the centennial anniversary of the surrender of the British at Yorktown. This was the first step in assembling the parts. The host was Senator Edouard de Laboulaye, and the site was the yard of Gaget, Gauthier et Cie. The American minister to France, Levi Parsons Morton, was given the honor of driving in the first rivet through the left foot, after which he addressed the crowd. This was fol-

lowed by a gracious response by Laboulaye. The assembled guests were invited to sign a parchment document richly ornamented with the portraits of the marquis de Lafayette, George Washington, and the count de Rochambeau.

Rogers, Frances (*b.* 1888, Grand Rapids, Michigan; *d.* 1974). Writer. Frances Rogers was the author of perhaps the first commercially successful book on the Statue of Liberty, *Big Miss Liberty,* published in 1938, just after Liberty's fiftieth anniversary. It is a charming tale written for children. Rogers had a long career in publishing, working for many years as an illustrator and designer of book covers; in 1933, she switched to writing. Her books include *5000 Years of Glass* (1937), *Old Liberty Bell* (1942), and *5000 Years of Stargazing* (1964).

Roosevelt, Franklin Delano (*b.* 30 January 1882, Hyde Park, New York; *d.* 12 April 1945, Warm Springs, Georgia). President of the United States, 1933–45. President Roosevelt transferred the Statue of Liberty National Monument to the National Park Service (NPS) in 1933 and the whole of Bedloe's Island to the NPS in 1937. Further, he rededicated the monument in Bedloe's Island ceremonies on 28 October 1936. In the address he made these remarks:

> Fifty years ago our old neighbor and friend from across the sea gave us this monument to stand at the principal gateway to the New World. Grover Cleveland, President of the United States, accepted this gift with the pledge that "We shall not forget that liberty has here made her home; nor shall her chosen altar be neglected."
>
> During those fifty years that covenant between ourselves and our most cherished convictions has not been broken.

In 1937 and 1938, President Roosevelt also presided over the first major restoration of

1980s Liberty restoration, torch work

the monument since its arrival in the United States. *See also* Anniversaries.

Roosevelt, Theodore (*b.* 22 September 1831, New York, New York; *d.* 9 February 1878, New York, New York). Glass importer and philanthropist. Roosevelt was a founding member of the American Committee, Franco-American Union, which raised funds for the Statue of Liberty's pedestal, and served on its subcommittee on contributions. A well-known philanthropist, he was instrumental in founding such organizations as the Children's Aid Society, the Metropolitan Museum of Art, and the American Museum of Natural History. He was a member of the Union League Club. His son, Theodore Roosevelt, served as president of the United States, 1901–09.

(opposite page, top) President Franklin Roosevelt delivering his Liberty Golden Jubilee speech on Bedloe's Island, 28 October 1936

(opposite page, bottom) President Roosevelt and motorcade on Bedloe's Island, 28 October 1936

(left) Theodore Roosevelt (oil on canvas; courtesy of Theodore Roosevelt Birthplace)

S

Saddles. U-shaped copper pieces that hold the skin to the armature. They fit around the armature bars on three sides and are flush-riveted to the skin. About 300,000 copper rivets hold the 300 hammered repoussé sheets of copper skin together. The saddle attachment technique avoids further penetration of the metal.

Scaffold. The aluminum scaffold, constructed in 1983, was designed and built by Universal Builders Supply of Mount Vernon, New York, which won the contract on 14 December 1982, with a required completion date of 27 April 1983. It was the tallest free-standing scaffold ever constructed. Its purpose was to allow direct access to the entire surface of the statue. The scaffold, which was attached to the pedestal, not the statue, rose 240 feet high (73.2 meters) and was 81 feet square (24.7 meters). It was provided with two independent stair towers and an external elevator. The topping-out ceremony was held, as promised, on 27 April 1983.

Schneider, Charles Conrad (*b.* 24 April 1843, Apolda, Saxony, Germany; *d.* 8 January 1916, Philadelphia, Pennsylvania). Civil engineer. Engaged as a consulting engineer, he supervised and inspected the construction of the interior puddled iron framework and the complete steel anchorage built by the Keystone Bridge Company of Pittsburgh. He worked under the supervision of General Charles P. Stone, the chief engineer. Schneider, a prominent bridge builder throughout the United States and Canada, constructed the New Niagara Bridge and, most notably, the George Washington Bridge in New York, between 1886 and 1889. Schneider immigrated to the United States in 1867. He was elected president of the American Society of Civil Engineers in 1905.

Schofield, John McAllister (*b.* 29 September 1831, Gerry, New York; *d.* 1906, Bar Harbor, Maine). Soldier and statesman. General Schofield, designated by President Cleveland, acted as the government's representative in making arrangements and plans for the inauguration of the Statue of Liberty in October 1886. Schofield distinguished himself in the Civil War, especially against General Hood at the Battle of Franklin, Tennessee. He later served as U.S. secretary of state, 1868–69, and commander in chief of the U.S. Army, 1888–95.

Schools. Several schools have been named to honor those instrumental in creating and exporting the Statue of Liberty to the United States. Among them are the sculptor Auguste

(left to right) Liberty scaffold, 1980s restoration; John M. Schofield

Bartholdi, who is honored with the Lycée Auguste Bartholdi in his native Colmar, Alsace, while in Paris, there is the Lycée Jules Ferry in the Boulevard de Clichy, named to honor the French prime minister who shipped the Goddess of Liberty to America free of cost.

Schuyler, Georgina (*b.* 1841; *d.* 1923). New York society woman and friend of Emma Lazarus. In 1903, Schuyler, with the help of several friends, paid for and donated the bronze tablet inscribed with the words of Lazarus's sonnet, "The New Colossus," which was presented to the federal caretakers of the Statue of Liberty. The tablet's existence has played a key role in making the sonnet and its author widely known throughout the twentieth century.

Schuyler and her sister Louisa were descendants of the Dutch Schuylers and also direct descendants of Alexander Hamilton. They had a privileged upbringing in New York City and on the family estate at Dobb's Ferry on the Hudson River; they were educated privately by governesses and tutors, summering at such fashionable resorts as Newport, Rhode Island. The girls' parents, who were involved in the Children's Aid Society of New York, introduced their daughters to elite charitable activities early in life. Louisa Schuyler (1837–1926) became one of the city's leading philanthropists and reformers.

Second Empire. French constitutional and political regime founded and ruled by Emperor Napoléon III, December 1852–September 1870. Although the regime was passionately opposed on constitutional and political grounds by legitimist monarchists, republicans, and liberals, it was nevertheless noteworthy for the development of large-scale industrialization, massive improvements in communications, and urban planning. The regime originated in a December 1851 coup d'état in which Prince Louis Napoléon overthrew the democratic Second Republic, of which he was the elected president. He obtained overwhelming approval of his act through a plebiscite of 21–22 November 1852.

Under the Second Empire, the emperor had dictatorial powers. Article 14 of the Constitution obliged all members of parliament and assemblies, ministers, officers, magistrates, and civil servants to take an oath of personal allegiance to the emperor. Title 3 declared him head of state and commander of the armed forces, and it granted him extensive executive authority: the power to make war and peace, conclude treaties and alliances, make all appointments, and write up all policies and decrees. He was also given extensive legislative power: "He alone can initiate laws" (Art. 8), and "he approves and promulgates laws and *senatus consultums.*" Article 7 stated, "Justice is administered in his name." The emperor also had the right of declaring a state of siege in one or more *départements.* Cabinet ministers were not members of parliament, but only imperial servants, carrying out the emperor's will.

Parliament consisted of three weak bodies, the popularly elected Corps Législatif (Legislative Assembly); the appointed Conseil d'Etat (the supreme administrative tribunal, with legislative functions); and the Senate (the keeper of the constitution and national security), which consisted of de jure imperial princes, cardinals, marshals, admirals, and others appointed to the body for life by the emperor.

Between 1867 and 1870, the emperor began to democratize the constitutional system. The Second Empire ended when the emperor was taken prisoner by the enemy during the Franco-Prussian War in 1870. It was eventually replaced by the Third Republic (1875–1940). *See also* Napoleon III.

Second Republic. French constitutional and political system, 1848–52. This period was characterized by widespread democratic ideology and led to the abolition of slavery in the French colonies, the establishment of universal manhood suffrage (retained in the Second Empire), and the temporary abolition of execution for political

A portion of the shackle at Liberty's foot

crimes. In the early days of the republic, labor troubles led to the bloody Paris insurrection 23–26 June 1848, which was suppressed by General Louis Cavaignac (1802–57). The constitution provided for the election of a four-year-term president (reeligible for another term only after a four-year gap) and a Legislative Assembly (similarly chosen), which nominated a Council of State. Prince Louis Napoléon Bonaparte defeated General Cavaignac in the 1848 presidential election and overthrew the Constitution of the Second Republic in his coup d'état of 2 December 1851. He formally replaced it with his new regime, the Second Empire, in December 1852.

Secrétan, Pierre-Eugène (*b.* 1834, France; *d. ?*). Metallurgist and industrialist. This entrepreneur made a fortune in the copper production business in the 1870s. He donated 64 tonnes of copper (or more) to the Franco-American Union for use in constructing the Statue of Liberty. The Union's members showed their gratitude by recommending Secrétan for the Legion of Honor, and Bartholdi made a portrait bust of him. Secrétan was also noted for his fine collection of pictures, including Jean-François Millet's masterpiece *The Angelus.* He had factories located at Dives. Secrétan's business was ruined when the British dumped copper on the international market, causing the copper crash of 1889. He wrote *La Vérité sur l'affaire des cuivres* in protest.

Sérurier, Count (*b.* 1812, France; *d. ?*). Prominent member of Laboulaye's political and intellectual circle. Count Sérurier was a member of the French Committee of the Franco-American Union and served as administrative officer and, later, vice president, 1883–86. His personal interest in honoring the United States on its independence stemmed from his grandfather, Jean, count Sérurier (1742–1819), one of Napoléon I's marshals, who had twice traveled to America with the marquis de Lafayette.

Shackle. The broken shackle and chain lies at the Statue of Liberty's right foot. The chain

disappears beneath the draperies, only to reappear in front of her left foot, its end link broken. In keeping with Liberty's political and philosophical theme, the broken shackle symbolizes American independence and the end of all types of servitude and oppression.

Sherman, William Tecumseh (*b*. 8 February 1820, Lancaster, Ohio; *d*. 14 February 1891, New York, New York). Soldier. In 1877, Sherman, on the authority of President Rutherford Hayes, chose Bedloe's Island as the site for the Statue of Liberty. He retained an interest in the project and later made a financial contribution toward the pedestal.

General Sherman was famous for his Civil War march through Georgia to the sea in command of 65,000 men. From his victory at Savannah, he moved on to another triumph, ultimately receiving the surrender of General Robert E. Lee at Appomattox, Virginia. Sherman was commander in chief of the U.S. Army, 1869–74.

Ships. The most powerful impressions of the Statue of Liberty have often been made on steamship passengers entering New York harbor, such as immigrants, military personnel (often Americans returning from service overseas), and foreign visitors. Those aboard ship obtain the ideal aesthetic view of the monument, which can be even more impressive if the vessel circles

(opposite page) View of Liberty's right shoulder from above

(below) Steamship passing Liberty, c. 1949

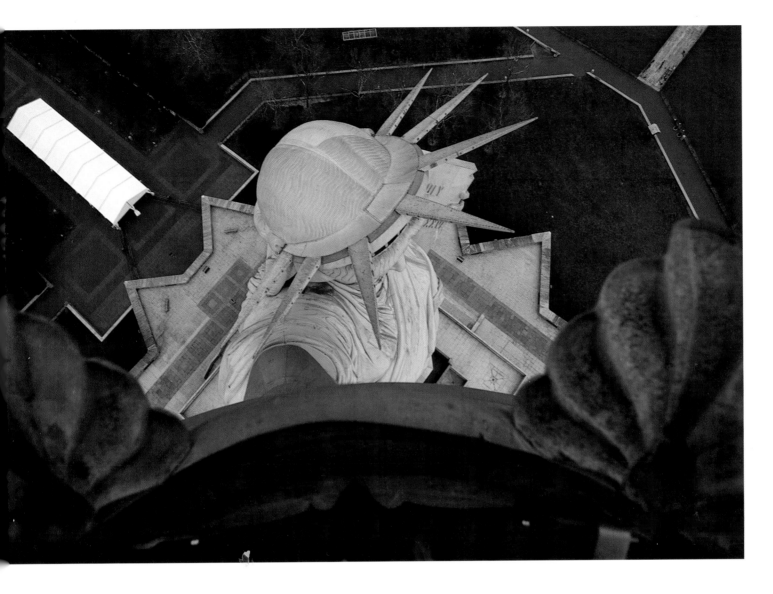

Liberty Island. From these views, the sculpture's pose seems to change at different approaches, giving it a curious sense of movement. Yet at the front view, the impressions of movement suddenly vanish, and the statue appears still.

Shoulder. During the 1980s restoration project, it was discovered that the shoulder frame is approximately 18 inches (45.7 centimeters) off from the axis of the pylon, showing that it was not constructed in accordance with Gustave Eiffel's drawings. Similarly, the head is offset by about 2 feet (0.6 meter). It is believed that this mistake was made during the construction of the statue in Paris.

Sightseeing. *See* Ferry; Statue of Liberty–Ellis Island Ferry; Visitation.

Simon, Marie (*b.* 1810?; *d.* ?). French sculptor. Auguste Bartholdi's indefatigable assistant who played a key role during the years of the Statue of Liberty project, 1871–86. He accompanied Bartholdi on his first visit to the United States in 1871. Viscount de Lesseps praised Simon at the presentation ceremony in Paris on 4 July 1884, observing, "We all of us would have wished to see him honored . . . by an official distinction."

Skeleton. Liberty's skeleton is composed of three parts: a 92-foot-high powerfully trussed tower known as the pylon, a lighter skeletal framework attached to the pylon, and a skin-support and attachment system. The first two parts of the skeleton are triangulated for rigidity. *See also* Interior.

Slavery. The Statue of Liberty is intimately connected to this social condition through its ties to the past, as well as to its political and philosophical symbolism. The creators of the monument were French liberals anxious to honor, and in a sense revive, ancient Rome's goddess of liberty in the modern world. As the classical personification of freedom, Libertas was patroness not only to those seeking relief from slavery but also to those seeking to do away with tyrannical government. The deity's modern revivers were aware of her symbolic power as an aid in pushing forward their aims. In 1865, Edouard de Laboulaye organized the French Anti-Slavery Society and joined with ordinary citizens in presenting a commemorative medal to Mary Todd Lincoln, widow of the slain American president, which hailed Lincoln for "abolishing slavery . . . and not veiling the Statue of Liberty." Laboulaye's abiding interest in American institutions and political life, as well as his determination to promote democracy in his own country, led him to propose presenting the Statue of Liberty to America as a celebration of that nation's one hundred years of independence. To him, the results of the Civil War (abolition of slavery and preservation of the Union) were proof that liberty had found a fertile soil in the United States. In New York City, Laboulaye was aided in his designs by the antislavery Union League Club whose members used their considerable political and social influence to smooth the way for the Statue of Liberty's acceptance. The dedication speeches at

the statue's inauguration in 1886 were eloquent in praising the newly unveiled goddess of liberty as a tribute to the Union victory and the abolition of slavery. And although no one seems to have remarked on it on that day, there lay a broken shackle at the statue's feet, eloquent in its silence for what liberty means. *See also* Civil War; Emancipation Movement; French Anti-Slavery Society; Laboulaye, Edouard de; Shackle; Union League Club.

Smith, Francis Hopkinson (*b.* 23 October 1838; *d.* 7 April 1915, New York, New York). Engineer, novelist, artist, and illustrator. Smith was a great-grandson of Francis Hopkinson of New Jersey, a signer of the Declaration of Independence. His firm of Smith, Magan and Drake constructed the masonry foundation of the Statue of Liberty for the American Committee. Smith also built Race Rock lighthouse in Connecticut, of which he was justly proud. His numerous published works include *Well-Worn Roads* (1886), *A White Umbrella in Mexico and Other Lands* (1889), *Colonel Carter of Cartersville* (1891), *Tom Grogan* (1896), *The Fortunes of Oliver Horn* (1902), and *Kennedy Square* (1911).

Soitoux, Jean-François (*b.* 1816, Besançon, France; *d.* 21 May 1891, Paris, France). Sculptor. Soitoux taught Auguste Bartholdi the art and techniques of sculpture around 1852. Having himself learned the art of sculpture in the ateliers of David d'Angers and Feuchères, Soitoux debuted at the Salon of 1850 with his heavily draped amazonian-like statue of the French Second Republic. Other well-known works of his include the statues of Montaigne, Erato, and Clio; the bust of Paul de Flotte; and his splendid bas-reliefs, which include *Force Génératrice*. Bartholdi designed Soitoux's tomb in the Montparnasse Cemetery.

Spaulding, Henry Foster (*b.* 24 April 1817, Brandon, Vermont; *d.* 7 July 1893, New York, New York). Merchant and philanthropist. Member of the American Committee, Franco-American Union, of which he was treasurer, 1883–86. Spaulding was a prominent member of the inner circle or executive committee, which included William M. Evarts, James Pinchot, Joseph Drexel, V. Mumford Moore, Frederick A. Potts, and others. As treasurer, he was confronted by dwindling donations, a persistent problem that was at last remedied by the vigorous fund-raising drive launched by Joseph Pulitzer, publisher of the *World*.

Spaulding arrived in New York City as a poor orphan in 1832. Beginning as a clerk, he rose to senior partner in a woolen importing firm. He later served as a president of the Central Trust Company and sat on the board of directors of the Continental Insurance Company and the Mechanics' National Bank. He was president of the Home for Incurables. His clubs were the Century Association, Manhattan, Reform, Country, and Downtown.

Spofford, Ainsworth Rand (*b.* 12 September 1825, Gilmanton, New Hampshire; *d.* 11 August 1908, Holderness, New Hampshire). Librarian of Congress, 1864–97. Spofford registered the copyrights and patents of the Statue of Liberty for Auguste Bartholdi (1876, 1878 [bust], 1879) and the pedestal for Richard Morris Hunt (1885). He was the author and editor of several publications, including *The Copyright System of the United States* (1892).

Spuller, Eugène (*b.* 8 December 1835, Seurre, France; *d.* 1896, Sombernon, France). Politician and editor. With Frédéric Desmons, Spuller was an official delegate of the Chamber of Deputies at the inauguration and dedication of the Statue of Liberty in October 1886. He also attended and delivered a speech at the dedication ceremony of the 36-foot replica of the Statue of Liberty, unveiled in Paris on 4 July 1889. Spuller was a close friend and political ally of radical republican leader Léon Gambetta, with whom he opposed the Second Empire (1852–70). He was also editor in chief of Gambetta's journal, *La République française*. He served as parliamentary deputy, 1876–92; minister of education, 1887, 1893–94; foreign minister, 1889–90; and senator, 1892–96.

Stamps. The first U.S. stamp depicting the Statue of Liberty was issued in 1922, with more stamps issued in subsequent years. France issued a commemorative stamp for the New York World's Fair with the Statue of Liberty on

Liberty's interior skeletal system

it in 1939. Further, following World War II, the French Republic issued its famous Statue of Liberty stamp bearing the words, *Aide aux Réfugiés* (Help to the refugees), while Liberty is depicted with her fiery torch held aloft, and on her tablet the word *Fraternité* ("brotherhood"). In 1954, France issued a Bartholdi commemorative stamp, depicting the sculptor and his two most celebrated works, *Liberty Enlightening the World* and the *Lion of Belfort*. Other nations depicting the Statue of Liberty and her torch on their stamps in the first half of the twentieth century include Spain (1930, 1937), Nicaragua (1940), Haiti (1941, 1949), Cuba (1945), Philippines (1946), Monaco (1947), Uruguay (1949), and San Marino.

Statue of Liberty–Ellis Island Centennial Commission. President Ronald Reagan established this commission to oversee the restoration of the two sites. On 17 May 1982, the president held a press conference in the East Room of the White House, announcing the appointment of Lee A. Iacocca as commission chairman. Veteran journalist J. R. "Tex" McCrary had suggested Iacocca to Garnet Chapin, an Interior Department official. Prominent members of the commission included Philippe Vallery-Radot of the French-American Committee for the Restoration of the Statue of Liberty and Philip Lax of the Ellis Island Restoration Commission.

Statue of Liberty–Ellis Island Ferry, Inc. Ferryboat excursion company. Founded in 1953 by Circle Line as a separate company, it holds the exclusive franchise to bring tourists to the Statue of Liberty, having replaced rival excursion boat operator B. B.Wills on 1 October 1953. In the spring of 1954, Circle Line brought into service *Miss Liberty,* a new three-deck boat. In recent years, it has added many new boats, including *Miss Ellis Island* and *Miss Gateway.* The company continues to be operated by descendants of some of the founders of Circle Line. It provided ferry services to Ellis Is-

land from 1976 to 1984 and resumed service after the opening of the Ellis Island Immigration Museum in 1990. *See also* Circle Line; Ferry service.

Statue of Liberty–Ellis Island Foundation, Inc. Originally founded by Richard Rovsek in 1981 as the fund-raising arm of the Statue of Liberty–Ellis Island Centennial Commission, this organization eventually took on a life of its own. In September 1982, Lee A. Iacocca became chairman and named J. Paul Bergmoser as executive director. Bergmoser then hired several directors: Steven Briganti in operations, Denver Frederick in fund raising, and Gary Kelley as comptroller. Iacocca was later succeeded by William May as chairman, and Briganti assumed the presidency. Due to Iacocca's prestige and popularity, the foundation has raised more than $350 million in donations.

Statue of Liberty Exhibit. Museum exhibition in the base of the pedestal, opened in July 1986. The exhibition tells the history of the Statue of Liberty from Edouard de Laboulaye's original idea to the dedication of the monument and its subsequent universal acclaim through historic artifacts, full-scale copper replicas of the statue's face and feet, illustrations (such as coins bearing the likeness of the goddess Libertas), replicas of Auguste Bartholdi's terra-cotta study models, a video documentary on the repoussé technique, a scale model of the Statue of Liberty, a Liberty postcard display, the original bronze tablet of Emma Lazarus's "The New Colossus" poem, Liberty advertisements and government posters, and other historic items and curiosities. The exhibit was established during the Statue of Liberty restoration in the 1980s. Its designers were the MetaForm/Rathe/D&P–The Liberty/Ellis Island Collaborative.

Statue of Liberty oral histories. Since 1973, the National Park Service has maintained an oral history interview project at the monument.

Employees and others connected with the site's history have been interviewed in a way similar to the Ellis Island interview project. Those interviewed include John Bowen, an army stenographer on Bedloe's Island, 1911–16; Marcelle Brunet, who maintained that her mother had been the model for the Statue of Liberty; Beulah Pennel, who had memories of Granger Brown, the man who gave the signal at the Statue of Liberty's inauguration in 1886; Evelyn Hill, who with her husband operated a food concession at Bedloe's Island; and Hill's son, James Hill, who was born on Bedloe's Island in December 1925 and continued as the concession owner at the island for many years. Other persons interviewed were Stanley J. Grogan (b. 1925), the son of an army captain who lived on Bedloe's Island, 1931–35; a 1930s WPA painter named Patrick Izzo; National Park Service employee Harry McManamy, who worked on the island, 1940–79; two World War II Statue of Liberty look-out Coast Guardsmen, Anthony Radomsky and William Saretsky; Charles DeLeo, the keeper of the flame, 1972–99; Park Service architectural historian Michael Adlerstein; Statue of Liberty deputy superintendent Thomas A. Bradley, who, with his wife and two children, lived on Liberty Island, 1988–95; and Brian Feeney, the Statue of Liberty's staff photographer during the 1980s restoration. *See also* Ellis Island Oral History Project.

Statue of Liberty story room. Museum exhibit established as part of the American Museum of Immigration on Liberty Island and opened to the public on 22 February 1970. The Statue of Liberty story room was destroyed by dynamite explosion in an act of sabotage in 1980.

Statuettes. Miniature replications of the Statue of Liberty as models or souvenirs. The first models were made by Auguste Bartholdi as purely artistic samples for Edouard de Laboulaye's approval (1871–75) and to show

Auguste Bartholdi's Liberty and *Egypt Carrying the Light* maquettes others. He also forwarded a study model to the Gaget and Gauthier foundry (1875). Next came Bartholdi's terra-cotta figures, which were used as presentation gifts, while 200 others were "touched up and signed" by the sculptor and provided to the Franco-American Union for fund raising. These were made from Bartholdi's 4-foot *modèle d'étude*. Each was numbered, inscribed "Modèle du Comité," and cold-stamped with the union's seal. Cast in Bartholdi's studio in about 1878, they were sold throughout France for 1,000 francs each and in the United States for $350 each. Bartholdi gave the unsold statuettes to French museums.

In 1878, he contracted the Avoiron foundry in Paris, known for its statuettes and candlesticks, to produce the first cast metal reproductions for public sale. Although it is known that the firm cast replicas in four sizes—of which one is known to have been 22 inches high—the number made remains unknown.

In 1885, the American Committee engaged the Newton Bottle Stopper and Britannia Company to manufacture Liberty statuettes known as the American Committee Model. These were cast in three sizes, with the 6-inch (152.4 millimeters) and the 12-inch (304.8 millimeters) sizes predominating. A few were 3 feet (about 1 meter) in height. The models were made in vast quantities and sold in shops and department stores throughout the country. The five dollar 12-inch model was the design of the French sculptor Max Baudelot, whom Bartholdi had engaged and sent to New York. Throughout the twentieth century, commercial firms produced millions of Liberty statuettes for tourists and collectors. *See also* Replications.

Stokes, Anson Phelps (*b.* 22 February 1838, New York, New York; *d.* 28 June 1913, New York, New York). Banker and philanthropist. Stokes, a Democrat, was a member of the American Committee, Franco-American Union, 1877–86.

American War. He resigned from the army with the rank of lieutenant in 1856 to go into banking in San Francisco, but the business failed and, in 1857, he was appointed chief of a private scientific commission that conducted a survey and exploration of Sonora, Mexico. He finished the job and in 1861 published his findings in *Notes on the State of Sonora*. That same year marked the start of the Civil War, and he returned to active military duty, first as a colonel in the District of Columbia Volunteers, next as an infantry colonel in the regular army, and finally as a brigadier general of volunteers. He was responsible for the safety of the president, the White House, and Washington, D.C. A brilliant career stood before him until ruin came on 21 October 1861 at the disastrous skirmish at Ball's Bluff, near Leesburg, Virginia. The Union troops suffered several casualties, including that of Colonel Edward Baker, a U.S. senator. Stone, whose popularity with the Confederates aroused suspicion, was suspected of treason and arrested in February 1862. He was held in solitary confinement in various forts in New York harbor, but no evidence could be found against him. Congressional intervention forced his release that August. In 1863, he returned to active duty in the Red River campaign, but he resigned from the service the following year.

After working from 1865 to 1869 as engineer and superintendent of the unsuccessful Dover Mining Company in Virginia, he accepted a position in the Egyptian army, becoming chief of staff and receiving the rank of lieutenant general from the Khedive Isma'il. The khedive also put Stone in the charge of the Department of Public Works. His duties included reconnaissance expeditions, explorations, and surveys, and he also established military schools for the War Office. He was fluent in French, Spanish, and German and understood Arabic. He worked for the Egyptians until 1883 and was given the title of ferik pasha in the Egyptian peerage. After returning to the United States, he worked for a year as chief engineer of the

(left) Liberty model, 1870s

Stone, Charles Pomeroy (*b.* 30 September 1824, Greenfield, Massachusetts; *d.* 24 January 1887, New York, New York). Soldier and engineer. Stone was the chief engineer in the construction of both the foundation and the pedestal of the Statue of Liberty, 1883–85. His assistants were Colonel Samuel Lockett and George Simpson.

Having graduated from the Military Academy at West Point in 1845, Stone served under General Winfield Scott in the siege of Veracruz and the capture of Mexico City in the Mexican-

Florida Ship Canal Company. General Stone, a Roman Catholic convert, seems to have been the only leading non-Protestant American to work on the Statue of Liberty project. Just months after the statue's inauguration, he died after a brief bout with pneumonia. *See also* Anchorage; Construction (United States); Foundation; Pedestal.

Storrs, Richard Salter (*b.* 21 August 1821, Braintree, Massachusetts; *d.* 1900, Brooklyn, New York). Congregationalist minister. Storrs led the opening prayer at the dedication of the Statue of Liberty in October 1886. A lively and intelligent man, he served as president of the Board of Foreign Missions, 1887–97, and was editor of *The Independent,* 1848–61. He was the author of *The Constitution of the Human Soul, The Declaration of Independence and the Effects of It,* and an autobiography, *Forty Years of Pastoral Life.*

Streets. Auguste Bartholdi lived at 38 Rue Vavin, Paris, for thirty-eight years, 1854–92. When the house was demolished and a new road was built, Bartholdi moved to 84 Rue d'Assas, where he lived until his death. Streets have been named to honor both Edouard de Laboulaye and Bartholdi: the Place Edouard de Laboulaye in Glatigny, France, and two Bartholdi avenues in New Jersey—one in Butler and one in Jersey City.

Strong, William Lafayette (*b.* 22 March 1827, Richland County, Ohio; *d.* 2 November 1900, New York, New York). Merchant, banker, and politician. Member of the American Committee, Franco-American Union; served on the Finance Committee, 1884–86. He founded W. L. Strong & Company in 1869, a highly successful dry goods business. Strong claimed to be a political reformer and was a Republican mayor of

New York City, 1895–97. His police commissioner was Theodore Roosevelt (1858–1919).

Suez lighthouse. *See* "Egypt Carrying the Light to Asia."

Superintendents. President Calvin Coolidge proclaimed the Statue of Liberty a national monument on 15 October 1924, and since then superintendents have administered the site. The superintendent has many responsibilities, such as preservation and protection, controlling the budget, hiring and supervising the staff, and providing public programs. The first superintendent of the Statue of Liberty National Monument was William A. Simpson, a civilian employee of the Army, U.S. War Department. His successors have all been employees of the National Park Service, U.S. Department of the Interior. The following is a complete list of superintendents. In some instances, they have held other titles due to occasional NPS regional reorganizations, most of which were not lasting. But the responsibilities of the people on this list, for practical purposes, have remained consistent: William A. Simpson (1925–34); George A. Palmer (1934–35); Oswald E. Camp (1935–37); George Palmer (1937–45); Charles S. Marshall (1945–47); Newell H. Foster (1947–64); Lester McClanahan (management assistant, 1964–67, and assistant superintendent, 1967–69); Arthur Sullivan (assistant superintendent, 1969–70); James Batman (assistant superintendent, 1970–73); Howard Crane (acting assistant superintendent, 1973–74); Luis García y Curbelo (unit manager, 1974–76); David L. Moffitt (1976–87); Kevin C. Buckley (1987–90); M. Ann Belkov (1991–96); Diane H. Dayson (1996–present). *See also* Camp, Oswald Edward; Moffitt, David L.; National Park Service; Palmer, George A.

A GIFT
FROM
THE PEOPLE OF THE REPUBLIC OF FRANCE
TO THE PEOPLE OF THE UNITED STATES.
THIS STATUE
OF
LIBERTY ENLIGHTENING THE WORLD
COMMEMORATES THE ALLIANCE OF THE TWO NATIONS
IN ACHIEVING THE INDEPENDENCE
OF THE
UNITED STATES OF AMERICA.
AND
ATTESTS THEIR ABIDING FRIENDSHIP.

AUGUSTE BARTHOLDI.
SCULPTOR.

INAUGURATED
OCTOBER 28TH 1886.

T

Tablet. The Statue of Liberty's symbol of the American Declaration of Independence and constitutional law. It is held in Liberty's left hand and, in keeping with the statue's symbolism as a Roman deity, it is inscribed with the date of the Declaration of Independence in Roman numerals. *See also* Dimensions.

Tablets and plaques. Aside from the tablet held in the Statue of Liberty's hand, several other commemorative tablets have been mounted for permanent public display at the Statue of Liberty:

• Sculptor's Tablet (bronze) dating from the 1880s, located just under Liberty's feet on its copper base. It bears these words:

Statue Colossale de la Liberté par Auguste Bartholdi, statuaire. Executeé en Cuivre Martelé par Gaget, Gauthier et Cie., constructeur à Paris. (Colossal Statue of Liberty by Auguste Bartholdi, sculptor. Executed in hammered copper by Gaget, Gauthier and Co., builder in Paris).

• Presentation Tablet (brass), bearing these words:

A Gift from the People of the Republic of France to the people of the United States. This Statue, Liberty Enlightening the World, commemorates the alliance of the two Nations in achieving the Independence of the United States of America and attests to their Abiding Friendship.

Auguste Bartholdi, sculptor. Inaugurated October 28, 1886

• American Committee Tablet (brass), which bears these words:

This Pedestal was built by voluntary contributions from the people of the United States. [A list of the names of fund-raising committees follows.]

• Cornerstone Tablet (bronze) given by the Freemasons, mounted outside the pedestal at its base.

There is also a bronze tablet, dating from 1903, which is engraved with the celebrated poem, "The New Colossus," written by Emma Lazarus. Since 1986 it has been displayed in the Statue of Liberty exhibit at the base of the pedestal; prior to the 1984–86 restoration, it had been mounted inside the pedestal. Next to it is a bronze tablet dedicated to the poet's memory by the Emma Lazarus Commemorative Committee in 1977. *See also* "The New Colossus."

Thiébaut Frères. Foundry in Paris noted for its decorative and ornamental sculpture cast in bronze. The firm produced the world's most noted replica of the Statue of Liberty, that which stands on the Ile des Cygnes in the River Seine in Paris. It was commissioned by the American colony in Paris as a gift to the city in 1884 and dedicated by President Sadi Carnot on 4 July 1889. Auguste Bartholdi provided the foundry with a study model. The completed bronze figure rises 36 feet in height. The foundry also made bronze statuettes as table ornaments for Bartholdi. It later produced four 9-foot statues of Liberty—one for a park (Jardin du Luxembourg, Paris) and the others for public squares in France (in Bordeaux, Lunel, and Saint-Affrique). The Germans melted the last three down for ammunition during World War II; the sole survivor is the one in the Jardin du Luxembourg. The distinguished firm of Thiébaut Frères was founded in 1789 and was still in operation in the early twentieth century. *See also* Replications.

Third Republic. French constitutional and political system, 1875–1940. After the fall of the Second Empire and defeat in the Franco-Prussian War (1870–71), France selected a moderate system of government—a sort of constitutional monarchy without a king. After failing to reach agreement to restore the legitimate Bourbon-Orléans monarchy (represented by two princes, the count of Chambord and the count of Paris), the National Assembly accepted the Wallon amendment (advocated by Henri Wallon, Edouard de Laboulaye, and others), which defined France's government as that of a republic (1875). The constitutional documents of the Third Republic (written by Edouard de Laboulaye and other constitutional experts) were democratic, providing for an elected Chamber of Deputies, an appointed Senate, a prime minister, a cabinet, and a president with largely ceremonial functions. The Third Republic ended when Nazi Germany conquered France in June 1940.

Torch. The Statue of Liberty's primary symbol of enlightenment, originally made of copper.

Designed by Auguste Bartholdi and Eugène Viollet-le-Duc, the torch, flame, and portion of the arm were constructed in Paris and unveiled at the Philadelphia Centennial Exhibition in 1876, where they were popular attractions. At the close of the fair in 1877, they were sent to New York City for display in Madison Square park and then shipped back to France in 1882. The torch was brought back to the United States in 1885 and assembled with the rest of the statue at Bedloe's Island and unveiled in 1886.

Initially the torch emitted just a faint glow, so efforts were made to improve its electrical system. Two rows of portholes were cut in 1886; in 1892, an 18-inch belt of glass and pyramid-shaped skylight of colored glass were installed; in 1916, following the Black Tom explosion, the American sculptor Gutzon Borglum gave the torch a new appearance, creating a "Chinese lantern" effect. The holes he made at the top of the torch allowed rain to enter and flow down the arm; this caused corrosion over the years (which was later corrected by building a new torch).

View of the torch

The torch and its flame have been an important worldwide symbol of enlightenment, liberty, and democracy. After a World War II blackout, the torch was relit for fifteen minutes on 6 June 1944 to celebrate the Allied invasion of Normandy, France. It was again illuminated on 7 May 1945 to celebrate Germany's surrender.

The torch and flame have had many caretakers over the years. The best known is Vietnam War veteran Charles DeLeo, the keeper of the flame, who bore the responsibility from 1972 until his retirement in September 1999. The old torch was taken down on 4 July 1984 and replaced by a new one with a gilded flame in 1986. The retired icon of freedom, escorted by mounted U.S. park rangers, was carried on the Hilton Hotels Float in the Tournament of Roses Parade in Pasadena, California, on New Year's Day 1985; the grand marshal of the parade was Statue of Liberty Centennial Com-

mission chairman Lee Iacocca. The old torch is now on permanent display in the entrance lobby of Fort Wood on Liberty Island.

Following are torch facts and figures:

Old Torch and Flame
Sculptor: Auguste Bartholdi.
Engineer: Eugène Viollet-le-Duc.
Year of construction: 1876.
Builder: Monduit et Béchet.
Place: Paris, France.
Metal of flame: Copper.
Years attached to Statue: 1886–1984.
Reason for removal: Corrosion caused by water leakage.
Present location: On display in the lobby of Fort Wood, Statue of Liberty.
Lighting power: Electricity.
Note: Portions of the copper flame were later cut away to improve lighting in 1886, 1892, and 1916.

New Torch and Flame
Sculptor: Auguste Bartholdi.
Engineer: Eugène Viollet-le-Duc.
Years of construction: 1984–86.
Builder: Les Métalliers Champenois (chief artisans: Serge Pascal and Jean Wiart).
Place: Liberty Island, New York.
Inner metal of flame: Copper.
Outer metal of flame: Gold.
Lighting power: Electricity.

Dimensions of Old and New Torches
Height: 16 feet, 5 inches.
Weight: 3,600 pounds.
Diameter: 12 feet.
From tip of flame to deck of catwalk: 12 feet, 6 inches.
From tip of flame to bottom of torch: 29 feet.
Circumference of deck: 36 feet.
From deck of catwalk to base of flame: 5 feet, 6 inches.
Circumference of flame (support column): 11 feet, 8 1/2 inches.

See also Dimensions; Enlightenment; Flame; Gold leaf; Lighting.

U

Union League Club (New York City). Exclusive political club, founded on 6 February 1863 as a local bulwark of Abraham Lincoln, the Republican party, and the Union cause. The club contributed vigorously to the Loyal Publication Society's propaganda campaign and raised three African American regiments in New York. Soon after the war, it gained a reputation for the promotion of art as well as that of patriotism. Its members were largely responsible for the successful fund raising drive for and construction of Liberty's pedestal. Edouard de Laboulaye (an honorary member of the Philadelphia branch) drew the institution into the effort to build the pedestal, following Auguste Bartholdi's selection of New York harbor as the site of the monument. It was a fortunate choice, for the club had the largest representation of elite society and business leaders in New York City as its members; the Manhattan Club (Democratic) had only one-fourth as many. Political scientist Gabriel Almond has studied the membership for the years 1863 through 1935, and found that 31 percent were business leaders, 8 percent were society leaders, and 15 percent were federal politicians.

Union League Club (Philadelphia). First of the exclusive Union League clubs, officially established on 27 December 1862 in response to the Civil War and as a "refuge of loyalty." It was founded and supported exclusively by wealthy Republicans, such as George H. Boker, Mayor Morton McMichael, John W. Forney, and Congressman William D. Kelley. Branches were established in New York, Boston, and Chicago. The league was dedicated to the preservation of the Union and the abolition of slavery. During the war, it raised new regiments (including the first African American one) and carried out a vigorous propaganda campaign for the Union and the federal government through its Loyal Publication Society. One of its foremost pamphleteers was the publisher Henry Charles Lea. Edouard de Laboulaye was a contributor in this effort.

After the war, the league was active in patriotic efforts to promote good citizenship and bring dignity to politics. Believing that education and art were essential elements of a civilized society, members established libraries and promoted civic art. The league sponsored important exhibitions of contemporary paintings and sculpture. Edouard de Laboulaye was exceedingly popular with the Philadelphia League due to his enthusiastic support of the unity of the United States, and was elected an honorary member of the body in 1863. The Union League Club's permanent home at 140 Broad Street was dedicated on 11 May 1865. Its motto is "Love of Country Leads."

V

Véron, Pierre (*b.* 19 April 1831, Paris, France; *d.* 2 November 1900, Paris, France). Journalist. Member of the French Committee, Franco-American Union. Véron was reputedly one of the most brilliant journalists of his time.

Veterans of Foreign Wars (Ladies Auxiliary). Military service and patriotic organization founded in 1914. The Ladies Auxiliary to the Veterans of Foreign Wars (VFW) was invited to join President Franklin D. Roosevelt and the National Park Service in celebrating the Statue of Liberty's Golden Jubilee in 1936. The auxiliary sponsored a national essay contest for American high schools in which some 100,000 students participated. The essay was entitled, "What the Statue of Liberty Means to America." The success of the Golden Jubilee convinced the Ladies Auxiliary to make what was to become a permanent commitment to return each year for Liberty's anniversary. During World War II, they participated in events honoring the Allied soldiers and sailors, which helped to strengthen bonds of camaraderie. In the 1950s, they raised funds to help build the American Museum of Immigration and, by 1962, had raised $50,000 in time for the laying of the cornerstone. Each year the Ladies Auxiliary

makes a gift to the park. Over the years these have included heavy-duty wheelchairs, public benches, American flags, a public address system, and a world globe for the library.

Vigsnes Mine (Norwegian: *Vigsnes Grubeområde*). This mine has been determined to be the source of the Statue of Liberty's copper based on a combination of scientific analyses of the copper and historical evidence. It is located on Karm Island (Karmøy), off the coast of Norway, in the North Sea. A fisherman from Jaeren discovered the incredibly rich copper deposits in 1865, and a Belgian-French mining company started working the mines shortly afterward. For many years, the mine's director was Charles DeFrance, a French engineer who had earlier been employed at Antwerp. By 1895, Vigsnes had become northern Europe's leading source of pure copper; it represented 70 percent of Norway's copper export. During these prosperous years, more than 3,000 people lived at Vigsnes, 750 of them miners. The mine went to a depth of some 2,500 feet (730 meters) below sea level. The mining company, concerned for the welfare of its workers and their families, operated a school and a hospital in the community. Mining ceased at Vigsnes in 1972. In recent

Eugène Viollet-le-Duc

years, an open-air mining museum was established at the site.

Villard, Henry (*b.* 10 April 1835, Speyer, Bavaria; *d.* 12 November 1900, Dobbs Ferry, New York). Railroad magnate and journalist. Villard and his business partner, Frederick Billings, donated $1,000 each toward building the State of Liberty's pedestal in the 1880s. He emigrated to the United States during the second great wave of German emigration in 1853. An effective railroad promoter, he owned the Northern Pacific RR.; he was a prominent Democrat and the son-in-law of abolitionist William Lloyd Garrison.

Viollet-le-Duc, Eugène Emmanuel (*b.* 21 January 1814, Paris, France; *d.* 17 September 1879, Lausanne, Switzerland). Architect. Restorer of ancient buildings in France, including the cathedral of Nôtre Dame in Paris and the Château de Pierrefonds. Auguste Bartholdi asked Viollet-le-Duc, under whom he had studied, to design Liberty's internal structure. Viollet-le-Duc's proposal was to construct sand-filled masonry compartments within the hollow statue: "In place of masonry there will be inferior coffers rising to about the level of the hips; these shall be filled with sand. Were an accident to happen, stonework would have to be dismantled; [but] with the coffers, simply open the flap valve affixed to the inner surface of each one and the sand will run out by itself." He also created a plan to secure the copper sheets together by means of armature bars and advised Bartholdi to use the repoussé technique in sculpting the statue's copper body. He assisted Bartholdi in the design of the torch and flame as well. Viollet-le-Duc's unexpected death altered the plan for the sand-filled compartments, for Bartholdi's new engineer, Gustave Eiffel, designed a new primary support: a central iron tower or pylon. Viollet-le-Duc's brilliant armature bar design for the copper sheeting and his other ideas were retained.

Tourism advertisement

Visitation. The visitor's experience at the Statue of Liberty has traditionally involved climbing the stairs inside the pedestal and the statue to the top. Until 1916, the highest point open to the public was the torch; however, access was closed following the Black Tom explosion that year. Since then, the highest a visitor may go is to the head, also known as the crown.

When the Statue of Liberty was under the jurisdiction of the Light-House Board (1886–1902), the American Committee was responsible for visitation. This organization provided ferry service to the island and maintained a caretaker to keep the oil lamps in the interior lit. The island was not attractive in the least. Most of it was still reserved as an army base and therefore off limits to visitors. People would land on a pier and proceed into the walls of Fort Wood, where they would see shanties in which cheap refreshments and beer were sold; they would sometimes catch sight of the army mule. After the army took over the statue in 1902, conditions were somewhat cleaner, and the Otis Elevator Company installed the first elevator, c. 1907–8. In 1924, the statue became a national monument. In 1931, an even newer cable elevator was installed in the pedestal. The year 1933 was an especially important one for the statue and its visitors, as the National Park Service took over responsibility for the monument. For the first time, educational programs were offered to visitors, and from 1939 to 1965, the Park Service achieved its long-term goals of making the island attractive through landscape gardening and the construction of attractive buildings, such as a Park Service administration building and a concession building containing a gift shop and cafeteria. More recent improvements were the 1982–86 restoration of the statue, the founding of the Statue of Liberty Exhibition at the base of the pedestal (1986), the installation of a hydraulic-powered elevator in the pedestal, improved programs given by park rangers, and increased staffing.

The War Department kept the following hours for visitation to the Statue of Liberty from 1915 to 1933, September 1–April 31: 9 A.M.–4.30 P.M. and May 1–August 31: 9 A.M.–8 P.M. Currently, the park is open 9 A.M.–5 P.M. every day of the year except for Christmas Day (25 December), when it is closed. The following is a list of visitations recorded annually.

1890—88,000 (estimated)
1902—44,000 (estimated)
1922—170,000 (estimated)
1928—450,000 (estimated)
1929—360,000 (estimated)
1930—no data
1931—280,000 (estimated)
1932—206,393
1933—155,715
1934—190,627
1935—252,556
1936—280,249
1937—319,042
1938—248,999
1939—428,081
1940—395,633
1941—446,334
1942—303,739
1943—321,761
1944—401,143
1945—501,040
1946—549,200
1947—565,927
1948—529,741
1949—504,023
1950—518,211
1951—591,587
1952—613,010
1953—714,345
1954—797,412
1955—739,364
1956—796,101
1957—850,270
1958—777,330
1959—767,206
1960—768,979
1961—763,499
1962—863,821
1963—847,959
1964—1,026,466

1965—1,064,516
1966—1,036,292
1967—1,071,479
1968—1,105,261
1969—1,140,130
1970—1,104,898
1971—1,078,084
1972—1,089,971
1973—1,125,339
1974—1,119,201
1975—1,144,075
1976—1,473,311
1977—1,334,289
1978—1,453,581
1979—1,605,422
1980—1,702,562
1981—1,817,926
1982—1,724,912
1983—1,598,829
1984— 637,180
1985— 190,172 (open January–July)
1986—1,923,692 (open July–December)
1987—3,092,686
1988—2,833,424
1989—2,655,797
1990—2,471,271
1991—2,488,614
1992—2,346,198
1993—2,568,602
1994—2,716,685
1995—2,846,472
1996—2,926,710
1997—3,100,525
1998—3,380,603

In an 1894 article, a *New York Herald* reporter described what Auguste Bartholdi would encounter as a visitor to the Statue of Liberty:

A United States artilleryman, spruce and trim, stands at arms beside the ticket chopper's box, into which the Statue Committee [*sic*] has the tickets of the visitors dropped as they leave the wharf. Several other United States regulars are sitting astride the stringers along the wharf, patiently fishing; they are off duty. Pick your way carefully there, M. Bartholdi, or you may step into one of those cigar boxes full of worms. . . . Let us follow him up the wooden steps that scale the rampart and down again on the inner side. Now we are within the walls of old Fort Wood, whose battlements form the walls about Liberty's pedestal. The board walk leads off to the left toward the iron shod doorways of the bastions that form the inner defences of the old fort. We start to follow the board walk. But what is that so peacefully browsing off to the right on the very slope of the rampart? Shades of Mars and Apollo! A young and frisky specimen of the army mule! There he is, tethered by an eight foot rope, comfortably cropping the few tufts of parched, stubby grass that grow between the muzzles of those frowning cannon. . . . Don't let a thing like that surprise you, M. Bartholdi. We glance with some surprise at the photographer's shanty and the shanties of the gentlemen who have the restaurant and bar concession for the island—concessions which they say they hold from the War Department. And then we note the "Ice Cold Beer" signs and the "Fresh Clam Chowder" signs all around us. It looks like Coney Island. . . . We trace our steps a few paces, past the frame containing eighteen of the photographer's specimen tintypes, which frame he has ingeniously suspended from a nail driven into the cement in the very masonry of the wall at the foot of Liberty's abiding place; past the peanut and fruit stand at the sally port of the old fort, where an elderly German matron, with Teutonic thrift, cries her wares in sublime disregard of all

French achievements, and then, once inside the granite battlements, we begin to mount a wooden stairway, and finally reach a spacious wooden platform, at the base of the pedestal proper. Both stairway and platform are just as they were when they were erected for the dedicatory ceremonies in 1886. They are not things of beauty, but luckily they are not visible to the spectator who gazes awe inspired from the bay. From a careful inspection of the island and the monument, I came away convinced that everybody else at the shrine of Bartholdi's Liberty emulates Tommy, the army mule, in his hours of leisure, and "does about as he pleases."

In 1898, American vaudeville comedian Cal Stewart (1856–1919) starred in *Uncle Josh at the Statue of Liberty,* an early sound recording on an Edison cylinder disc. In the two-minute recording, Uncle Josh comments on his boat ride and, above all, his long, tiring climb to the top of the statue.

Famous visitors to the Statue of Liberty have included King Olav V of Norway (1975); Queen Margrethe II of Denmark (1999); Prime Minister Prince Dlamini of Swaziland (c. 1990); Vietnamese political leader Ho Chi Minh (1912); novelist Fannie Hurst (1947); and French singer Edith Piaf, with American actors Franchot Tone and Burgess Meredith (who came to participate in a special RKO "Hands Across the Sea" radio broadcast to Paris in 1950). *See also* American Committee; Army; Crown; Dimensions; Ferry service; Hill, Aaron and Evelyn; Interior; Interpretation; Landscape and vegetation; Manhattan skyline; National Park Service; Observation balcony.

Actress Betty Grable (at right) and her friend Chiquita on the observation balcony, c. 1939

W

Waddington, William Henry (*b.* 11 December 1826, Saint Rémy-sur-Avre, France; *d.* 12 January 1894, Paris, France). French statesman and archaeologist. Member of the French Committee, Franco-American Union. His grandfather, an Englishman, had settled in Normandy in 1780, where he established cotton manufactories and eventually took French citizenship. The family remained Protestant. Waddington was a member of the National Assembly, 1871–76, and a senator, 1876–93. He twice served as minister of education, 1873 and 1876–77. As foreign minister, 1877–79, he distinguished himself at the Congress of Berlin (1878) by winning acceptance of French dominance in Tunisia. Impressed with this, President Jules Grévy appointed him prime minister in 1879, but Waddington's government collapsed after only nine months in office, due to Education Minister Jules Ferry's adoption of a controversial anti-Catholic national education policy. From 1883 to 1892, he served as ambassador to Great Britain. He was the author of *Voyage archéologique en Grèce et en Asie Mineur* (1866–77). He lost his Senate seat in the 1893 elections. In 1873, William Waddington married an American, Mary Alsop King, a granddaughter of U.S. vice president Rufus King.

Wallon, Henri Alexandre (*b.* 13 December 1812, Valenciennes, France; *d.* 13 November 1904, Paris, France). Historian, politician, and professor at the Sorbonne, Paris. A close political ally and friend of Edouard de Laboulaye, Wallon is known as the Father of the Third Republic, due to the passage in the National Assembly of his Wallon amendment, which described France as a republic. A member of the Chamber of Deputies, 1849–50, and the National Assembly in the 1870s, he later served as minister of education and religion, 1875–76, and was the author of many books, including *De l'esclavage dans les temps modernes* (1847), *Histoire de l'esclavage dans l'antiquité* (1848), and *L'Emancipation de l'esclavage* (1861).

War Department. *See* Army.

Wars. The adoption of the Statue of Liberty as the universally accepted American national icon dates from World War I. Following the installation of the new floodlighting system at the Statue of Liberty in time for her thirtieth anniversary in 1916, President Woodrow Wilson and French ambassador Jules Jusserand came to New York City to celebrate it. In an eloquent speech, Wilson identified the goddess of liberty (Libertas) with the goddess of peace (Pax), and emphasized the united desire of the United States and France for peace in Europe. A few months later, the United States entered the war as France's ally (April 1917). The popular war slogan was "Lafayette, here we come," and the federal government, in launching its Liberty Loan campaigns, chose the Statue of Liberty as its symbol; the nation responded generously. At the end of the war, steamers bearing thousands of young American soldiers returned from the fighting fields of France, entered New York harbor, and enthusiastically greeted the first familiar sign of home: the Statue of Liberty. In about 1918, Mole and Thomas, of Chicago, Illinois, took a remarkable aerial shot of eighteen thousand officers and men standing together in the form of a "Human Statue of Liberty" at Camp Dodge, Des Moines, Iowa. The commander was Colonel William Newman, and Colonel Rush S. Wells directed it.

In 1936, the Ladies Auxiliary of the Veterans of Foreign Wars began its yearly tradition of joining the National Park Service in celebrating the statue's 28 October anniversary in public ceremonies on Liberty Island. They continued to hold these events at the island during World War II, bringing over large numbers of American service men and women, including Allied personnel from the British Empire, the Soviet Union, and Brazil. Also, large numbers of evacuated British subjects, as well as other Europeans, were brought over and cheerfully waved a greeting to the icon of liberty. Wartime fear of sabotage and a secret "fifth column" of enemy agents and plotters led to a blackout of the electric lighting at the statue. The torch was relit only twice before the war's end (and only for a few minutes each time): to celebrate the successful D-Day landing of Allied forces in Normandy, France (6 June 1944) and to celebrate Victory in Europe, when Nazi Germany surrendered to the Allies (7 May 1945). *See also* Liberty Loan.

(left) Bundles for Britain campaign poster

(opposite page) British evacuees salute the Statue of Liberty, c. 1940

Washburne, Elihu Benjamin (*b.* 23 September 1816, Livermore, Maine; *d.* 22 October 1887, Chicago, Illinois). Politician and diplomat; U.S. minister to France, 1869–77. Washburne represented the United States at the French Committee's kick-off fund-raising banquet for the Statue of Liberty given at the splendidly redecorated Hotel du Louvre on 6 November 1875. It was an enormously successful event that raised 40,000 francs—one-tenth of the cost of construction. In the magnificent dining hall, Minister Washburne delivered a toast to Marshal MacMahon and France in response to Henri Martin's grand toast to President Ulysses S. Grant.

Washburne became prominent as an attorney in Illinois, which he represented as a Whig and then a Republican in Congress from 1853 until 1869. President Grant appointed him U.S. secretary of state in 1869, but Washburne resigned the following week; Grant then named him minister to France. Washburne spent his last years in Chicago pursuing his scholarly interests and was president of the Chicago Historical Society, 1884–87. His memoirs, *Recollections of a Minister to France, 1869–77,* were published in New York in 1887.

Weston, Theodore (*b.* 9 October 1832, Sandy Hill, New York; *d.* 6 May 1919, New York, New York). Engineer and architect. Member of the American Committee, Franco-American Union, and chairman of its Pedestal committee. Weston was associated with the construction of the Genesee Valley Railroad, 1853–55, and was assistant engineer for the New York State Canals, 1855–57. As an architect, his most important work was the Metropolitan Museum of Art, 1884–90. He was a member of the Union League Club.

White, Steven Van Culen (*b.* 1 August 1831, Chatham County, North Carolina; *d.* 18 January 1912, Brooklyn, New York). Stockbroker and politician. Member of the American Committee, Franco-American Union; served on the Finance Committee, 1884–86. White served for many years as a park commissioner before serving a single term as a Republican congressman, 1887–89.

Whittier, John Greenleaf (*b.* 17 December 1807, near Haverhill, Massachusetts; *d.* 7 September 1892, Hampton Falls, Massachusetts). Poet. Called the "bard of freedom," Whittier was already a famous icon of American literature when he paid glowing tribute to the Statue of Liberty in his poem "The Bartholdi Statue," which was dated from his Oak Knoll residence on 22 October 1886:

> The land, that, from the rule of Kings,
> In freeing us, itself made free,
> Our Old World Sister, to us brings
> Her sculptured Dream of Liberty:
>
> Unlike the shapes on Egypt's sands
> Uplifted by the toil-worn slave,
> On Freedom's soil with freemen's hands
> We rear the symbol free hands gave.
>
> O France, the beautiful! To thee
> Once more a debt of love we owe:
> In peace beneath thy Fleur de lis,
> We hail a later Rochambeau!
>
> Rise, stately symbol! Holding forth
> Thy light and hope to all who sit
> In chains and darkness! Belt the earth
> With watch-fires from thy torch uplift!
>
> Reveal the primal mandate still
> Which Chaos heard and ceased to be,
> Trace on mid-air th' Eternal Will
> In signs of fire: "Let man be free!"

This poem, published in *The Independent* on 28 October 1886, was also printed on the last page of the commemorative booklet describing the inaugural ceremonies on Bedloe's Island.

The meaning of liberty was very close to Whittier's heart, for he was an ardent Quaker and abolitionist. His writings in the 1830s reflected a stalwart opposition to the institution of slavery, and this was especially noticeable in his

World War II ceremony on Bedloe's Island, 1940s

fiery pamphlet, *Justice and Expediency* and the poems "The Moral Warfare" and "Massachusetts to Virginia." A man of broad talent, he produced many fine works, including the poem "Maud Muller," with these enduring lines: "Of all sad words of tongue and pen / The saddest are these: it might have been." He also wrote the novel *Leaves from Margaret Smith's Journal* (1849). Quaker settlers named Whittier, California, in his honor in 1887.

Whittredge, Thomas Worthington (*b.* 1820, Ohio; *d.* 1910, Summit, New Jersey). Landscape painter. Member of the American Committee, Franco-American Union, and the Union League Club. Settling in New York in 1860, Whittredge's early work reveals the strong influence of the Barbizon school of painting, which he had learned in Europe. He was later a prominent painter in the Hudson River school. In his last years, the value of his many paintings declined, and he died in relative obscurity.

Williams, Jonathan (*b.* 26 May 1750, Boston, Massachusetts; *d.* 16 May 1815, Philadelphia, Pennsylvania). Merchant, soldier, and superintendent of the defenses of the inner harbor of New York, where he supervised the construction of most of the forts and batteries, including Fort Wood, Fort Columbus, Castle Clinton, and Castle Williams. Williams also served as the superintendent of the U.S. Military Academy at West Point, 1802–3 and 1808–12. He was the author of *The Use of the Thermometer in Navigation* (1799) and the translator of the French military engineering manual, *The Elements of Fortifications* (1801), and Tadeuz Kosciuszko's *Manoeuvres of Horse Artillery* (1808). After a disagreement with the War Department, Williams resigned from the army in 1812 and returned to his home in Philadelphia. There, he served as vice president of the American Philosophical Society, 1814–15 and was elected to Congress in 1814. Williams was a grandnephew of Benjamin Franklin. One of the forts he constructed

(and formerly under his command), Castle Williams, located on Governor's Island, was named in his honor.

Wilson, (Thomas) Woodrow (*b.* 28 December 1856, Staunton, Virginia; *d.* 3 February 1924, Washington, D.C.). President of the United States, 1913–21. President Wilson, in inaugurating a new floodlighting system for the Statue of Liberty in 1916, made the following remarks:

It was the hope of those who gave us this Statue and the hope of the American people in receiving it that the Goddess of Liberty and the Goddess of Peace were the same.

The grandfather of my old friend the French Ambassador, and those who helped him make this gift possible, were citizens of a great sister republic established on the principle of the democratic form of government. Citizens of all democracies unite in their desire for peace. Grover Cleveland recognized that unity of purpose on this spot thirty years ago.

He suggested that Liberty enlightening the world would extend her rays from these shores to every other nation.

Today that symbolism should be broadened. To the message of liberty which America sends to all the world must be added her message of peace.

Windom, William (*b.* 10 May 1827, Belmont County, Ohio; *d.* 29 January 1891, New York, New York). Secretary of the treasury, 1881, 1889–91. In 1890, Windom unsuccessfully attempted to select Bedloe's Island as the site of the first federal immigration station, but public outrage (largely incited by Joseph Pulitzer's *World*) forced him to settle on Ellis Island.

Originally an Ohio lawyer, Windom moved his legal practice to Minnesota in 1855. As a member of the Republican party, he represented Minnesota as a congressman, 1859–69, and U.S. senator, 1870–81. Windom was rated highly during his two brief terms at the Treasury department.

Winthrop, Robert Charles (*b.* 12 May 1809, Boston, Massachusetts; *d.* 16 November 1894, Boston, Massachusetts). Statesman, lawyer, and orator. Member of the Boston Committee, Franco-American Union. Active in the Whig party and an outspoken critic of slavery, Winthrop served as U.S. congressman, 1841–50, and was Speaker of the House of Representatives, 1847–49. He succeeded Daniel Webster as senator, 1850–51. He was the author of *Washington, Bowdoin, and Franklin* (1876).

Witt, Cornélis de (*b.* 1828, Paris, France; *d.* ?). Politician and historian. Member of the French Committee, Franco-American Union. Noted for his strong monarchist views, Witt was elected to the National Assembly and served 1871–76. He briefly served as deputy minister of the interior, 1874–75. He was the author of several books on U.S. history, including *Histoire de Washington et de la fondation de la république des Etats-Unis* (1855) and *Thomas Jefferson* (1861). These works endeared him to liberals, although he remained an inflexible monarchist in French politics. Witt's wife, Pauline (also a historian), was the daughter of former prime minister François Guizot.

Wolowski, Louis François Michel Raymond (*b.* 31 August 1810, Warsaw, Poland; *d.* 14 August 1876, Gisors, France). Economist, politician, and editor. A member of the French Committee, Franco-American Union, 1875–76, he attended the highly publicized inaugural banquet for *Liberty Enlightening the World* given at the Hôtel du Louvre in November 1875.

Wolowski had fled to France as a political refugee following the abortive Polish rebellion of 1830, in which he had been deeply involved. He obtained French citizenship in 1834 and in the same year founded the periodical *Revue de législation et de jurisprudence.* His friendship with Edouard de Laboulaye began when the latter began contributing articles to the journal; shortly after, Wolowski invited him to sit on its editorial board. As publisher and editor in chief of the journal, Wolowski supported Laboulaye in his call for changes in legal education, specifically concerning the legal training of administrators, diplomats, and economists. Wolowski was appointed professor of industrial legislation at the Conservatory of Arts and Vocations in 1839 and was elected president of that institution in 1848. In the same year, he was elected to a seat in the French Constituent Assembly. Adhering to his left-of-center views, he indignantly retired from politics after Prince Louis Napoléon's coup d'état abolished the Second Republic in 1851. Twenty years later, Wolowski made a successful comeback in politics when he was elected a deputy in the newly created National Assembly. He was elected a life senator in 1875.

Wood, Eleazer Derby (*b.* 1783, New York, New York; *d.* 17 September 1814, near Fort Erie, Upper Canada). Soldier. Fort Wood, whose walls surround the base of the Statue of Liberty, was named in honor of this hero of the War of 1812. Educated at the Military Academy at West Point, New York, Wood was commissioned a second lieutenant in the Army Corps of Engineers in 1806. He assisted Colonel Jonathan Williams in the construction of Castle Williams on Governor's Island.

The War of 1812 gave Wood the chance to show his mettle. He won praise for his heroic defense of Fort Meigs in Ohio and as the artillery commander in the Battle of the Thames.

Brevetted to major, he was transferred to the forces engaged in the invasion of Canada and there he played a role in the capture of Fort Erie, for which he was cited for bravery and brevetted to lieutenant colonel. Colonel Wood was killed by the British while leading a sortie from Fort Erie.

Besides Fort Wood, Wood County, Ohio

230,220.
The Average Circulation of THE SUNDAY WORLD is Larger than that of any other Newspaper Published on the Western Hemisphere.

The World.

230,220.
The Average Circulation of THE SUNDAY WORLD is Larger than that of any other Newspaper Published on the Western Hemisphere.

VOL. XXVI., NO. 8,757.　　　NEW YORK, TUESDAY, AUGUST 11, 1885—WITH SUPPLEMENT.　　　PRICE TWO CENTS.

THE SPECTRE IN GRANADA.

CONDITION MORE HORRIBLE THAN THAT OF NAPLES LAST YEAR.

Cholera Victims Decaying in the Streets—Three Hundred Deaths in Marseilles—Missionaries Massacred by Black Flags in Tonquin—Fatal Fall of an English Railway Station Roof.

MURDERED IN HIS HOME.

A WEALTHY BROOKLYNITE SHOT DOWN BY A HIDDEN FOE.

Albert M. Herrick, Whose Place of Business is at No. 60 William Street, His City, Dies Before He Can Tell Who Fired the Fatal Shot—The Police Without a Clue.

ONE HUNDRED THOUSAND DOLLARS!

TRIUMPHANT COMPLETION OF THE WORLD'S FUND FOR THE LIBERTY PEDESTAL.

Story of the Greatest Popular Subscription Ever Raised in America—How the Republic Was Saved from Lasting Disgrace—An Event for Patriotic Citizens to Rejoice Over—A Roll of Honor Bearing the Names of 120,000 Generous Patriots—The Flags of France and the American Union Floating in Sisterly Sympathy—Over $3,500 Received Yesterday—The Grand Total Foots Up $102,006.39—A Generous Lady Pays $130 for the Washington Cent.

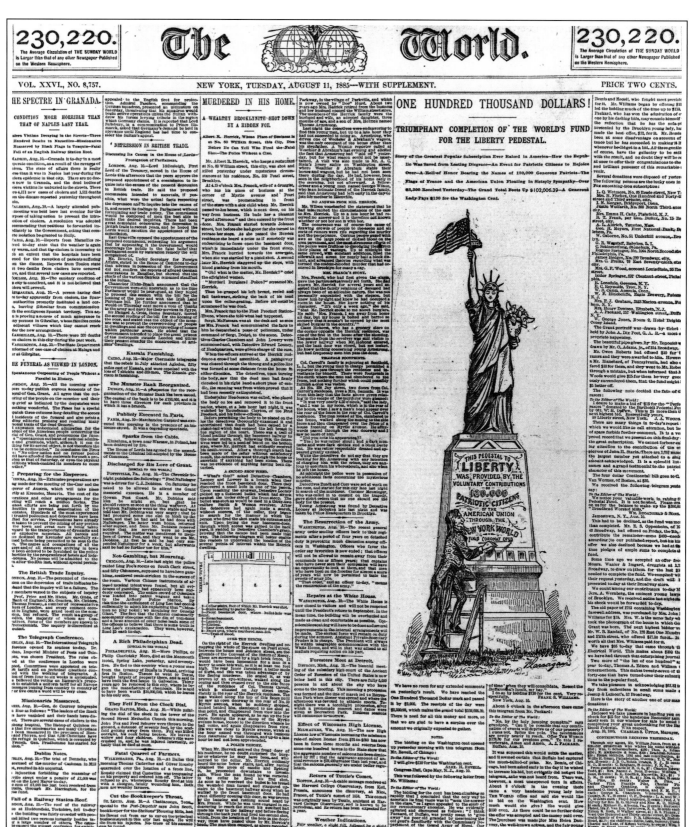

THIS PEDESTAL TO LIBERTY WAS PROVIDED BY THE VOLUNTARY CONTRIBUTIONS OF 120,000 PATRIOTIC CITIZENS OF THE AMERICAN UNION THROUGH THE NEW YORK WORLD. FINIS CORONAT OPUS.

(where Fort Meigs stood), was named in his honor. A memorial to him was also built at West Point.

World. New York newspaper founded in 1860. Joseph Pulitzer purchased it for $346,000 from the unscrupulous financier Jay Gould in 1883; he promptly changed the name from the *New York World* to the *World.* Pulitzer was to expand this newspaper considerably and make it one of the truly great newspapers of New York. In 1931, it was taken over by the Scripps-Howard chain and merged with the *New York Telegram* to become the *New York World-Telegram.* In 1950, it took over the old *Sun,* becoming the *World-Telegram and Sun.* In 1966, it combined with the *New York Herald Tribune* and the *New York Journal American,* and adopted the *World-Journal Tribune* as its final name before the news organization's complete dissolution in 1967. During much of its existence, this famous periodical was published at 125 Barclay Street, Manhattan. *See also* Pedestal campaign; Press; Pulitzer, Joseph.

Announcement of the triumphant completion of the *World*'s fund-raising campaign for Liberty's pedestal, 11 August 1885

Zouaves. These colorfully dressed soldiers marched in the Statue of Liberty inaugural parade in Manhattan on 28 October 1886. The unit was composed of soldiers who had served in the Civil War. The Zouaves were originally infantry in the French army, usually composed of Algerians who were dressed in Middle Eastern fashion.

BIBLIOGRAPHY

Acton, Lord. *The History of Freedom and Other Essays*. London, 1907.

Adkins, Lesley, and Roy Adkins. *Handbook of Life in Ancient Rome*. New York: Facts on File, 1994.

Aguila, Dani (comp. and ed.). *Taking Liberty with the Lady, by Cartoonists from Around the World*. Nashville, Tenn.: Eagle Nest Press, 1986.

Ainé, Alkan. *Un Fondeur en caractères*. Paris, 1886. (Includes a bibliography of Laboulaye's works)

Almond, Gabriel A. *Plutocracy and Politics in New York City*. Boulder, Colo.: Westview Press, 1998.

Andersen, Hans Christian. "Laboulaye." *Appleton's Journal of Literature, Science and Art* 11 (1874): 150–151.

Appleton's Cyclopaedia of American Biography. New York: D. Appleton & Company, 1888.

Arnaud, René. *The Second Republic and Napoleon III*. Translated from the French by E. F. Buckley. New York: G. P. Putnam's Sons, 1937.

Austone, Lionel. *Liberty Enlightening the World*. Santa Ana, Calif.: Gold Stein Press, 1986.

Axtell, Harold L. *The Deification of Abstract Ideas in Roman Literature and Inscriptions*. Chicago: University of Chicago Press, 1907.

Baboian, Robert, E. Blaine Cliver, and E. Lawrence Bellante (eds.). *The Statue of Liberty Restoration*. Houston: National Association of Corrosion Engineers, 1990.

Baker, Paul R. *Richard Morris Hunt*. Cambridge, Mass.: MIT Press, 1980.

Bartholdi, Frédéric-Auguste. *La Statue de la Liberté éclairant le monde*. (Edited notes of the sculptor's lectures to his lodge in November 1884 and May 1887). In Conférences prononcés à la loge Alsace-Lorraine, Paris, 1891.

———. *The Statue of Liberty Enlightening the World*. New York: North American Review, 1885.

Bellas, R. C. *Mother of Exiles*. Baltimore: Xavier Press, 1986.

Bernard, Fernand. *The First Year of Roman Law*. Translated from the French by Charles P. Sherman. New York: Oxford University Press, 1906.

Besel, Uli, and Uwe Kugelmeyer. *Fräulein Freiheit*. Berlin: Transit, 1986.

Betz, Jacques. *Bartholdi*. Paris: Les Editions Minuit, 1954.

Bigelow, John. *Retrospectives of an Active Life*. New York: Baker & Taylor, 1909–1913.

———. *Some Recollections of the Late Edouard Laboulaye*. New York: G. P. Putnam's Sons, 1889.

Bigot, Charles J. *De Paris au Niagra: Journal de voyage d'une délégation*. Paris: A. Dupret, 1887.

Boime, Albert. *Hollow Icons: The Politics of Sculpture in Nineteenth Century France*. Kent, Ohio: Kent State University Press, 1987.

———. *The Unveiling of the National Icons: A Plea for Patriotic Iconoclasm in a Nationalist Era*. Cambridge: Cambridge University Press, 1998.

Bouju, Paul M., and Henri DuBois. *La Troisième République*. Paris: Presses Universitaires de France, 1965.

Boutmy, Emile. *Taine, Scherer et Laboulaye*. Paris: Armand Colin, 1901.

Buckland, W. W. *The Roman Law of Slavery*. Cambridge: Cambridge University Press, 1908.

Cable, Carole. *The Statue of Liberty: A Selective Bibliography of Literature on Her Construction, History and Restoration*. Monticello, Ill.: Vance Bibliographies, 1986.

Camp, Oswald E. "A Brief Pictorial History of the Statue of Liberty and Its Interesting Surroundings and Approaches." Unpublished manuscript. Washington, D.C., and New York: National Park Service, 1937.

Castries, Duke of. *La France et l'indépendance américaine*. Paris, 1975.

Causel, Laurent. *Bartholdi and the Statue of Liberty—Centennial Commemoration*. Strasbourg, France: Editions de la Nuée Bleue, 1984.

Champlin, John Denison (ed.). *Orations and Speeches of Chauncey M. Depew*. New York, 1910.

Chastenet, Jacques. *Histoire de la IIIe République*. Vol. 2. Paris: Hachette, 1952–1963.

Clapp, Margaret A. *Forgotten First Citizen: John Bigelow*. Boston: Little, Brown, 1947.

Completion of the Mammoth Statue of "Liberty Enlightening the World." Banquet given by

Mr. Henry F. Gillig in Honour of M. Auguste Bartholdi, the Sculptor, Wednesday evening, May 21, 1884. Paris: Waterlow and Sons, Publishers, 1884.

Cudahy, Brian J. *Around Manhattan Island and Other Maritime Tales of New York.* New York: Fordham University Press, 1997.

Depew, Chauncey M. *My Memories of Eighty Years.* New York: Charles Scribner's Sons, 1922.

———. *Oration by the Honorable Chauncey M. Depew at the Unveiling of Bartholdi's Statue of Liberty Enlightening the World.* New York: De Vinne Press, 1886.

Dillon, Wilton S. *Gifts and Nations: The Obligation to Give, Receive and Repay.* The Hague: Mouton, 1968.

Dillon, Wilton S., and Neil G. Kotler (eds.). *The Statue of Liberty Revisited: Making a Universal Symbol.* Washington, D.C.: Smithsonian Institution Press, 1994.

Edwards, George. *Alsace-Lorraine.* Philadelphia: Penn Publishing Company, 1918.

Elderkin, John. *A Brief History of the Lotos Club.* New York: Lotos Club, 1895.

Engelhard, R. *De personificationibus, quae in poesi atque arte romanorum inveniuntur.* Germany, n.d.

Flowers, Charles. *The Tall Ships: A Salute to Liberty.* New York: Vendome Press, 1986.

Fox, Nancy Jo. *Liberties with Liberty: The Fascinating Story of America's Proudest Symbol.* New York: Dutton, 1986.

Gaillard, Jean-Michel. *Jules Ferry.* Paris: Fayard, 1989.

Gavronsky, Serge. *French Liberals and the American Civil War.* New York: Humanities Press, 1968.

George, Michael. *The Statue of Liberty.* New York: Abrams, 1985.

Gibson, Henry. *The Gift: The Illustrated History of the Statue of Liberty.* El Cajon, Calif.: Blackthorne, 1986.

Gilman, Daniel Colt. *Bluntschli, Lieber and Laboulaye.* Baltimore: J. Murphy & Company, 1884.

Girard, Louis. *Les Libéraux français.* Paris: Aubier, 1985.

Goubert, Pierre. *The Course of French History.* London: Routledge, 1991.

Gray, Walter D. *Interpreting American Democracy in France: The Career of Edouard Laboulaye, 1811–1883.* Newark, Del.: University of Delaware Press, 1994.

Grueber, H. A. *Coins of the Roman Republic in the British Museum.* London, 1910.

Gruen, Erich S. *Culture and National Identity in Republican Rome.* Ithaca, N.Y.: Cornell University Press, 1992.

Gschaedler, André. *True Light on the Statue of Liberty and Its Creator.* Narbeth, Penn.: Livingston Publishing Company, 1966.

Guhl, E., and W. Koner. *The Romans: Their Life and Customs.* Reprint. London: Studios Editions, 1994.

Hageman, Samuel M. *"Liberty"–Delivered to the Goddess at Her Unveiling in the Harbor of New York, October 28, 1886.* Brooklyn, N.Y.: Author, 1886. (Poetry)

Harrison, Constance Cary. *Recollections Grave and Gay.* New York: Charles Scribner's Sons, 1912.

Hayden, Richard Seth, and Thierry W. Despont. *Restoring the Statue of Liberty: Sculpture, Structure and Symbol.* New York: McGraw-Hill, 1986.

Hayne, Robert Y. *Fêtes de l'inauguration de la statue de la Liberté éclairant le monde, dans le baie de New-York en 1887.* Paris: Imprimerie nationale, 1887. (Colonel Laussédat's address in Paris delivered to the Lafayette Guards, post 140, Grand Armée de la République, November 10, 1886)

Hendrick, Welland. *A Brief History of the Empire State.* Syracuse, N.Y.: C. W. Bardeen, Publisher, 1892.

Holland, H. Ross. *Idealists, Scoundrels and the Lady: The Memoirs of an Insider in the Statue of Liberty–Ellis Island Project.* Urbana: University of Illinois Press, 1993.

Hugins, Walter. "Short History of the Statue of Liberty." Unpublished manuscript. New York: Statue of Liberty National Monument Library, 1956.

Jackson, Kenneth T. (ed.). *The Encyclopedia of New York City.* New Haven, Conn.: Yale University Press, 1995.

Johnson, Tristam B. *The Statue of Liberty Enlightening the World.* New York, 1986.

Jordan, Donaldson, and Edwin J. Pratt. *Europe and the American Civil War.* Boston: Houghton Mifflin, 1931.

Jordan, Michael. *Encyclopedia of Gods.* New York: Facts on File, 1993.

Kallop, Edward L., Jr. *Images of Liberty: Models and Reductions of the Statue of Liberty, 1867–1917.* New York: Christie, Manson & Woods, 1986.

Krensky, Stephen. *Maiden Voyage: The Story of the Statue of Liberty.* New York: Athenaeum, 1985. (Juvenile)

Kubler, Ludwig. *Friedrich-August Bartholdi und seine Vaterstadt Colmar vor 1870.* Zabern: A. Fuchs, 1912.

Kushner, Ellen. *The Statue of Liberty Adventure.* New York: Bantam Books, 1986. (Juvenile)

Laboulaye, Edouard de. *Etudes morales et politiques.* Paris, Charpentier, 1871.

———. *Histoire des Etats-Unis.* Paris: Charpentier, 1868.

———. *L'Etat et ses limites.* Paris: Charpentier, 1864.

———. *La Liberté religieuse.* Paris: Charpentier, 1858.

———. *Le Parti libéral.* Paris: Charpentier, 1871.

Lapidus, Ira M. *A History of Islamic Societies.* London: Cambridge University Press, 1988.

Lazarus, Emma. *The Poems of Emma Lazarus.* Boston: Houghton Mifflin, 1888.

Lehmann, Yves. *La Religion romaine.* Paris: Presses Universitaires de France, 1981.

Lesbazeilles, Eugène. *Les Colosses anciens et modernes.* Paris: Hachette, 1876.

Levine, Benjamin. "History of Bedloe's Island." Ph.D. dissertation, New York University, 1952.

Levine, Benjamin, and Isabelle F. Story. *Statue of Liberty National Monument.* Washington, D.C.: National Park Service, 1952.

Longfellow, Samuel. *Final Memorials of Henry Wadsworth Longfellow.* Boston: Ticknor and Company, 1887.

Ludmann, Oscar H. *Quand? or Liberty née Bartholdi.* New York: Vantage Press, 1965.

Martin, Edward Sandford. *The Life of Joseph Hodges Choate.* New York: Charles Scribner's Sons, 1920.

Mattingly, H. *Coins of the Roman Empire in the British Museum.* London, 1923.

Mauss, Marcel. *The Gift.* Glencoe, Ill.: Free Press, 1954.

Morton, Brian N. *Americans in Paris.* Ann Arbor, Mich.: Olivia & Hill Press, 1984.

Moses, Claire Goldberg. *French Feminism in the Nineteenth Century.* Albany: State University of New York Press, 1984.

O'Brien, Maureen C. *In Support of Liberty: European Paintings at the 1883 Pedestal Art Loan Exhibition.* New York: Parrish Art Museum and National Academy of Design, 1986.

Pahlen, Kurt. *De Wereld van de Opera.* Haarlem, The Netherlands: Uitgeverij J. H. Gott.

Palmer, George A. "Recollections of the First NPS Superintendent of the Statue of Liberty." Unpublished manuscript. New York: Statue of Liberty National Monument, 1984.

Passy, Frédéric. *Edouard Laboulaye, Conférence faite à la Societé du Travail.* Paris: Librairie Guillaumin, 1884.

Patterson, Lillie. *Meet Miss Liberty.* New York: Macmillan, 1962.

Pauly, Wissowa, and Kroll Pauly. *Real-Encyclopädie der classische Altertums-Wissenschaft.*

Penick, Ib. *The Story of the Statue of Liberty.* New York: Holt, Rinehart and Winston, 1986. (With movable illustrations in three dimensions)

Perrault, Carole L. (comp.). *The Statue of Liberty and Liberty Island: A Chronicle of the Physical Conditions and Appearance of the Island, 1871–1956.* Boston: North Atlantic Historic Preservation Center, National Park Service, 1984.

———. "Statue of Liberty National Monument Historic Resources Study." Draft manuscript. Lowell, Mass.: Northeast Cultural Resources Center, National Park Service, 1997.

Plessis, Alain. *The Rise and Fall of the Second Empire, 1852–1871.* Cambridge: Cambridge University Press, 1989.

Price, Willadene. *Bartholdi and the Statue of Liberty.* Chicago: Rand McNally, 1959.

Provoyeur, Pierre, and June Hargrove (eds.). *Liberty: The French-American Statue in Art and History.* New York: Harper and Row, 1986.

Reagan, Ronald. *An American Life.* New York: Simon & Schuster, 1990.

Rémond, René. *Les Etats-Unis devant l'opinion française, 1815–1852.* 2 vols. Paris: Presses Universitaires de France, 1962.

Rémusat, Count Charles de. *Mémoires de ma vie.* 5 vols. Paris: Librarie Plon, 1958–1967.

Reuss, Rodolphe. *Histoire d'Alsace.* Paris: Furne-Boivin, 1912.

Rio, Michel. *La Statue de la Liberté.* France: Le Seuil, 1997.

Roosevelt, Franklin D. *Nothing to Fear: The Selected Addresses of Franklin Delano Roosevelt, 1932–1945.* Edited by B. D. Zevin. Boston: Houghton Mifflin, 1946.

Schappes, Morris U. (ed.). *Emma Lazarus: Selections from Her Poetry and Prose.* New York: Cooperative Book League, International Workers Order, 1944.

Schimpf, Jean-Paul, and Robert Muller. *Parlons alsacien.* Paris: L'Harmattan, 1998.

Schmitt, Jean-Marie. *Bartholdi: Une Certaine idée de la liberté.* Strasbourg: Editions de la Nuée Bleue, 1985.

Scullard, H. H. *Festivals and Ceremonies of the Roman Republic.* Ithaca, N.Y.: Cornell University Press, 1981.

Seager, Frederic H. "The Alsace-Lorraine Question in France, 1871–1914." In *From the Ancien Régime to the Popular Front.* Edited by Charles K. Warner. New York: Columbia University Press, 1969.

Shapiro, Mary J. *Gateway to Liberty: The Story of the Statue of Liberty and Ellis Island.* New York: Vintage Books, 1986.

———. *La Statue de la Liberté, histoire de sa construction.* Paris: Flammarion, 1986.

Shapiro, William E. *The Statue of Liberty.* New York: Franklin Watts, 1985. (Juvenile)

Shlepakov, Arnold Nikolaevich. *Biografiia Statui Svabody.*

Simon, Jules. *La Liberté politique.* Paris: Hachette, 1881.

———. *Thiers, Guizot, Rémusat.* Paris: Calmann Lévy, 1885.

Sitzmann, Edouard. *Dictionnaire de biographie des hommes célèbres de l'Alsace.* Rixheim, 1912.

Stambaugh, John E. *The Ancient Roman City.* Baltimore: Johns Hopkins University Press, 1988.

Stone, Ross Conway. *A Way to See and Study the Statue of Liberty Enlightening the World.* New York: Bullion Press, 1887.

Taeger, F. *Untersuchungen zur römischen Geschichten und Quellenkunde: Tiberius Gracchus.* Stuttgart, 1923.

Talansier, Charles. *La Statue de la Liberté éclairant le monde.* Paris: Le Genie Civil, 1883.

Trachtenberg, Marvin. *The Statue of Liberty.* New York: Viking Press, 1976.

U.S. General Accounting Office. *The National Parks: Restoration of the Statue of Liberty.* Washington, D.C.: GAO, 1986.

Veyne, Paul (ed.). *Historie de la vie privée: De l'Empire romain à l'an mil.* Paris: Editions du Seuil, 1985.

Vidal, Pierre. *Frédéric-Auguste Bartholdi: par la main et par l'esprit.* Lyon, France: Les Créations du Pélican, 1994.

Waddington, Mary King. *Letters of a Diplomat's Wife, 1883–1900.* New York: Charles Scribner's Sons, 1903.

Wallon, Henri. *Notice sur la vie et les travaux de M. Edouard Laboulaye.* Paris, 1888. (Includes a bibliography of Laboulaye's works).

Warner, Marina. *Monuments and Maidens: The Allegory of Female Form.* New York: Atheneum, 1985.

Weighley, Russell F. (ed.). *Philadelphia: A Three-Hundred Year History.* New York: Norton, 1982.

Wirszubski, Chaim. *Libertas as a Political Idea at Rome During the Late Republic and Early Principate.* London: Cambridge University Press, 1968.

Wissowa, Georg. *Religion und Kultus der Römer.* Munich, 1902.

Yvert, Benoît (ed.). *Dictionnaire des ministres de 1789 à 1989.* Paris: Librairie Académique Perrin, 1990.

INDEX

INDEX

253